Great Times Down South

Great Times Down South

DEEP SOUTH TOURISM PROMOTION IN THE CARTER ERA

Giuliano Santangeli Valenzani

The University of Georgia Press

ATHENS

Published by the University of Georgia Press
Athens, Georgia 30602
www.ugapress.org
© 2025 by Giuliano Santangeli Valenzani
All rights reserved
Set in 10.25/13.5 Minion Pro Regular by Mary McKeon

Most University of Georgia Press titles are
available from popular e-book vendors.

Printed digitally

Library of Congress Cataloging-in-Publication Data

Names: Valenzani, Giuliano Santangeli, author.
Title: Great times down South : Deep South tourism promotion in the Carter era / Giuliano
    Santangeli Valenzani.
Other titles: Politics and culture in the twentieth-century South.
Description: Athens : University of Georgia Press, [2025] | Series: Politics and culture in the
    twentieth-century South | Includes bibliographical references and index.
Identifiers: LCCN 2024049473 (print) | LCCN 2024049474 (ebook) | ISBN 9780820373317 (hardback) |
    ISBN 9780820373324 (paperback) | ISBN 9780820373331 (epub) | ISBN 9780820373348 (pdf)
Subjects: LCSH: Advertising—Tourism—Southern States—History—20th century. | Advertising—
    Tourism—Social aspects—Southern States. | Place marketing—Southern States—History—
    20th century. | Culture and tourism—United States—History—20th century. | Southern
    States—Public opinion—History—20th century.
Classification: LCC HF6161.T63 V36 2025 (print) | LCC HF6161.T63 (ebook) | DDC 659.19/917504926—
    dc23/eng/20250218
LC record available at https://lccn.loc.gov/2024049473
LC ebook record available at https://lccn.loc.gov/2024049474

To Mom and Dad

CONTENTS

FIGURES

INTRODUCTION

As an Italian, and a European, my first trip to the South was a time of reflection as well as of sincere entertainment and appreciation. I instinctively realized that I was in a completely different America than the one shown on TV and in the movies I grew up with, which formed my mental picture of the country. In early 2014, I went to Richmond, Virginia, to conduct research for my master's thesis, but I also had enough time to be a tourist and experience something of the South. At that time, I was naïve enough to be impressed with a shop full of Confederate paraphernalia, as well as with the Confederate flags flying in the beautiful city cemetery. As a Civil War history buff, I could not help but get a little excited in front of Pickett's grave or under the giant statues of Confederate heroes. I remember that the first thing I asked myself was whether or not tourists went there just to see such things. That question evidently awakened something in me, because in 2017 I returned to the South, this time to write my PhD dissertation on the promotion of tourism in the Deep South during the Carter era. Therefore, for three months, I had the chance to see something—too little, unfortunately—of Alabama, Georgia, South Carolina, and Mississippi. This time, I was confronted with a different kind of South: a beautiful landscape that could sometimes turn eerie. If Virginia had been a bit alienating for me, the Deep South was much more so.

Given that my research was about the promotion of tourism in the late 1970s, it was impossible not to reflect on how tourism had impacted the places I was visiting, which images local promoters had wanted to put in the foreground and which not, or what processes had led to the formation of the particular touristic landscape we still see today. That trip provided me with many insights. As a foreigner, for example, I was jarred by the absence of the city as the ideal center of the landscape. And I could not help but be surprised, despite being prepared by then, at civil rights monuments and museums side by side with Confederate statues. I was also quite surprised by the words of two different tour operators in Alabama and Mississippi who admitted to me that I was the first Italian visitor they had met in their states. To peak my curiosity, they advertised mostly two things: (1) local food and breweries and (2) clubs with live music—not exactly what a European with little southern experience might expect, I thought. But I was wrong, of course, because I had not yet realized how little the stereotypical image of the South that still exists outside the United States (and I suspect even within the United States) actually corresponds to reality. To understand this, I first had to immerse myself in the world of 1970s tourism promotion and recognize how deeply this era was marked by a transition from the old to the modern.

By the end of my trip, the overall impression I had of the Deep South was of a region whose landscape is plainly shaped by the force of tourism, a place where just a casual passage through the territory can unveil fragments of themes and memories. The suspicion remains that such things are easier to notice when you are a foreigner; I would not be surprised if an American tourist would say the same thing when returning from a trip to Rome, Italy. Eventually, however, I wrote my dissertation, which, a couple of years later, after many revisions, became a book in Italian published by Roma TrE-Press (of the Università Roma Tre). It was a history book about the shifts in the touristic image of the South that occurred between the late 1970s and the early 1980s. The book you are now reading is in fact a translation of that book into English. However, I have also added several pieces that I believe will interest an American audience much more than an Italian one. That being said, I must try to give an answer to a complicated and long-debated issue: Why should a history book take tourism and the promotion of tourism as its main elements of analysis? The answer is that tourism has proven a particularly significant force in the construction of the southern United States as we know it, although its role appears to be somewhat overshadowed by more clearly visible and historically distinctive processes. Tourism and tourism promotion offer a fundamental key for understanding society. Analyzing the ways and means by which a place displays and communicates its past, its peculiarities, and its main characteristics to outsiders is a particularly effective way to better grasp the people's self-perception, as well as the processes of removal or modification taking place in their collective memory. As Richard Starnes wrote, historians should look at tourism as a "causal force in history," a lens through which to examine the past, to study culture, and to investigate national as well as regional identities.[1] This seems to be the case especially in the southern United States, a region with a long history as a tourist destination dating back to the colonial period and spanning the entire nineteenth century, interrupted by the onset of the Civil War, only to be swiftly revived in its aftermath. The construction of the "southern myth" within American culture also stemmed from a deliberate attempt by local elites to exploit precise promotional themes, usually accentuating the diversity and uniqueness of the South from the rest of the country. These very same themes have, for better or worse, marked the reputation of the South to this day. Whether one sees them as myths, misconceptions, or clichés, the images commonly associated with the region are closely linked to a set of ideas actively used to attract both visitors and investments.

In the broader context of southern studies, the relationship between the South's tourism, image, and history has received little attention, and only in the last twenty years have there been significant contributions on the subject, making this issue the center of a profound reflection on the transformation of southern society and identity. The volumes edited in 2003 and 2012 by Richard Starnes and Karen Cox,[2] in particular, are essential to understanding the full potential of this field of research. Yet, both books are collections of essays by various authors, often focused on very specific times and places, which might limit the overall perspective in favor of individual case studies. Nevertheless, both remain fundamental contributions to which this research owes much.

In *Dreaming of Dixie,* Cox addresses once again the historical ties between commercial (as well as touristic) promotion and the establishment of the southern image.[3] On the subject of the South as a brand and the creation of a touristic image, *Dixie Emporium* by Anthony Stanonis should also be mentioned.[4] This edited work includes another remarkable essay by Karen Cox that is of critical importance for comprehending how the market exploited the mythical image of the South between the nineteenth and twentieth centuries. On the theme of southern economic elites manipulating the local image and thus impacting tourism, the recent contributions of Rebecca McIntyre and Reiko Hillyer are also worth mentioning.[5] Occasionally, other volumes have referred to the important role of tourism in shaping the image of the South.[6]

Current studies, however, have focused either on narrow chronological periods or, conversely, on a much broader one, from the late nineteenth to the twenty-first century, devoting little attention to specific analysis of the region's different historical phases. Another aspect that appears to have been overlooked by historical studies on southern tourism is state-sponsored advertising. The existing literature on tourism in the South is centered on fairly limited contexts: a single city, a single county, one or more specific attractions (such as antebellum homes or beach resorts, for example), and their relationship with the tourism industry or the way in which they conveyed specific narratives to visitors. This has led to a focus on advertising produced at a local level, that is, regarding a single city or attraction. Scholars have not usually considered the general promotional material produced by the states themselves, yet this is a valuable tool for investigating the self-representation of these entities and their relationship to the classic idea of "the South." Historical research can benefit greatly from adopting certain categories and analytical methods specific to tourism studies, and the concept of destination image introduced in chapter 1, as well as its evaluation through state promotional material, will prove of particular importance throughout this volume.

The central argument of this book concerns the idea that in the second half of the 1970s, economic forces, image problems, and internal revolutions within the American advertising industry initiated a fragmentation of the perception of the South. The regional tourism industry not only profited from this fragmentation, but also contributed to it and showcased it. Admittedly, the origins of the process went all the way back to the post–World War II boom, when tourism became an important part of the economy of many southern states. Yet it was only in the 1970s that all the elements seemed to fall into place to make explicit this shift in the touristic image of the South.

As such, it seems doubly important to draw a connection between tourism and regional transformations in order to observe points of contact and mutual influence. As the former Confederate states evolved economically, politically, and socially, they also changed their physical landscape, their interpretation of the past they presented to visitors, and their style of self-representation. Advertising played an important role, conveying the idea of an ongoing transformation, of a changing region. The promotion of tourism, though, also helped initiate and realize this very change.

It is quite surprising that among the many works dedicated to the changes that occurred in the self-image of the South, none explicitly addresses the evolution of southern tourism promotion in its various historical phases. In general, existing studies have focused their attention either on the first half of the twentieth century—the moment when the process of reestablishing the southern image for tourism-economic purposes first began—or on a much more recent period, in order to observe elements of continuity or rupture with the classic imagery. Chapter 1 will provide an overview of this complex subject, drawing a quick historical picture of the evolution of southern tourism imagery and then focusing on the importance of the 1970s as a catalyst for changing the perception of the region. The election of Jimmy Carter, of course, played an important role, which will be discussed, with a particular eye on the cultural rapprochement between the ideas of the South and the North, or the Nation. What will emerge is that in the evolution of the touristic imagery of the South in the twentieth century, there is both a point of origin and a point of arrival, so to speak. The former is an image that is commonly referred to as "classic," centered on the rural, antimodern South and its fascination with moonlight and magnolias, Scarlett O'Hara and the Confederacy. This remained predominant for a long time, only to evolve into the undefined, indefinable South of today, a region of indistinct boundaries that accommodates countless themes and ideas, though none appear truly fundamental or unique. It is clear a transition did take place, but no one has yet attempted to view it through the lens of tourism.

What happened to elicit this shift, and more importantly, when did it happen? This book will try to answer these questions, identifying and analyzing the moment when this process, which is still far from being complete, became fully apparent.

These questions are not just about advertising or tourism in themselves. Neither do they concern only the South. Rather, they involve American culture tout court and the evolution of its relationship with the South. An analysis of the promotional advertising strategies implemented by the southern states can actually provide valuable insights into the myth of the "New South" that reemerged after the Second World War, and into the much-celebrated economic and cultural reintegration of the South into the Union during the 1970s. Also, the way southern promotional efforts were received by American culture says something about the United States in general: whether the divisive myth of the Old South still held in the 1970s or whether, instead, the negative perception of the region had been overcome. The search for new methods of asserting an identity strongly united the South and the United States in the 1970s and 1980s. It would be a mistake to try to disconnect the activity of southern tourist promoters from the broader American cultural context.

In the second chapter, I will focus on the southern tourism industry of the 1970s to understand not only its needs but its available resources. A very complex picture will emerge, as many of the problems inherited from previous decades contrasted with a modernity that in many ways had already taken over the traditional South. The reality of tourism in the South at that time—that is, the real attractions it could count on to attract visitors—will also be analyzed. The somewhat stereotyped image of a region where people traveled only to visit antebellum homes and nineteenth-century historical sites gives way to a South where urban destinations, entertainment, and sports are far more widespread and widely promoted.

This book will focus on a rather narrow timeframe, namely, the years between 1976 and 1981, which are seen as a moment of passage and transformation both in terms of the South's image and, more specifically, in terms of its style of tourism promotion; the processes are profoundly intertwined. This time span corresponds propitiously to the presidency of the southerner Jimmy Carter and, therefore, also to a moment of renewed interest for the region. Indeed, it is striking how little attention scholars have dedicated to the evolution of official advertising in southern states during a period broadly recognized as critical in developing the image and perception of the South. The touristic image of the South during that period has been described at times as a substantial extension of earlier messages, guided by a white-centric narrative and based on the old promotional discourse of the antebellum South.[7] This perspective seems to erase from the overall picture the active role that state tourism offices played in making the local image more complex and multifaceted.

The second half of the 1970s holds significant importance, as it witnessed extensive debates around the place of tourism in the United States' national economy. Between 1978, the year when Carter proposed the closure of the U.S. Travel Service (USTS), and 1981, when newly elected U.S. president Ronald Reagan signed a bill compromising with the tourism sector, media, academia, and state governments all had to address the issue of tourism as they had never done before.[8] This inevitably led to certain advantages in obtaining documentation, as tourism reports, congressional hearings, and academic essays on the travel industry proliferated during the 1970s. During these years, the foundations were also laid for the great achievement of 1981: a shift in the balance of international tourism. For the first time in history, more foreigners visited the United States than Americans did countries abroad, which had profound repercussions on the promotional activities of the individual states of the Union. At the end of the 1970s, in fact, even the smaller states, including those examined here, began promotion programs abroad, eager to carve out a slice of an increasingly attractive market.

Finally, it should be noted that the 1970s also saw an increase in the number of people living within the confines of the South, many of whom were workers fleeing the decline of the northern rustbelt. While for some states such as Florida and Texas this was a process that had already begun in earlier years, for other southern states it constituted an entirely new phenomenon. Georgia, Virginia, North and South Carolina, and even Tennessee actually received newcomers from other parts of the country. By the end of the 1970s, the U.S. Census Bureau confirmed this trend: more people were now arriving in the South than were leaving. In addition, between 1975 and 1980, the South received a considerable influx of African American migration from the Midwest, the Northeast, and the West. Immigration from other areas of the world, especially Asia and Europe, also intensified during the same period. Thus, by the end of the decade, the traditional social fabric of the South, composed primarily of southern-born white Protestants and African Americans, had become richer and more multifaceted.[9]

While this explains my decision to limit the time frame of this analysis to the years between 1976 and 1981, the choice of states requires further clarification. The study sample was intentionally kept to a select number of cases, albeit one still large enough to draw useful considerations valid for the South as a region.

This book, then, focuses on Alabama, Georgia, Mississippi, and South Carolina. These states will be analyzed in detail in chapters 3 and 4, as I opted to study them in pairs, drawing parallels between Alabama and Mississippi and then between Georgia and South Carolina. The goal, in fact, is to make the analysis as comparative as possible. The states selected are not only geographically and culturally compact, but also markedly different from one another, making the analysis more meaningful. Each of these four states, moreover, has distinct peculiarities within its tourism industry that, combined, help give a representative sample of the entire region.

Alabama and Mississippi, in particular, had the least developed tourism sector in the 1970s. In addition, Alabama represents an especially fascinating case because of the long-lasting leadership of Governor George Wallace, a deeply complex political figure. South Carolina, meanwhile, is another interesting case both because it contains a significant internal imbalance, with a highly touristic coastal area and a scarcely visited hinterland, and because of the presence of Charleston, a city that has made historical tourism one of its economic pillars since the turn of the nineteenth century. Even though South Carolina was far from becoming a major national destination, its reputation as a tourist spot, especially the Grand Strand, was another major difference with other parts of the South. The themes that were exploited in its promotion—mainly related to beach tourism, family fun, and purely recreational activities, which clearly shows the influence of Florida—were also unique among states in the Deep South.

Georgia, of course, proved to be an obvious choice, being President Jimmy Carter's home state and the main beneficiary of his election, in terms of both tourism and visibility. In 1976–1977, Georgia was probably the southern state best known to the general public, thanks to the relentless media campaign that followed Carter's candidacy and victory. If Mississippi in some way represents the negative parameter of this analysis, that is, as the most backward state both economically and in terms of image, Georgia stands at the opposite end of the spectrum. As far as tourism is concerned, moreover, the so-called Peach State ranked first among the Deep South states, with the city of Atlanta representing another unique asset. The only true metropolis of the Deep South, Atlanta and its hinterland were an important component of what Georgia offered to its visitors.

Of course, other southern states, far more established as national and international destinations, could have been added to the study. My goal, however, was to analyze the tourism promotion offices of states that were still developing and establishing their tourism industry during the 1970s. This explains the choice to leave out Louisiana and Florida, both destinations with well-established tourism sectors and fairly delineated tourist promotional images. Nonetheless, Florida in particular will recur frequently in the book, because its importance as a southern tourism destination makes it a model of emulation and an obligatory standard of comparison for all other states in the region.

New Orleans (and Louisiana in general) would undoubtedly have been another enthralling case, especially because of its multiethnic tradition and French-speaking heritage. However, precisely because of this uniqueness and its reputation as a tourist destination, it has already been the subject of much historical and tourism research. Anthony Stanonis, in particular, scrutinized the establishment of the city's tourism industry in the early twentieth century.[10] The period between the 1970s and the 1980s is also sufficiently documented. Specifically, Mark Souther's study of the development of the New Orleans image through tourism promotion represents a significant contribution to which little more could be added.[11]

One last word about the use of archival material. In addition to the official promotional literature published by these four states (brochures, pamphlets, posters, and so on), my primary research includes bureaucratic documentation produced by the state tourism offices, including internal reports, evaluation sheets, personal correspondence, and the strategic plans of advertising agencies that worked in the tourism sector, the latter a source rarely considered from a historical perspective. With these resources, it has been possible to trace a detailed picture of state tourism in the Deep South in the late 1970s and early 1980s. Analysis of promotional material alone would, in fact, have been less meaningful without reference to the context and the manner in which such material was conceived and produced.

A historical analysis of tourism advertisement can therefore shed light on a South in a moment of change, caught, as it were, between its old image and the need to overcome it. When modernization and globalization burst in on the placid image of a rural South, the former Confederate states appeared committed to rethinking their official image and offering it not only to the rest of the country, but to the world. This process, however, did not end during the 1980s, and in a sense it still has not yet reached its conclusion, in part because American culture has not ceased to reflect on the idea of South. Thus, this will necessarily also be a history of the relationship between the United States and its own understanding of one of its quintessential regions, at a moment when the nation was already speedily progressing toward the dramatic cultural transformations of the last decade of the millennium.

Great Times Down South

CHAPTER 1

The Tourist South, Jimmy Carter, and the Southernization of America

Destination Image: An Introduction

The term "destination image" will recur frequently throughout this book, and while it might seem like a relatively simple and straightforward concept, it actually remains one of the most complex subjects in the field of tourism studies. Indeed, one fundamental question driving academic research on the issue of tourists' thinking and behavior concerns the process by which people choose one destination over another. To quote Robert Dilley, "Why do tourists go where they do for their vacations?"[1] Although there exists no single answer and the matter remains open to debate, most authors currently believe that tourists choose a destination based on their preexisting images and ideas of the place.[2] The connection between image and destination choice has been the subject of numerous studies based on the notion of *tourism destination image* (TDI). While this remains a fairly broad concept, with as many definitions as there are authors who have written about it, John Crompton has formulated perhaps the clearest and most comprehensive, describing TDI as "the sum of beliefs, ideas, and impressions that a person has of a destination."[3]

Advertising a tourist destination is not simply promoting a place, but rather selling a narrative of it.[4] In other words, tourism advertising must constantly create, modify, correct, and keep alive the story of the destination being promoted. This task partly involves some form of coordinated effort. If a single destination were, in fact, to project different or conflicting images, the result would be an image fragmentation that could negatively impact its TDI.[5]

What is more interesting, however, is that destination images do not necessarily have to be realistic or accurate. On the contrary, often, the more unrealistic they are, the greater their commercial success. As Olivia Jenkins writes, "Whether an image is a true representation of what any given region has to offer the tourist is less important than the mere existence of the image in the mind of the person."[6] Consider the South. It is neither historically true nor accurate that in the nineteenth century Dixie was a magnificent garden populated only by gracious belles, brave cavaliers, and happy, singing Black slaves. Yet this is the destination image that the southern tourism industry projected for decades. And Americans liked it. In fact, it was what they expected to experience below the Mason-Dixon Line.

Developing and promoting positive images of a destination is the job of so-called *destination marketing organizations* (DMOs). These can take the form of regional or state tourism offices, advertising agencies, national governments, and city councils, for instance. However, DMOs are not the only producers of TDI. Clare Gunn, the first scholar to explore the question of destination image more deeply, divided it into two levels: *induced image* and *organic image*.[7] An induced image is crafted and managed by the tourism industry's DMOs, through advertising and promotional publications. An organic image, on the other hand, consists of all other non-tourism-related and nonpromotional forms of communication, such as novels, movies, newspapers, and music. In other words, the image and view people have of a particular place is only partly the result of direct promotion.

Once again, consider the South. Television programs such as *The Dukes of Hazzard*, for example, were responsible for a new interest in the region that probably surpassed the promotional efforts of southern travel bureaus. The music industry can also have this effect. Many have argued that bands such as Lynyrd Skynyrd and the Allman Brothers strongly influenced perceptions of the 1970s South, especially abroad. Political events can contribute as well. The elections of Jimmy Carter and Bill Clinton increased tourism in Georgia and Arkansas. However, it is cinema that has the strongest influence on tourists' choice of a destination and on the organic imaginary. Enthusiasm for *Gone with the Wind* did more for the South than any form of advertising campaign. Of course, organic imagery can also be unfavorable. Images of the beatings of Civil Rights activists in the South during the 1960s have long remained a stain and a mark of disgrace for several southern states.

In this book, however, the focus will be on induced images. Of all the different kinds of official promotional literature, travel brochures (or booklets, depending on their size and volume) are the most academically studied, since they appear to play the most fundamental role in the formation of an induced image.[8] This was especially so in a predigital era, when tourists could not make use of the internet to choose a destination. Historians should pay close attention to this type of printed promotional material, above all in cases when there were no other means of planning a trip. It could be argued that the further back in time one goes, the more influence induced images have on the overall destination image of a location.

Visual and textual elements have a strong correlation in brochures. In order to fulfill their communicative-promotional function, these materials use persuasion strategies linked to verbal-visual codes to evoke certain impressions in the reader. This means that in brochures and booklets, illustrations and photos are more than just a descriptive tool to show what is mentioned in the text. Tourism images are never limited to presenting what is "out there."[9] Similarly, the text uses verbal images to depict the intangible object of promotion, whether it is an abstract notion of the destination ("this place is beautiful" or "this place is rich in history"), a myth, or a local narrative.[10] Photos in promotional literature act on two different levels: on the surface they portray a clear and direct subject, but on a deeper level they also convey a message through the very way the subject is represented. Consider, for instance, the classic depiction of an antebellum home, so common in traditional southern promotion. In most cases, advertisements depict it as an immaculate object, separated from the rest of the landscape and without human figures. This representation acts on two symbolic planes: it is of course the image of a historical building, but it is also a visual cue that immediately conjures all the ideological paraphernalia of the Lost Cause of the Confederacy, i.e., a pseudo-historical narrative that romanticizes and mythologizes the southern cause in the Civil War. Or think of the long tradition of portraying African Americans primarily as waiters and waitresses. Superficially it stated, "Here tourists will be served with all comforts," but on a deeper level it meant, "Here *white* tourists will be served with all comforts." Even a photo collage is more than just a list of possible attractions, but rather a way to imprint in the visitor's mind the idea of abundance and richness in entertainment: "Here you will find everything." The same model can be applied to language, which in advertising is always emphatic, hyperbolic, and exciting.[11] It was through these promotional elements, both visual and textual, that images of the antebellum South continued to permeate American society well into the 1960s and 1970s.

It is obvious that tourism in the South was not exclusively focused on attractions related to the Lost Cause and the antebellum period. Nevertheless, that was the general destination image, the broad promotional framework in which southern DMOs operated for nearly half a century. Things gradually began to change once segregation was dismantled and the region opened its doors to globalizing forces that had been at work since World War II.

The Relationship between the South and Its Tourist Image

According to some, the South was always innately predisposed to become destination for leisure travel—the quintessential American destination. Cindy Aron sees in the southern cult of hospitality and slow living a natural inclination toward leisure and recreation, as opposed to the puritanical hard-work ethic of the North.[12] In any case, one thing is certain: the image and popular perception of the South have historically been linked to the development of its tourism.

Karen Cox advised southern historians to pay special attention to tourism, as "much of what the general public learns about the history of the American South is a result of a tour to a historic site."[13] Historic sites are, in fact, places where memories become associated with a particular space, thus helping to determine the conditions for a collective understanding of the past. To use a term introduced by Pierre Nora, these sites are "places of memory," that is, material and/or symbolic places that certify reality, or rather, certify one reality among many possible ones, allowing us to understand and rationalize past events.[14]

Just as the past loses its meaning without the places, people, and historical sites that confirm and convey it,[15] similarly the myth of the antebellum South would not have taken root in American society as it did if the southern landscape had not been overflowing with those "shrines to white heroes" mentioned by W. Fitzhugh Brundage.[16] Antebellum homes, Civil War battlefields, plantations, museums, and even generic attractions or gift stores have all contributed significantly to shaping a certain image of the American South. The South's landscape, too, has been in some ways a particularly significant architect of southern memory, as Carole Crumley has pointed out.[17] The myth of its rural land has always had a central place in southern identity, in an American society where the cultural elite and mainstream have long been connected to a more urban, industrial setting. Today as much as in the past, people envision the countryside within a temporal and spatial framework separate from everyday life—characterized by closer proximity to nature, flourishing community ties, and a more authentic life.[18]

For much of the twentieth century, the placid agricultural landscape of the South has also been closely associated with the idea of white supremacy. On this theme, Susanne Dietzel introduced the concept of the "southern garden imaginary," that is, the persistent induced image of the South as an idyllic rural garden, a fantasy built around the myth of the plantation as a place of social and implicit racial harmony.[19] In short, the mythical southern landscape is in itself a place of memory, and for much of the twentieth century this place of memory was filtered through the mainstream American idea of the South, namely a white, Protestant, and romantically antimodern region.

Hence, to comprehend the enduring presence of the classic nineteenth-century postcard image of the South in the popular imagination, it is essential to take into account the South's relationship to tourism as one of the contributing factors. Early twentieth-century tourism played an incisive role both in altering the perception of the South for Americans and in changing the image southerners had of their region. Local society was quick to adapt to the expectations and desires of visitors from the North or West.[20] In a circular manner, the southern economic elite has always used the popular perception of the South to its advantage, but at the same time, this perception has often been shaped by a precise agenda conceived by the very same elite.[21] In other words, the ideas usually associated with the South for most of the twentieth century were largely developed as bait for tourists. In a sense, this appears as a further evidence corroborating James Cobb's suggestion that southern identity results mainly from "myth and invention."[22]

Clearly, elites are key agents of memory within societies, as they play an active role in perpetuating the interpretation of the past considered dominant and in choosing which aspects of historical memory to highlight and which to eliminate.[23] These agents are engaged in defining and interpreting past events (i.e., establishing the "truth") and, at the same time, are constantly involved in a battle over the meaning of the past, pitted against other memory agents who propose counternarratives or opposing views.[24]

In the South, this manipulation of the reins of historical memory by the local elite is well recorded. Prior to the Civil War, the cotton aristocracy promoted a myth of their society and their values, as a defense mechanism (as W. J. Cash called it) against the negative image that slavery cast on them.[25] Even before this, the South had a long-established legacy as a unique place that local elites had actively helped shape. During the colonial period, the region appeared to the new Anglo-Saxon settlers as a different, exotic, and at times mysterious place. To some extent, people also perceived it as a land where life could be more pleasant. This idea is found especially in the illustrative pamphlets produced during the colonial era, which praised the South to Europeans, glorifying this territory where the climate and landscape provided idyllic living conditions. In short, it was a form of proto-advertising, aimed at attracting new settlers by inventing an overly optimistic image of the area and its climate.[26] It was not until the nineteenth century, however, that tourism became a regular activity, especially during the Reconstruction period in the aftermath of the Civil War, when the so-called New South started to reap the benefits of the burgeoning travel industry.

The Civil War profoundly affected the perception and image of the southern states. In the decades following the conflict, an impressive combination of denialism and rewriting of the past by southern whites succeeded in providing America with a coherent and imaginative narrative of the traumatic events of the war, greatly changing the perception of the South and making it inseparable from slave society and the Confederacy. Thus, between the 1880s and the beginning of the twentieth century, the Lost Cause was established as the dominant ideology and memory of the South, promoted by the political elite and shared at every social level by the white population. As has been pointed out, the Lost Cause was not just a set of myths and apologetic fantasies involving the Confederate experience, but a genuine attempt to rationalize the profound implications of the war and conceal its more problematic aspects. Alan Nolan made this very clear when he argued that the real victim of the Lost Cause was history, which was replaced by a legend in America's national memory.[27]

As a result, during and after Reconstruction, the new white southern culture created an even more idyllic and romantic vision of the past than in the prewar period, categorically excluding African American society from this process.[28] In doing so, southern whites, invoking the Lost Cause, were able to reassert the alleged superiority of their race and culture, while at the same time affirming the existence of a bygone golden age of daring cavaliers, beautiful ladies, and grand mansions.[29] This was the southern past that had to be sold to visitors, which had major repercussions on local tourism. Inevitably, travel activities were intertwined with the promotion of the Lost Cause. The romantic, pro-Confederate narrative did not override the region's wilder appeal, but rather fell in smoothly alongside it. Until the 1930s, as described by Cox, the region was predominantly perceived as quaint and antimodern, representing the most remote part of America. In a sense, this seems to be true even today, at least for some parts of the Deep South.[30] Although the picturesque and "timeless" southern aura is currently addressed in local promotion through glamorous, friendly imagery, there is no doubt that something of the old antimodern appeal still lingers and, at times, takes over. A small 2018 ad from a Louisiana parish, for example, ventures to promise a place where locals "never meet a stranger."[31]

Clearly, over the past century, not all visitors traveling to the South were necessarily driven by antebellum fascination. The appeal of the South has gone beyond that. One must also keep in mind that tourism changes over time. Historically, the first elements of attraction of the South were its climate and natural landscape, or environmental tourism, soon followed by forms of destination tourism, that is, the search for specific attractions or places to visit (seaside resorts, New Orleans during Mardi Gras, a certain fair, and so on). Finally, cultural and heritage tourism began to develop.[32] According to Brundage, this is closely connected to the spread of the automobile as a means of travel: "Automobile tourism has led to a commercially oriented celebration of Southern architecture, landscape, and history, and, in turn, historical memory in the South has come to reflect the ubiquitous influence of tourism."[33] In other words, this form of tourism did arise until the 1920s; before then, it was primarily the environment and landscape that drove visitors to travel beyond the Mason-Dixon Line. Tom Selwyn sees in this national passion for rural and remote areas a search for the preindustrial American myth. Crossing the Mason-Dixon line from North to South also meant escaping the hectic, urban, industrialized life of the cities and experiencing the allure of an imaginary, premodern world that, at some point, became tied to the Confederate image.[34] Because of this, when industrialization took over the country in the late nineteenth and early twentieth centuries, the advertising industry found it easy to promote the South, or rather old Dixie, for tourism, consumer goods, and everyday items.[35] Aided by the great boom in commercial advertising during the Roaring Twenties, images of the South spread rapidly. Karen Cox identifies the period between 1890 and 1930 as the era of the "selling of the American South," that is, the moment when the greatest commercial diffusion of the Dixie/South brand took place.[36] In addition to tourism, countless consumer items were advertised by southern companies with references to Confederate symbolism and southern heroes. Northern companies also exploited southern imagery for commercial purposes, favoring idyllic plantation scenes and racial stereotypes over images directly related to the rebellion, demonstrating the extent to which the idea of a placid white man's paradise appealed to both the South and the North.

By this time the South had become a commercial brand in its own right. The main theme was the romantic idea of an old, orderly, gallant, and implicitly white world, a theme that suited the South well since it was still largely agricultural and sparsely urbanized, and would remain so until after World War II. Moreover, exploiting the image of a rigid and stereotypical white master–Black slave relationship was a viable strategy in order to reach beyond the confines of the South to a part of white society deeply nostalgic for that bygone social order. Studying the tourist imagery of Atlantic City, New Jersey, in the first half of the twentieth century, Bryant Simon noted how the idea of being served by a Black man had become an important indicator of social advancement for white, middle-class American tourists.[37]

The spread and commercialization of southern images, therefore, did not overtly trouble the rest of the country. On the contrary, the popular use of typical aspects of southern tradition was one of the most evident signs of the reconciliation between the two sides in the aftermath of the Civil War. As David Blight convincingly explains, it was the South that dictated the terms of rapprochement.[38] By accepting the southern view of the war and its causes, the nation mended the rift caused by the conflict, but at the expense of the African American population, entirely forgotten by the narrative that emerged from the cauldron of reconciliation. It was an obviously supremacist and racist vision of the past that celebrated the Civil War as a chivalrous clash between brothers, between equals, between two different ways of understanding the same American patriotism. Slavery was no longer listed as a cause of the conflict, while Confederate generals were celebrated as heroes and romantic idealists in the national pantheon. Along with achieving this historical revisionism, the Lost Cause also succeeded in inserting into the American landscape a collection of monuments, civic celebrations, and public rituals that profoundly affected its appearance and would become one of the pivots around which southern heritage tourism revolved.[39] This allowed the Confederate cause and its heroes to populate the American imagination tout court, while the antebellum landscape established itself as a place in the collective memory.

Indeed, antebellum homes and plantations were among the most cherished and celebrated attractions in the twentieth-century South, often combined into a single attraction. They soon became American symbols, physically located in the South but conveying a narrative accepted by all Americans. Antebellum homes are almost ubiquitous in twentieth-century southern promotional material, and they once were prominent public sites in certain states; today they still remain popular tourist sites. Although the narrative and interpretation of the past offered by these locations has dramatically changed over time, this change occurred slowly and tentatively. There was very little difference between the 1930s, when antebellum homes first became tourist attractions in Mississippi, eventually spreading to other parts of the South, and the late 1970s, when they remained one of the region's most popular attractions.[40] Indeed, Robert Janiskee identifies the 1970s as a time of exponential increase in events such as tours, reenactments, and historical festivals that used historic homes either as attractions or simple scenographic backdrops.[41] The author provides no explanation for this phenomenon, but it could be attributed in part to a general increase in leisure travel and a wave of historical nostalgia that occurred during the 1970s and 1980s.[42]

The tourism industry had something to do with the trend. Because of developing anxieties about American purpose and mission, between the 1970s and 1980s U.S. society experienced a period of renewed interest in its past and in historical landmarks. Seeking reassurance, Americans resorted to a selective use of history to escape the complexity of the present. Heritage is in fact an ambiguous and complex concept. Michael Kammen defines it as "an impulse to remember what is attractive or flattering and to ignore all the rest. Heritage is comprised of those aspects of history that we cherish and affirm,"[43] while Fowler states that heritage is that part of the past which is not "emotionally neutral."[44] Yet the term does refer merely to the relationship between the present and the past. It includes culture. Heritage, in fact, is pervasive, including not only landmarks or historical sites but also "the entire landscape of the region with its geographic base" and a wide range of intangible assets, such as festivals, cultural events, food, music, idioms, and customs.[45] In short, it is a set of ideas assembled from memories, artifacts, and spaces, with the aim of addressing contemporary needs.

Moreover, as Jim Week rightly pointed out, the American postwar cult of heritage—or "heritage obsession," as Kammen defined it—has been widely cultivated and driven by the economy. The market helps create and select the past to meet the public's demand for nostalgia, and the tourism industry has obviously played a very important role in this process.[46] Thus, to speak of antebellum homes as historic sites would be misleading. Historicity, in fact, has never been their main function; they are not educational sites in the strict sense, despite their intentions. Using the terminology proposed by Vida Bajc, it would be better to call them "heritage sites," i.e., places that aim to be a "cultural space of memory," where visitors can experience "life as it was."[47] In the case of the South, this presents another problem. What tourists see staged in antebellum southern homes is not life as it was in the nineteenth century, but rather a representation of what someone imagines life was like back then. The representation of the past that these sites still promoted in the 1970s was evidently connected to the Lost Cause, since slaves were omitted from the narrative offered to visitors. Sometimes these sites were (and still are) used for larger events, true celebrations of the antebellum South at a city, county, or state level. The most famous of these events, the Spring Pilgrimage, has been held in Natchez, Mississippi, since the early 1930s. It is a full-blown celebration of the antebellum South that at one time included costume dances, parades, tours of homes, and a contest to elect Mr. and Miss Confederacy. All in all, a true "performative embodiment of whiteness."[48] Significantly enough, the highlight of the event was the Confederate Pageant, a costume reenactment. (It was not until 2001, in the wake of mounting criticism, that the event was renamed, more neutrally, the Historic Natchez Pageant). A Black woman who attended in the 1960s reported her impressions of disgust at the sight of the show, which featured African Americans only as cheerful cotton pickers.[49] It comes as no surprise that in 1965, civil rights activists took it upon themselves to contest this event, an effort that would cost them six arrests and charges as "agitators."[50]

White supremacist undertones frequently characterized southern tourism in the twentieth century. This, however, was not just a southern problem. Rather, it was American heritage tourism itself that had for too long been disinterested in nonwhites.[51] Yet in the South this was more evident, as the landscape was littered with monuments and historic sites designed specifically to celebrate white society. The heritage market, however, is also always necessarily segmented, since different groups or social entities select and recognize different elements of tradition and the past as valuable. In the South during the late 1970s, a Black heritage industry was on the rise, and it would soon turn into a tourist commodity. The first timid signs of a change in the racial attitude of southern tourism were thus possible only with the development of a mass tourism industry interested in more in maximizing revenues than in preserving the traditional social hierarchy.

The Second Postwar Period and the Boom of Mass Tourism

The period following World War II was generally positive for tourism in the South. The economic boom allowed more people to spend money on travel, with the result that the local tourism industry began to focus on promoting middle- and lower-class tourism, a phenomenon that would eventually be known as mass tourism. New accommodations and attractions were built and new state bodies were founded solely to coordinate promotional and tourism policies.[52] Overall it was a period of general growth for the tourism industry in the United States. To describe this progress in the context of the South, authors frequently reference a statement from the mayor of Knoxville, Tennessee, in the early 1950s: "It's easier to pick up a tourist, than it is a bale of cotton,"[53] a line that effectively describes the shift from a purely agricultural economy to something more modern and service oriented. By the 1950s, the overall southern tourism landscape had even become more multifaceted, as state leaders and tourism developers had already initiated a "variety Vacationland," adding new establishments and amenities to the traditional natural and historical-cultural attractions to enhance the South's appeal to tourists.[54] This was an obvious response to the increase in visitor numbers.

Susan Sessions Rugh identifies the entire period between 1945 and 1973 as the so-called Age of Family Vacation, a phenomenon bolstered by postwar prosperity and the rise of the middle class.[55] This growth in tourism was supported in part by the creation, in the early 1940s, of the first state travel bu-

reaus, agencies dedicated to the promotion and management of tourism resources.[56] Traveling within the country also allowed Americans to assert or
reassert their status as citizens of the United States; visiting national monuments and the most symbolic sites of national culture helped cultivate a sense
of identity and a renewed attachment to American history.[57] Picking up on the
concept of the post-1945 tourist boom, Emily Nelson recognized in it a process of national identity building that occurred "through patriotic pilgrimages
and landscape appreciation."[58] Spending money along the way on motels, historical sites, and attractions was akin to an act of patriotism, as it allowed you
to get to know and explore your country, far from the domestic areas to which
one was accustomed. Recent tourism studies have extensively discussed this
topic, investigating the role of cultural attractions in relation to the construction of national identity.[59] In the years following World War II, as the tensions
between the East and West escalated in the Cold War, nationalism became an
important aspect of American society.[60]

But traveling to the South, visiting its landscape and historic sites, actually meant more than just experiencing the region's past and traditions. In the
twentieth century, visiting the "Lost Cause South" also became an occasion for
expressing one's *Americanness*. While this might appear like a contradiction
on the surface, it is not. Something very similar happened also with the myth
of the Wild West. As Richard Aquila suggests:

> The pop culture West also served as a mirror and a matrix for American attitudes
> toward gender, race, ethnicity, and class. The pop culture West frequently served
> as a metaphor for the superiority of white, Anglo-Saxon, Protestant culture, ide-
> alizing middle-class Anglo males at the expense of women, new immigrants, His-
> panics, Indians, and other people of color.[61]

Indeed, the picturesque antebellum South should be considered as part of the
collective American memory tout court. By accepting the Lost Cause as part
of its official narrative, the United States had implicitly incorporated it into its
cultural mainstream. The antebellum South, after all, was a symbol that appealed to Americans of different backgrounds. Just as the myth of the West
celebrated the image of the adventurous white frontier male as the symbolic
hero of America's manifest destiny, in the same way the Lost Cause was also
a way of reaffirming, or rather conjuring, certain aspects of classic American
national identity: racism, traditionalism, ruralism, nostalgia for the past, and
gender subordination.[62] Just as Mount Rushmore symbolizes and conveys to
its visitors a narrative centered on American values and the American way
of life, so a visit to southern antebellum homes can equally represent something inherently American. The same happened, for example, when Alabama

participated in the 1981 presidential patriotic parade in Washington, D.C., by sending fifty southern belles in antebellum costume.[63] In doing so they were celebrating not simply the South, but part of American history, through a certain idea of the region.

As previously mentioned, postwar growth also affected the South, triggering profound changes. Yet the relationship between whites and African Americans remained nearly identical to that of the post-Reconstruction era. Even the favorable attitude of American national culture toward the southern Confederate appeal had not faded. Christopher Bates observed how the "favorable conception of the South and the Confederacy" in America remained virtually intact until at least the 1950s and 1960s.[64] It was not until the middle of the century, when scenes of violence perpetrated by white southerners against civil rights activists began entering American homes through newspapers and television, that something in the southern myth was irreversibly damaged. The old Confederate symbols in particular acquired a new negative, racist, and oppressive meaning that, paradoxically, the Lost Cause had managed to remove in the years following the Civil War.[65] The South still appeared antimodern, but no longer in the good-natured, reassuring, charming way of fifty years before. As Bruce Schulman evocatively points out, "The cotton fields of Alabama seemed scarcely less foreign than the jungles of Vietnam or the steppes of Russia—and no less un-American."[66]

Confederate symbols were still present in the South but now openly used as a sign of protest and resistance to social change. The centennial of the Civil War, celebrated between 1961 and 1965, was clearly a moment for reflection, a reconsideration of the events of the past, but it was also, to a large extent, a triumph of southern regionalism marked by reactionary overtones. The South openly celebrated the Confederacy rather than honoring the shared memory of the conflict. Therefore, the Confederate battle flag established itself also a symbol of resistance to desegregation. As remarked by Harry Golden in a 1962 article in the *Saturday Evening Post*: "There were more Confederate flags sold during the first year of the Civil War Centennial [1961] than were sold throughout the South during the war itself."[67]

Despite the ambiguous reputation the South was gaining, local tourism continued to exist and develop. Thomas D. Clark, for example, noted how in the late 1950s, at the height of the civil rights struggles, the tourism sector in many southern states surpassed agriculture in economic importance.[68] Moreover, most visitors came from within the region, traveling from state to state, and thus represented a tourist flow largely unaffected by the dark national reputation of segregation. Yet the leisure industry also became a battleground in the broader context of the civil rights struggle, as recreational facilities such as golf courts, pools, spas, and beaches became the target of integration efforts by African Americans, especially after the U.S. Supreme Court's ruling in *Brown v. Board of Education*.[69] Travel- and leisure-related businesses, fearing huge losses, soon began to press local and state governments to end the unrest and tensions in one way or another. This seems to have happened especially in those areas most affected by tourism from other parts of the country, such as the Atlantic coast. As stated by Anthony Stanonis, southern beach towns in particular were the "Achilles' heel of Jim Crow," i.e., places where the racial status quo was less rigid than inland and could be challenged with more ease. When international media began to cover the situation in the South, coastal-area businessmen pressed state legislators to intervene, after several beach resorts lost revenue because visitors were afraid of the situation.[70] Although tourism in the South quickly rebounded after the most acute phase of racial tensions had passed, something in the region's image had been broken for good, forcing the southern states, in the decades that followed, to come to terms with their tarnished image.[71]

Eventually, after nearly three decades of postwar prosperity, even the family vacation boom came to a halt in the early 1970s under the blows of the energy crisis and recession. This, however, was not a setback for tourism, but rather a boon. Travel habits changed, as did tourists, and the industry flourished. The country's economic state was only one of the causes. Social change also contributed to changes in the habits of American travelers. New social upheaval, such as the Sexual Revolution, student Vietnam protests, and feminist movements, helped remove the "white middle-class suburban" stereotype as the main target of the tourism industry.[72] By 1974 long family road trips were already "a thing of the past," as Georgia's tourism director put it.[73] More and more people were travelling alone, with one partner, or in small groups, including older couples or teenagers without parents. An increasingly negative view of mass tourism spread.

In the "Me Decade," even leisure travel became a more reflective, personal, and intimate activity than in the past. As mentioned earlier, many were now traveling mostly to reconnect with an American heritage that allowed them to overcome doubts and distrust regarding the country's current situation. The national bicentennial celebrations at mid-decade further stimulated interest in the past. Others also sought a direct and deep connection with the land in America, as a reaction to the problems of modern life. Thus, attitudes and movements inspired by the idea of a "return to nature" that developed in the late 1960s and early 1970s also generated new business opportunities for the tourism industry. Outdoor recreational activities were booming, thanks in part to a host of media sources and publications that celebrated the outdoors and promoted many different forms of activities to be enjoyed in a natural environment. Some of these emerged right in the wake of the 1970s outdoor recreation boom, including the popular *Outside* magazine, which published its first issue in 1976. Local music, food, and crafts, although still in embryonic form, were also becoming important assets for reaching new niches in the market. During the late 1960s, many Americans, especially the young, disillusioned with the mass conformism of the present, became interested in early Americana, and traditional food, antiques, or local artifacts were widely sought.[74]

In short, by the 1970s, going on vacation was no longer associated only with the idea of relaxing with the family in some charming location, and the tourism industry began to acknowledge the existence of different niche interests. Ads were no longer limited to describing a product or a vacation destination, as in the past; they now wanted to be personally inspiring and appealing through slogans, evocative photographs, and promotional themes that would stick in the mind of the public.

This led to another major turning point in the world of advertising. As legendary Madison Avenue executive Carl Ally said in 1977, "Ads must be fitted to the audience, not the other way around."[75] In the 1970s, also in reaction to the "creative revolution" of the previous decade, advertising used increasingly scientific methods, based more and more on studies and market researches. The focus was on understanding the lifestyles and psychological variables of the public, in order to identify consumer niches that could be targeted by advertisements.[76] If the target audience of the tourism industry was no longer the generic postwar American family, then advertising also had to address the needs of new travelers attracted by specialized recreational activities, thus promoting not only the state, city, or county as a whole, but also focusing on certain themes and peculiarities. In the 1970s, the trend was to direct ads toward narrow markets: historical tourism, sightseeing, local folklore, sport, music, beach activities, luxury lodgings, nightlife, fishing, hiking, and various other types of tourism. Until then, the tendency had been to create general advertisements that could fit everyone. Now, each segment of the market deemed profitable corresponded to a specially designed advertisement. Undoubtedly this process, caused mostly by internal innovations in the world of advertising, contributed to the need to make promotional images more multifaceted and less monothematic than before. In the 1970s, tourist brochures were still probably the most important means of promotion, along with newspaper ads. During these years, however, tourist brochures became more sophisticated, definitely evolving from earlier formats and allowing for more articulate, complex messages.[77]

However, it is at this point in the story, between the end of the civil rights era and the dawn of a renewed New South, that we somehow lose sight of the region's tourism narrative. There is no doubt that tourism was a vibrant industry in the 1970s, and in fact, it was in a phase of expansion, despite the end of the family vacation era. With regard to image building and tourism promotion, however, things are not as clear. We do know that by the late 1970s the bucolic image of a white man's paradise remained. Brundage is in no doubt when he states that columned mansions, white belles in hoop skirts, and Civil War shrines "were the icons of Southern tourism during the 1970s."[78] To be sure, this picture-postcard South was still a great promotional weapon in the hands of the economic elite of the former Confederate states. Nonetheless, some innovations were already underway and beginning to be noticed. As we will see in the following chapters, these included a first tentative depiction of African American society in the overall picture of some southern states. More importantly, however, a broad attempt was made to situate the antebellum appeal within a larger, more modern, more multifaceted promotional image. In this sense, Brundage's statement seems too reductive and narrow.

Rather than a time in which old patterns and promotional images were simply repeated, the 1970s appear as a moment of transition from the old, classic narrative to something new. More recent analyses have highlighted the culmination of this process. Ted Ownby, for example, notes that the tourism sector's representation of the South in the first decade of the twenty-first century was little more than a jumble of different, often conflicting themes and images with no clear common thread: "According to the tourism industry, the South of the twenty-first century has no particular identity: it has numerous identities, gained from the land and climate, from some parts of history, from modern economic change, from cultural creativity, and from other sources as well."[79]

If we look at promotional booklets in four Deep South states from 2018, Ownby's early observations seem to be confirmed: the rigid approach is a thing of the past, and the new imagery ranges from food to music, with a strong focus on Black heritage and civil rights tourism, while the epic of the Confederacy and the Lost Cause are now reduced almost to a distant memory.[80] Therefore, something must have happened between the 1970s and the turn of the century. Something caused the monolithic image of the romantic South to dissolve, making way, albeit confusedly, to a whole series of new, less distinguishable features.

Not surprisingly, the origin of these new ideas can be traced back to the 1970s, a moment of historical importance for the South. This does not mean that the old classic attractions had stopped drawing visitors—on the contrary.

But it is clear that, at least from a promotional point of view, this type of imagery was no longer suitable to represent the South and, in fact, even risked proving counterproductive for the regional image and economy.

"We've Got Carter. Now We Can Rejoin the Union": The South in the 1970s

Between 1950 and the early 2000s, the South changed so much that it became almost unrecognizable, and the 1970s marked a pivotal moment in the region's evolutionary transition. It is no coincidence that the decade came essentially halfway along the fifty-year-long transformation process that Alfred Eckes effectively outlines in his essay "The South and Economic Globalization."[81] As James Gregory suggests, the change could not have been more remarkable: "The region that had once been considered the least healthy section of America—a land of boll weevils and pellagra, of enervating heat, deadly pests, and fevers—reemerged as the warm and attractive Sun Belt."[82] Clearly, the end of segregation and the beginning of less strained racial relations also made the South more appealing, significantly modifying the overall perception of the region.[83]

The agricultural sector was replaced by industry and services as the driving force of southern economy. At the same time, local society was also transformed, becoming more diversified and complex, thanks mainly to new national and international migratory flows that developed over the course of the decade. Even in terms of landscape and daily life, the 1970s had revolutionary implications for the South. Cities grew, new air routes allowed travelers to reach the region quickly and conveniently, and the popularity of air conditioning made the torrid southern heat easier to bear. Satellite television dealt a decisive blow to regional isolation and facilitated the integration of the South with both the rest of the country and the rest of the world.

From a cultural point of view, the 1970s set in motion a process of total (or almost total) remodeling of the regional image with profound repercussions for tourism promotion as well. In the late sixties and early seventies, the South found itself embroiled in a complex situation from which it needed to seek new defining myths to understand itself and explain this new reality and status quo.[84] What would the identity of the region be based on now that the old southern lore was beginning to lose its importance? No one seemed able to provide a clear answer. As George B. Tindall stated in 1976: "We now live in a post–New South that nobody has yet given a name."[85] Willingly or not, the white South had changed, and more and more voices were calling for the Lost Cause and the myth of the Old South to be left behind, as they were no longer representative, and indeed were detrimental to the future of the region.

This situation intertwined with anxiety about an alleged loss of southern regional identity that had been persisting since the 1950s. In his book *An Epitaph for Dixie*, Harry S. Ashmore presented a series of reflections on the future of the South, a region that appeared to be on the verge of a transition "at the expense of the qualities that made the South distinctive."[86] A fear tinged what was essentially a conservative gaze on the social changes taking place. According to some authors, the South was losing its distinctive characteristics to become the so-called "No South."[87] In 1971, Joseph B. Cumming Jr. famously announced in Esquire that "the South is over."[88] Expressions such as "the disappearing sectional South" or "the vanishing South" were commonplace throughout the 1960s and early 1970s,[89] until most observers became convinced that it was the South that had taken hold culturally, economically, and socially at the expense of the North. This was the picture that emerged from the two conferences on the vanishing South held in 1972 and especially from John Egerton's seminal work *The Americanization of Dixie: The Southernization of America*.[90] By the mid-1970s, in short, the consensus was that the South was experiencing a complete comeback, and this assumption unquestionably contributed in generating a deep reflection on the meaning of the South and its core cultural themes

Thus, when Carter won the presidency in 1976 the region appeared to most as a true "New America."[91] It was also the closing year of the United States' bicentennial celebrations, which made the new alleged North-South reunification all the more significant. The former Confederate states responded with enthusiasm to the national celebrations, promoting about 24 percent of all activities and events dedicated to the anniversary.[92] The process of healing historical sectional animosities advanced when President Ford, in 1975, chose to reinstate full citizenship for Confederate general Robert E. Lee, and it was further strengthened when President Carter approved the congressional pardon of Jefferson Davis in November 1978. Both measures clearly had their roots in the need to mend dangerous internal divisions within the country in the aftermath of Watergate and Vietnam. In signing the bill restoring full citizenship to the former rebel president, Carter called for national unity: "Our Nation needs to clear away the guilts and enmities and recriminations of the past, to finally set at rest the divisions that threatened to destroy our Nation and to discredit the great principles on which it was founded."[93] According to many observers, however, by the end of the 1970s there had not only been a reunification between North and South, but a real establishment of the South as the driving force of the country.

To many, Carter's victory showed that it was not Dixie that had become similar to the rest of America, but rather the opposite. Both David Donald and

Merle Prunty saw it in much the same way: "The recent [Carter] campaign may not signify that the South has rejoined the rest of the nation as much as it may mean that a lot of the nation wants to join the South."[94]

In reality, the change taking place in the North-South relationship went far beyond that and was identified with particular acumen as early as the mid-1970s by John Egerton and C. Vann Woodward. They saw in the newfound American interest in the South an attempt to make contact with a previous historical experience that seemed to be very close to Americans. In the 1970s America was in the midst of a crisis (which Carter himself defined as a real crisis of confidence), rooted in the military defeat of Vietnam, the Watergate scandal, and the energy shortage. During that time, the defeated region par excellence in American history was seen in a new light; its past crises recalled the country's current struggles. Thus American culture (and especially American pop culture) looked for the first time to the South for answers, searching for a "cultural antidote" to the nation's problems.[95] But there was more. America had recently discovered that racial problems were not confined to the South and that the North itself had an embarrassing system of de facto segregation.[96]

Some believe that what really lightened racial tensions in the South was not the end of prejudice per se, but rather the growing recognition that this problem was not confined to the region alone.[97] Not surprisingly, in a South so deeply in search of its own distinct new identity, a "myth of the biracial South" was also taking shape, that is, the idea that the South had the potential to offer a truly integrated society characterized by harmonious and peaceful racial relations.[98] In other words, Dixie now appeared as less culturally distant, while remaining reassuring in its simplicity and rustic folksiness. Not only did the process of rehabilitation as part of the Union appear finally complete, but the region seemed poised to become a model for an America crippled by a deep crisis.[99] The South had passed through secession, military defeat, Reconstruction, Jim Crow, and desegregation and was seemingly emerging stronger than ever.

Following these trends, the South was once again becoming a commercial brand. In the 1970s, movies, music, and television mediated a new appeal for everything that was (or appeared to be) genuinely southern. Pop culture and art also revived the southern landscape as an ideal setting for stories that appealed to the country's consciousness. Over the course of the decade, even the "redneck," the stereotypical caricature of an ignorant and bigoted working-class man, had become for many white Americans the emblem of all that was good, honest, and sincere in the American tradition.[100] Clearly, the redneck fad reflected the country's growing disillusionment with government and politics in general; the redneck, after all, was and still is the quintessential anti-government figure, the farthest thing from Washington, D.C., that one can imagine. Newspapers began to talk about "redneck chic," a new way of being that transcended the regional barrier of the South. In the 1970s there were self-proclaimed rednecks just about everywhere, from California to New York. The "new American redneck" was both an antisystem rebel and also a conservative. He was conservative in a very southern fashion, i.e., bound to family values, religion, and his regional roots. Its *raison d'être* was, once again, to pose as a cultural antidote to the changes taking place in the 1970s. That the term redneck had come to signify something positive, albeit folkloristic, even in tourism promotion is evidenced by the fact that in 1978 Howell Raines of the New York Times renamed the strip of coastline between Alabama and Florida as the *Redneck Riviera*.[101]

Most importantly, however, the cultural background of the 1970s also produced a decisive change in the perception of the southern landscape. An article in a Florida newspaper, for example, directly related the newly elected southern president to the discovery of an allegedly "real" southern landscape. With traditional images put on the sidelines, now the South was described as rustic, down-to-earth, folksy: "This is the dirt-road, railroad-track, pickup-truck South. It is a region that has shouldered its miseries with hard work, church-going, porch-sitting, hunting hounds, Hank Williams and suppertime. Now, finally, it is being discovered."[102] The focus on rural scenery remained important for tourism promotion, though it was no longer confined to cotton fields and white-columned mansions. Instead, southern rural areas now aimed to appeal to tourists by highlighting their more natural and genuine qualities, with Carter serving as an ideal representation of this renewed rustic charm. Plains, Georgia, Carter's small hometown, obviously became a central element in this process of reshaping of the southern landscape, as Charles Reagan Wilson suggests.[103] Not only did Plains perfectly embody the rustic but good-natured southern rural feel, but it was also a familiar and domestic setting, being home for Carter's large family and his brothers, uncles, cousins, and grandparents, thus conveying that sense of strong family ties and identity widely popular in 1970s America.[104]

These kinds of images that came from the South during the 1970s also contributed to the development of the small-town imagery for American tourists, with its colorful country towns full of friendly smiles and rustic charm. More broadly, this was clearly also one of the effects of the end of the unbridled American self-confidence and the desire to return to envisioning the country through older, more reassuring ideas. In the late 1970s United States, the simple, rural American town was a strong symbol. From these small towns emerged a feeling of connection to traditional values, which many Americans wanted to reestablish. A sense of community was rooted in a simple, unpretentious way of life, removed from the influences of Washington, D.C., and full of a genuine, homely charm. Richard Francaviglia and Wayne Franklin have examined why small towns continue to captivate people by presenting them as a constant that stands out amid the rapid social and political transformations around the world.[105] The idea of small-town America as a model for the nation, however, was already in circulation well before Carter's election, with the most significant example being a tourist attraction: the 1955 opening of Disneyland, where Walt Disney portrayed an idealistic vision of an American Main Street.[106] Small-town America was thus already part of the national imaginary when Carter won the presidency, and Plains thus became a southern-style reaffirmation of a myth already present in American culture. This is why in 1976 the *Washington Post* could describe Carter's hometown as something "more like a Hollywood set than a real town."[107] Others were less enthusiastic about the stereotyped imagery. By the mid-1970s, the passion for small southern towns was so widespread in American cinema that the *Orlando Sentinel* wrote, "Are you folks getting weary (and wary) of movies about the wild life in small Southern towns? Boy, are we."[108]

Small-town America imagery, however, obviously had strong repercussions for the leisure industry, becoming a key asset for tourism in the South. As Valene Smith suggests, the quest for the picturesque and for "real" local color is indeed an important part of cultural tourism. Looking for an off-the-beaten-path experience, visitors swarm into small villages that have been purposefully converted into tourist sites and that offer such things as homespun fabrics, horse- or ox-drawn carts and plows, handmade crafts, home-cooked meals in rustic inns, and folklore performances.[109] "Many of our small towns, especially the county seats, were built around a central town square. Most are still the hub of activity for these rural, agricultural communities," announced an official South Carolina brochure in 1981.[110] Thus, not surprisingly, when Carter became a figure of national relevance, Plains immediately became the quintessential southern and American small town, or the "most famous small town in America," as the official tourist booklet produced in 1978 called it.

The new relationship the nation developed with the image of the South clearly did not lack conservative and even reactionary undertones. The rustic, down-home southern image appealed to a populist side of America that by the end of the 1970s had become a political force. The region's familiar, tradition-bound imagery was well suited to convey antigovernment and antiwelfare sentiments without resorting to explicit racist overtones. Those who protested or were frightened by the magnitude of major social changes taking place, such as the legalization of abortion, women's rights, integrated busing, gay rights, and general civil rights, had a source of reassurance in the idea of a rustic, religious, incorruptible South.[111]

Optimism about the alleged southern rebirth lasted throughout the 1980s, although more cautious views were always present. In the early 1990s, Joe Dunn summarized these ideas in his introduction to *The Future South*. Economic growth had been uneven in the region, with industrial, urban, socially progressive districts developing alongside large rural areas that were socially conservative and economically underdeveloped, where access to education was still problematic, especially for the Black population.[112] Alfred Eckes noted that the more rural areas of the Deep South (Alabama, Arkansas, Louisiana, and Mississippi) had been much less affected by the great economic growth of the region.[113]

As early as the late 1970s, however, an author like Walker Percy could look at his home region with disappointment, seeing it as nothing more than a subordinate extension of a "Los Angeles-Dallas-Atlanta axis" founded on an "agribusiness-sport-vacation-retirement-showbiz culture." It was Percy who provocatively introduced the concept of the "Losangelization" of the South.[114] Some authors reopened the debate over the demise of the region's identity even before the close of the decade. The South, according to Percy, had already dissolved within a new and culturally insignificant macro region: the Sunbelt. It is interesting to note, however, that among the factors responsible for the dispersal of southern singularity, Percy includes the "vacation-retirement culture." Indeed, among the many differences that had marked the progress of the Sunbelt was a fairly uneven growth of the tourism industry across the various subregions. While some former Confederate states had become (or continued to be) capable of attracting significant flows of visitors (Florida, Texas, New Orleans, and even Tennessee to some extent), others remained in the background or out of the tourist business altogether. Florida maintained its role as the trailblazer for southern tourism and retirement resorts, although new centers of some significance emerged during the 1970s.[115] Tourists were not just bringing in dollars; they were directly helping to lead some areas of the South out of economic underdevelopment and racial backwardness. Alfred Eckes rightly places this new flow of visitors—tourists, businessmen, workers, students or researchers—among the globalizing forces that changed the face of the South over the past half century.[116]

Then, at the end of the 1980s, the South as it had been known was once again given up for dead by some.[117] Yet again, it was mostly the South's blurred, undefinable new image as a cultural region that worried many. Some older elements persisted, while others had been added during the previous decade, thanks in part to the tourism industry. Yet no viable alternatives to previous traditional images and myths had been found.

Southern and American Tourism in the 1970s

Without a doubt, the 1970s and early 1980s were a time of particular importance for tourism in the United States. From a purely quantitative point of view, during that period, a considerable increase in the number of visitors from abroad was recorded. In the first six months of 1966, more than 600,000 foreigners had arrived in the country; by 1977 there were over 18,000,000.[118] Between 1965 and 1975, annual growth in entries was about 10 percent; between 1977 and 1982 it reached 18 percent, nearly doubling the previous record.[119] The decade ended with an active balance of the percentage of tourists to and from the United States: in 1981, for the first time ever, there were more foreigners who visited the United States than Americans who traveled abroad. The growth, however, was short lived, lasting from 1970 to 1981 and then declining.[120]

Several causes were behind this positive trend. A 1977 article in the *U.S. News and World Report* covered them in detail: good economic conditions in Europe and Japan led to higher wages and consequently a greater inclination to travel, cheaper flights, and a weaker dollar. But most importantly, the origin of this interest in America was to be found in the soft power of U.S. culture: "While America's political prestige may be declining in some areas of the world, this nation's reputation as a cultural leader is at an all-time high and still growing."[121] The article pointed out how many foreign nations were exposed to the captivating cultural model of America through the media. Internationally, the 1970s was a decade of constant doubt about America and its role in the world, a period in which the unanimous consensus on the "American century" was shattered and the American way of life strongly contested by various segments of western society. Nevertheless, the international media continued to be a vehicle for American imagery. This was also the result of the major role played by the American advertising industry, which, in the aftermath of World War II, was able to impose its language and style on the western world, together with its slogans and aggressive ad campaigns, which fueled and sometimes shaped the desires and needs of the non-American public. The great achievement of the United States was to make America the common standard within its vast global market empire.[122]

Although the 1970s were a time of crisis for the United States, the country was in no way perceived as dangerous or backward, nor was it considered unsafe for travel. Politically there were challenges, but there does not seem to have been any particular impact on tourist arrivals. It is true, of course, that the racial issues had represented an embarrassment for the United States, tarnishing its reputation since World War II and seriously undermining its role as leader of the western bloc.[123] By the 1970s, however, new problems had emerged; the war in Vietnam had ousted domestic racism as the main stain on the American image abroad. In other words, segregation had ceased to represent the United States in the common imagination.

In the mid-1960s, the United States Information Agency (USIA) released a report stating that the "treatment of the Negro seem to have comparatively little effect on general opinion of the U.S."[124] As Mary Dudziak pointed out, by that time American promotional policies and soft power had already succeeded in convincing international opinion that the situation of Black Americans was steadily improving and that the problem had almost been resolved, thus succeeding in redirecting public indignation and disapproval toward more specific targets: "The target of blame is now largely a white supremacist minority."[125] In other words, the buck was passed to an aggressive minority and not to the entire South.

At the same time, it has yet to be proven that segregation and the struggle for civil rights were ever actually a problem for tourism in America. Foreign entry data in statistical abstracts by the U.S. Census Bureau, for example, shows a steady growth in the years between 1955 and 1979. Undoubtedly, the reputation of a segregated South had resonated with international public opinion since the 1950s, but if anything, it merely discouraged travel to the South, not the United States as a whole. The South remained a primarily domestic tourist destination, the majority of its visitors coming from within the region—that is, southerners traveling across the South. Foreign tourists were only a small part of the market, and most of these were Canadians, certainly more accustomed to American racial mores than overseas tourists. This allowed the region to develop a tourism market without being particularly affected by local issues. However, when the Deep South states began to promote themselves to a broader international audience, they had to deal directly with the issue of their negative reputation. Still in 1981 the director of Alabama's tourist bureau had to reassure the British public that her state was no longer the same one they had seen on television news reports in the sixties.[126]

In the quest for tourist money, each state worked individually. There was very little action on the part of the federal government to promote national tourism. National campaigns aimed at selling the United States as a travel destination were very few, limited in scope, and far behind those of many European and Latin American countries.[127] The 1970s, and particularly the Carter era, were a time of great debate on the role of tourism in the national economy.

In 1981, tourism consultant Bernetta Hayes admitted that although the United States was a highly industrialized country at the forefront of many western nations, it was also "somewhat underdeveloped with regard to tourism."[128] The problem lay in a weak national tourism policy, managed by the USTS, a relatively young government office (founded only in 1961) with limited resources. This demonstrates, if nothing else, that the steady growth of international visitors to the United States during the 1970s can really be attributed to favorable conditions and soft power rather than to any specific national promotional strategy.

With this in mind, it is not surprising that the South occupied a marginal position in the promotional work of the USTS. The Travel Service designed few promotional items altogether, allocating little or no space to the region even in these rare publications. As mentioned above, each state had to take care of its own tourism promotion for both the domestic and international markets. The South partly overcame this lack of top-down national coordination by founding in 1965 a regional tourism organization, the Southern Travel Directors Council (STDC), better known as Travel South USA, through which member states promoted themselves in America and Canada (and only later abroad) as a distinct unified region:

> The guiding philosophy of STDC since its inception has been that member states can sell themselves effectively to travelers if the south as a region is sold; that the traveler is not interested so much in state boundaries, but in specific places, attractions and events.[129]

In other words, the group's charter recognized that in order to develop its potential, the South needed to promote itself as a region through its *specific places, attractions, and events*. However, until the mid-seventies Travel South USA hardly ever engaged in international promotion, with the exception of Canada, the country that generated the largest foreign tourist flow to the South.[130]

It is difficult to determine how many international tourists actually arrived in the South during this period. It is known that in 1977 there were about 3.2 million, corresponding to about 17 percent of the total number of visitors to the United States.[131] Of these, nearly 60 percent were from Canada, 35 percent from overseas countries, and 8 percent from Mexico. In 1980 Travel South USA attempted to calculate an average and estimated about 16,500 foreign visitors moving through the region every day.[132] Canada remained the main country of departure, especially in the coastal South. By the early 1970s, for example, about 35,000 Canadians were arriving in South Carolina's Grand Strand each March. Already during the 1960s, Canadian tourism was such an important asset for the southern travel industry that some tourist areas began launching targeted promotional initiatives such as Canada Days (Myrtle Beach) or Canadian Holiday (Virginia Beach) to capitalize on that market.[133]

Even more challenging would be to determine which travel locations were preferred by foreigners in the South. Without a doubt Florida appears as the main destination. In 1980, 327,000 British visitors (not counting Canadians and other nationalities) were estimated traveling to Miami Beach alone.[134] To give an idea of the gap between Florida and the other Deep South states, it is sufficient to note that in 1981 South Carolina considered it a success to have welcomed 17,000 tourists from outside national borders, 6,000 of them from the United Kingdom.[135] Even in Atlanta, the South's main international port of entry, just over 15,000 foreigners had landed in 1980 (not counting Canadians).[136]

In 1979, however, the USTS clearly stated that the South was the third largest region in terms of the number of international visits, but second only to the Far West in terms of the "preference" of foreign tourists—that is, the areas that they indicated as their ideal destinations in the United States.[137] The legendary Wild West was indeed a favorite stop for foreign travelers, though few actually visited it.[138] This fact is especially illustrative of how pop culture, movies, television, and even commercial advertising can influence the perception of an entire region and its destination image. For many, the desire to experience the Wild West was (and still is) more a desire to participate in a myth than to visit a real place. Therefore, it is not surprising that the interest of such individuals did not materialize into actual tourism. As Paul Christensen reminds us, this is as true for foreigners as it is for Americans themselves.[139] Incidentally, the region that was visited by the largest number of foreigners was the Eastern Gateway, i.e., the New York City area. While this was by no means the most "desired" destination, it was arguably the easiest to reach (thanks to direct flights) and the area with the highest concentration of attractions. The South, however, was preferred as an ideal. Non-Americans recognized the South as unique and were attracted not only to the beaches of Miami, but to something more picturesque and fascinating, often glimpsed through media. The 1939 film *Gone with the Wind*, for example, was a true international cult phenomenon that largely contributed to the establishment of a mythical image for the South in the rest of the world. Still, the lure of the myth did not necessarily translate into a trip to the region.

Material on the South produced by the USTS during the 1970s is scarce and not particularly elaborate. In 1977, the Travel Service published a list of the promotional posters that they had distributed nationwide. One poster, titled *The South*, exclusively depicted an "antebellum plantation and young girl"[140]—another repetition of the old belle and plantation theme, further evidence that the national tourism office also helped promote this kind of imagery, considering it a true American symbol. There were also two small-format brochures, one on Florida, the other on New Orleans. However, the antebellum plantation remained the only image of the South as a region. These brochures created by the USTS demonstrate another interesting point: none of them focused exclusively on the South as a whole, despite the fact that they were designed in the midst of the 1970s southern fashion frenzy. Another brochure was dedicated to *Atlanta and Georgia with North and South Carolina* and one to *New Orleans and the South*.[141] This shows how both Atlanta and New Orleans were identified as major southern tourist destinations (in addition to Florida, of course), while Alabama, Arkansas, Mississippi, and even Tennessee were placed in a subordinate role, apparently less easy to advertise and almost unknown to foreign audiences (as well as more difficult to reach). Nevertheless, a change seems to have occurred from the previous decade. In the list of material published by the USTS in 1968, there is no presentation of the South as a region, and only occasional posters of individual states were produced, including one from South Carolina depicting the usual antebellum mansion.[142]

Tourism promoters also knew that the antebellum home had attained immortal fame through *Gone with the Wind*, reaching a wide international audience. As late as 1980, the USTS openly advised South Carolina to exploit the popularity of *Gone with the Wind* for its promotion in Europe.[143] It was the southern equivalent to the classic cowboy-and-Indian theme used to promote the West. There was no particular difference from the early twentieth century: the old antebellum South remained the main reference of the southern destination image, a picture that appealed to international audiences no less than to Americans. This promotional activity was, however, entirely internal to the national tourist bureau, and the southern states had little or nothing to do with it. Thus, the USTS seemed to maintain a stereotypical view of the South, treating it as a thematic region on par with the Far West. We will see later on that the image southern states promoted for themselves in those same years, both through the collective organization Travel South USA and individual advertising, was far more complex.

Meanwhile the southern tourism industry seemed to flourish. By the mid-1970s, and especially in the second half of the decade, the general consensus was that the region was experiencing a tourism boom that had never been seen before. In 1976, *The South Magazine* published an article triumphantly titled "Tourism: A '76 Gold Rush."[144] According to the piece, there were five reasons that explained this influx of visitors: (1) an increase in vacation packages and tours promoted and sold by the travel industry; (2) more conventions and meetings held in the South; (3) the growth of southern nightlife; (4) new theme parks ("undoubtedly the country's major theme park focus is southern"); (5) a trend toward more frequent but shorter trips. All of these causes pointed to the economic growth and general increase in domestic travel across the Sunbelt. In those years, articles and editorials dedicated to this growing number of visitors were common and often particularly enthusiastic: "There's a new war between the states, but this one is limited to the South and the objective is the Yankee and Canadian tourist."[145]

The election of Jimmy Carter played a minor role in the burgeoning southern tourism industry. It certainly benefitted Georgia—where, while his popularity endured, visitors flocked to visit the president's hometown of Plains— but the overall impact on tourism in the South seems to have been minimal. Governor George Busbee was well aware that "the president and the Carter family are, very definitely, an attraction at the present time," but this so-called "Carter mystique" did little to increase the number of arrivals in the rest of the South.[146] In fact, no mention of the 1976 election can be found in the tourism bureau records of Alabama, Mississippi, or South Carolina.

Without a doubt, the new president briefly gave free publicity to the region, but this effect was too short lived to quantify within the local tourism industries. It can be said that the Carter mystique faded even before the end of the presidential term due to the president's growing unpopularity. It must also be remembered that the American (and southern) tourism industry eventually saw Carter as an antagonist rather than a potential ally. The conflict began when the administration in Washington was prepared to close the weak national tourist office permanently. In 1978, the Office of Management and Budget (OMB) lobbied to eliminate the USTS as a separate and distinct entity within the Department of Commerce. The reason was clear: the growth of tourism in the United States was not considered the result of government promotional programs, making the USTS appear essentially useless. The private sector was fully capable of handling it in a much more efficient manner (as in fact it was already doing). Foreign advertising produced by American airline companies and hotel chains generated far more visits than Travel Service promotional material. For the OMB, the obvious conclusion was that the six foreign offices of the USTS should be closed as soon as possible.[147] Among the many voices within the tourism industry raised against the Carter administration's decision was that of Travel South USA, which had developed a successful relationship with the USTS since 1967, especially with regard to overseas promotion.[148]

Optimism, however, remained strong. "The South Rises Again—as Draw for Tourists," stated the *Orlando Sentinel* in 1977; three years later *Travel Trade* ran almost the same headline.[149] Growth was steady, and in 1979 the *Southern*

Traveler reported a record year for southern tourism.[150] The following year, figures published by Travel South indicated that 26 percent of all tourists in America were in the South, certainly a remarkable percentage for a region that covered only about 13 percent of the nation's surface.[151]

In 1976, an internal ranking of the region was attempted by *The South Magazine* based on state tourism office budgets and the dollars spent by visitors in individual states. The results obviously had Florida in the lead, followed by Georgia and Virginia. Alabama, Arkansas, South Carolina, and Mississippi were at the bottom of the list.[152]

The most significant data on southern tourism, however, concerns the origin of domestic visitors passing through the region. For the year 1979, Travel South USA produced a report where it calculated how many millions of people came to the South from the various areas of the United States.[153] The results showed that the majority of visitors, about 60 percent, were from southern states: "In sum, Travel South residents prefer their own region to any other for their travel by nearly four to one."[154] According to Census of Transportation data for 1967, the situation had changed since the previous decade. During 1957, in fact, about 73 percent of "leisure" travel from the South had come from within the region.[155] It is true, then, that southerners now traveled more outside their region, but they still constituted the majority of local visitors.

The fact that a large part of tourists were local does not mean that the South ignored the rest of the country in its promotional activities. The advertisements produced by state tourism offices were often the same, whether they were to be circulated within the region, within the state itself, or across the rest of the country. In short, promotional materials were almost never designed to appeal exclusively to (white) southern society. Even the moonlight-and-magnolias South, with its picturesque and timeless charm, was all the more appealing the farther one strayed from Dixie's geographical boundaries.

One question for the tourism industry was what kinds of visitors came to see certain specific attractions. Who, for example, were the tourists who visited antebellum homes? Were they southern whites, whites from other parts of the Union, or people from abroad? The answer, as will be fairly clear by now, is that such sites were favored destinations especially for white tourists from outside the region's boundaries. Stephen Birdsall conducts an interesting analysis of travel articles about the South that appeared in the *New York Times* between 1950 and 1980. Despite being based in the North, even during the civil rights years the *Times* continued to publish articles celebrating the romantic antebellum South and historical sites related to the Civil War. Ironically, Birdsall concluded that "the only reason the *Times* could tell its readers to go to Mississippi was to experience the serenity and graciousness of that state's rebuilt plantation estates."[156] Meanwhile, Governor Finch of Mississippi launched a campaign in 1977 specifically aimed at encouraging residents to visit their state as tourists: "In our beautiful countryside, we have numerous attractions such as water mills, Indian mounds and *antebellum homes that Mississippians seldom see.*"[157]

The Rise of African American Tourism

The seventies were also marked by the emergence of African American tourism. There is no need to point out how segregation made the act of traveling not only nearly impossible, but also physically dangerous for African Americans. Since the nineteenth century, "Jim Crow travel" had stood out as one of the most despised forms of subordination among African Americans, serving as a potent catalyst for their ongoing struggle to assert their rights and secure freedom of movement. As Mia Bay shows, there was no means of transportation, not even the automobile, that was exempt from race-related concerns.[158] This was not just a southern problem. De facto segregation and plain intolerance were experienced even beyond the South's regional borders. In the aftermath of the World War II the National Association for the Advancement of Colored People (NAACP) newspaper *The Crisis* complained that Black people could not travel safely across the country.[159] As one Mississippi man wrote to the *Pittsburgh Courier*, a Black newspaper, in October 1961, problems also occurred when traveling in the North and the West.[160]

From 1936 until 1966, the renowned *Negro Motorist Green Book* was published, the existence of which is itself a testament to the difficulty that Blacks had in being actual "tourists." It consisted of a travel guide containing lists of establishments that did not discriminate against Blacks as well as a series of tips to make travel safer. As late as 1965, African American author John A. Williams wrote in his book *This Is My Country Too*: "I do not believe white travelers have any idea of how much nerve and courage it requires for a Negro to drive coast to coast in America."[161] The reportage of his journey through the South is a vivid account of the anxieties and dangers that a Black man faced when crossing the Mason-Dixon line. It was not uncommon for African American travelers simply to disappear along the way or to run into a sundown town.[162]

By the mid-1960s, the South remained a problematic destination for Black America, despite high expectations for a new South. Just four months after the passage of the Civil Rights Act of 1964, the *St. Petersburg Times* sent an African American reporter, Samuel Adams, and his wife on a road trip through the twelve southern states to report on the effect of the legislation on Black tourism.[163] Although they tended to be optimistic, their weekly reports did not fail to point out the problems a Black person encountered in the South.

The situation, however, changed rapidly between the late 1960s and early 1970s. The Black tourism market was expanding and the desegregation of public facilities helped open the South to visitors of all races. In 1972, an editorial in *Black Enterprise* announced that African American tourism was an $800,000,000-a-year business, and predictions for the future looked just as bright.[164] The following year, a headline in the *Detroit Free Press* read, "Black Tourist Boom: A Sleeping Giant Rouses."[165] Once they regained the freedom they had long been denied, Blacks began to travel extensively, both across America and abroad. Tourism is itself a "totem of freedom," as the act of traveling represents a "ritual" associated with being a free member of a free society.[166] African Americans' interest in travel and tourism was growing so much and so rapidly that by the mid-1970s the tourism industry began taking notice of this new and expanding market.[167]

Where did African Americans go on vacation? Black tourists in the seventies chose such destinations as Africa (especially after the popular TV series *Roots*), the Caribbean, and to a lesser extent Europe, all areas where African Americans felt safe from racial prejudice. In the USA, on the other hand, their main destinations were Los Angeles, Miami Beach, San Francisco, Atlantic City, and New England.[168] Even the major tourist destinations in the (urban) South were being visited by an increasing number of Black tourists. A 1979 travel article claimed that the cities with most Black tourism were Atlanta, New Orleans, Miami, Houston, and Dallas.[169]

It is difficult to say how widespread Black tourism actually was in the Deep South, beyond the celebratory and often exaggerated statements found in Black newspapers of the time. Undoubtedly, Black tourism existed and represented a sizable portion of the market even in the 1970s. This was not only because many African Americans had their roots in the Deep South and therefore tended to return there, but also because civil rights tourism soon became a lucrative business for Black travel agencies. Moreover, the attitude of Black society toward its history had also changed greatly. The humiliation and shame over the past of slavery had been overcome. Beginning in the mid-1960s, new powerful ideologies of Black American pride were developing in parallel with Black nationalism, especially what Kamari Clarke refers to as the "slavery narrative" and the "African nobility-redemption narrative."[170] These were new ways of interpreting their past and experience, accepting and even finding pride in the hardships experienced by their ancestors. Africa became a great homeland for African Americans and the place to visit to trace one's roots. Many historical and cultural heritage sites in the United States also benefited from the influx of Black visitors in search of their past. Not surprisingly, the American tourism industry quickly saw a lucrative opportunity in Black heritage tourism and acted accordingly. During the travel boom of the 1970s, the tourism sector looked to the newfound interest in African and African American history and culture to create and market new products to Black audiences.[171]

It would have been extremely naive and counterproductive for the southern states to pretend that none of this was happening. And they did not. That is why this rapid irruption of the Black world into the tourist market should be regarded as one of the forces that undermined the univocal interpretation of the southern landscape as an antebellum garden. After all, the southern economy had already demonstrated its ability to mediate between conservative white traditionalism and the acceptance of a new status quo, a lesson learned between the 1950s and 1960s: Jim Crow was not good for the economy.

The 1970s also represented a pivotal moment in the relationship between Black society and the South in a deeper sense. This is noted by James Cobb when he reports data from a series of surveys taken between the mid-1960s and 1970s: in 1964 only 55 percent of Blacks (southerners and non-southerners) responded that they had "warm feelings toward southerners"; by 1976 it was 80 percent.[172] At the same time, the self-identification of Black southerners as *southerners* was growing, as was their inclination to travel to the region. In 1977, a travel article about the South in *Black Enterprise* summed up this new scenario when it announced, "Now the South has changed."[173]

Let us be clear: the initial impact of Black tourism on tourist promotion in the seventies South should not be overstated. State promotion, even in the early eighties, was almost entirely white-centered. Only in the 1980s and 1990s did political motivations and economic interests finally change this situation.[174] It was not until 1983, for example, during George Wallace's last term as governor, that Alabama became the first state in the former Confederacy (and the United States) to publish a tourist guide dedicated exclusively to African American tourists.

Nor was this enough to solve the underlying problems of a tourism system often divided by skin color. Bringing African American history and experience to bear on the classic white southern narrative remained a complex problem. It ran the risk of creating two touristic worlds that ran parallel without meeting, promoting attractions "for Blacks" and attractions "for whites" in a reproposition of the segregationist idea. Some, in fact, criticized Alabama's 1983 tourist guide as an attempt to segregate tourism.[175] The problem is far from trivial, and even today there are signs of a similar debate. When looking at contemporary guidebooks, it is impossible to ignore the tendency to use photographs of Black tourists at Civil Rights or Black heritage tourist sites, underrepresenting them in images of other activities, as if to say that these sites are actually "Black attractions" more than historic or heritage sites for all.[176]

By the 1970s, however, state travel offices were slowly adapting to the growing number of Black travelers. More and more southern states began placing advertisements in major Black American magazines. Up until 1976, only sporadic ads appeared in the monthly magazine *Ebony* by the offices of Florida, Virginia, Tennessee, and Louisiana; in 1979, Georgia joined their ranks, and in 1981 even Alabama placed one of its ads in the magazine.

While all this was indicative of a new phase, in the late seventies most Black tourism seems to have been completely disconnected from the activities of state travel offices, as it depended mostly on private travel agencies, especially those run by African Americans. It is no coincidence that a report by the National Tourism Resources Review Commission showed that between 1968 and 1972 the number of Black tourism agencies in the United States doubled from 65 to 120.[177] Some Black heritage tours and packages existed in the South during the 1970s, but they were not officially managed or structured by any state office.

The problem of underrepresentation also reflects the American advertising industry's attitude toward African American society, a widely examined subject.[178] Research has shown how Blacks have historically been subjected to misrepresentation in advertisements, often portrayed in subordinate positions with very light skin tones or "white" facial features. By the 1970s this trend had mostly disappeared, but the underrepresentation of Blacks in the overall picture continued, whether in ads, pamphlets, or brochures. This was true, of course, of ads designed for the mainstream public, i.e., white people, which was the target audience for all the major publications produced by state travel offices. All of the ads (both tourist and nontourist) that appeared in magazines for African Americans, on the other hand, portrayed people of color. This is another example of these two worlds proceeding in parallel. Yet something was about to change on a deeper plane, precisely because during this period state tourism offices began to reflect on the issue of minority inclusion, recognizing it as a problem to be addressed.

One of the most interesting aspects of Black tourism concerns those historical and cultural attractions that African American society "shared," so to speak, with white society. An important feature of a number of southern plantations and heritage sites is that in the 1970s they began to be visited by Black tourists as well, despite the fact that their narrative setting was usually entirely white-centric. This was certainly a small percentage of visitors, at least in proportion to the total, but it is still important in helping us understand how a counternarrative view of an event or a place could strip the Lost Cause of its interpretation of the past, to the benefit of that part of the society that did not participate in the dominant discourse. In the 1970s two of these sites were Fort Sumter in South Carolina and the Atlanta Cyclorama in Georgia, which will be discussed in more detail in chapter 4. Clearly, when visiting a given historic/heritage site, African Americans may not have been looking for the same experience as non-Black visitors. In many cases they had another narrative and another past to confirm through their visit, different from the one officially conveyed by the site in question. A plantation thus became not a place of antebellum nostalgia but a site of Black heritage and roots tourism; a Civil War battlefield was a site to commemorate the sacrifice of African American Union soldiers; and so on. Moreover, sites that celebrated the Lost Cause could be interpreted by Blacks as places of so-called dark tourism or dissonant heritage.[179]

What is most important to note here, however, is how the growth of Black heritage tourism coincided with the establishment of multiple civil rights memorials in the South, eroding, essentially for the first time, the white-centric landscape of the South. In other words, a clash over the interpretation of regional history reflected an internal clash within southern cultural tourism.[180]

The 1970s were undoubtedly the moment in which a reflection on the meaning of the past and its transmission first began in America. Important progress was made, albeit slowly, on the inclusion of minorities in historical memory. In 1970, the National Park Service initiated a program to designate a number of important Black heritage sites as national historic landmarks. Initially, thirteen were chosen, but sixty-one more were added by 1977.[181] At the same time, Black history became a field of study and research in many universities, forcing a critical rethinking and reevaluation of American history as a whole. These were all fairly recent innovations, to which the tourism industry adapted slowly and with difficulty.

CHAPTER 2

The Tourism Industry in the Deep South of the 1970s

Problems, Targets, and Resources

Travel South USA and the Destination Image of the South

In 1965, in order to overcome existing promotional issues such as inadequate funding, intense competition among neighboring states, and lack of logistics, eleven southern states founded a regional association with specific competencies in the field of tourism promotion. This was the Southern Travel Directors Council, or Travel South USA, which grouped together Virginia, North Carolina, South Carolina, Georgia, Florida, Kentucky, Tennessee, Alabama, Arkansas, Mississippi, and Louisiana. Texas, regionally projected toward the West, was not part of this group, while Kentucky was included despite the fact that it usually did not fit the classic definition of the South. Upon payment of an annual fee by each member state, the association would streamline promotional efforts, purchase advertising space in newspapers and magazines—often several large-size color pages—and allow the states to present themselves as one region at conventions and during travel trade shows. Each state had its own space in Travel South's ads and promotional articles, although not all participated on every occasion. The consortium operated primarily in the domestic market, promoting the South across the United States, but it was also able to reach other countries. The foreign market of reference was Canada, with several ads published in local newspapers in the areas of Toronto, Montreal, and Ottawa.[1] Later, between 1977 and 1981, the association began to test the ground in Europe through a series of missions, including conventions and meetings in West Germany, France, the United Kingdom, Denmark, and Sweden.[2]

An important step forward for regional tourism promotion happened in 1974, when Travel South adopted a five-year plan whose goals were to increase the visibility and awareness of the South as a tourist destination for the general public and to establish the South as a promotionally minded region. Among the different strategies to achieve the goals were a list of promotional themes to bring into focus: the music of the South, history and scenery, theme park development, natural attractions, and special events.[3] The southern tourism industry, in other words, was working to create a single coherent destination image for the region, based on many different themes suitable for the modern tourist market. The challenge was not so simple, because the participating states had major differences among themselves, and finding elements to build a unified image required some deep reflection on the postintegration South. A 1975 Travel South insert rhetorically asked what united the South and answered that it was mostly its past: "What ties Alabama, Arkansas, Florida, Georgia, Kentucky, Louisiana, Mississippi, North Carolina, South Carolina, Tennessee, and Virginia into a regional unit as cohesive as any in the country is a shared legacy of Civil War, Reconstruction, and a set of controversial social customs that perished only a decade ago." But now, as the region is "striding energetically into the forefront of late 20th-Century American life," the ad continues, "it's in traditional music and food, perhaps more than in any other categories, that the legendary South lives on."[4] It is worth noting that while music and food are today key assets for the southern recreational industry, in the 1970s they were just beginning to develop as viable tourism themes. New elements were thus being discovered to set the South apart from the rest of the country and to unite it under one coherent destination image.

The magazines in which Travel South placed its ads are indicative of the promotional strategy the group intended to pursue, even though these did not change significantly over time. In fact, since 1973, the earliest date for which publication records are available, the magazines have remained the same with few additions. These ranged from periodicals aimed at a female audience, such as *House Beautiful, House & Garden,* and *Modern Bride,* to men's sports magazines, including *Golf Magazine, Field & Stream,* and *Tennis.*[5] Clearly, in keeping with the idea that tourism was made up of various niche aspects, different types of advertisements were designed for different magazines. Thus, in sports magazines, one finds Travel South ads dedicated exclusively to golf courses or tennis clubs in the South, while in women's periodicals like *House Beautiful* the focus was on southern romance and scenic beauty.

On other occasions, a more general promotion was carried out, describing and selling the idea of the South in its entirety. A 1977 Travel South promotional piece sums up the logic behind this sales strategy. The South was "a region with a unique past, an exciting present, and a predicted future of unprecedented achievement." The region was beautiful, romantic, and blessed with a singular past and history, combined with an ideal landscape and climate for a perfect seaside or mountain vacation—a culture, according to the ad, bound to traditions but "advancing into a bright future."[6] The penchant for the past now interacted with an equally vibrant present aimed toward modernity and the future.

The idea of a South caught in the middle of a dynamic transition and therefore already modern was, paradoxically, an old one. In the mid-1960s, an association involving Arkansas, Louisiana, and Mississippi known as Middle South, which also focused on tourism, invited readers to "come see the Changing Middle South, where the legacy of beauty, charm and history blends so remarkably with the growing, dynamic present."[7] The photo was emblematic: a girl in a nineteenth-century Scarlett O'Hara costume, posed in front of the usual columned mansion, but leaning against a luxurious modern car. Likewise, as early as 1941, Alabama ran its own advertisement inviting people to visit a "Romantic and progressive Alabama," where "the old South blends with the new."[8]

Therefore, this extremely generic notion of a natural coexistence between old and new was already part of the southern promotional strategy. What changed, if anything, was that by the 1960s this concept appeared to be largely disconnected from the actual condition of the local tourism landscape. Despite the slogans, the proposed attractions were for the most part the same old ones. When earlier ads extolled "progress" and the "new," however, their main purpose was actually to present states as suitable for economic investment and industry rather than as attractive tourist destinations. Thus, for example, a promotional ad produced by Mississippi in 1948 stated that "Mississippians today turn a proud ear to the hum of farm machinery being echoed by the busy noise of nearby factories."[9] In the tourist material of the 1970s, on the other hand, the idea of modernity was more closely linked to purely recreational activities, such as through city nightlife, elegant beach facilities, fashionable hotels and resorts, and classy restaurants. So in the 1977 promotional text produced by Travel South, the emphasis on the modern, cosmopolitan nature of the South was much less generic than before. The claim that the region was changing or that the future had arrived was not unfounded. There was a marked insistence that in the South it was now possible to experience "bustling, big-league cities, filled with modern hotels and international dining and shopping," as well as to embark on comfortable first-class travels thanks to new "ultra-modern facilities." The traditional antebellum, rural, and antimodern South, though visible as a watermark in the text, was now only part of the overall picture.

Granted, the South described by Travel South still left no room for nonwhite culture or tradition, lacking any reference to African Americans or Native-related historical sites or attractions, the region was presented through a kaleidoscope of different themes—from music and landscape to water sports and city nightlife—already appearing as that tourist South described by Ted Ownby in the early 2000s: rich in everything, but confusing and indeterminate. The antebellum theme figured as a subsidiary element in the 1977 script and was never directly mentioned. Antebellum homes were referred to only twice in about 120 lines of text, and only on one occasion was reference made to the Civil War, cited as "the awesome War Between the States," a name rooted in the Lost Cause that seemed to locate the conflict somewhere between the monumental and playful, presenting it as a spectacular rather than tragic past event.

In 1979, for the first time, Travel South USA published its own promotional booklet titled *Come to the Warm*.[10] Once again, a multitude of different messages and promotional ideas were contained. The most important, also highlighted by the romantic photo of a red sunset by the sea on the brochure cover, was that of the beautiful southern landscape and mild weather. The Lost Cause appears in the text, but is certainly not predominant. The Confederate generals portrayed on the side of Stone Mountain, for example, are referred to as "Southern legends," and the Civil War is still cited as the "War Between the States." Nevertheless, the antebellum charm is only a small part of the many attractions offered to readers. More space is devoted to beaches, scenic tourism, excursions, hiking, parks and general attractions, and even southern music. When an antebellum home is mentioned in the section on Mississippi, the reference is accompanied by the words of the local site manager who explains how "one of our purposes is to lend historical accuracy *to an often over-romanticized segment of southern history*."[11] On this occasion the myth is explicitly denied. This is not to say, of course, that all antebellum houses in the South shared the same mission, but it is relevant to note that the official Travel South booklet chose to promote one specific antebellum home using that precise message. *Come to the Warm* portrays a constant sense of irreversible change in the South. The Old South seems to be fading away while still maintaining that "romantic personality of an aging South." On this occasion the section on southern music also features a Black artist, the legendary "Father of the Blues," W. C. Handy.

Ultimately, the themes were many and all equally represented in order to engage a tourist market that was no longer structured solely around long, relaxing family trips. Promotion had to be designed for specific niche interests (seaside tourism, historical tourism, outdoor activities, sports, vacation spots for retired couples, and so on). In short, the South needed to make itself attractive in the eyes of outdoor and sports enthusiasts as well as music and entertainment aficionados, providing them all with the most modern comforts. It is also interesting to note the total absence in both the 1977 piece and the 1979 booklet of any reference to food tourism or southern cuisine in general. Only a few sporadic mentions of this theme appeared in some smaller inserts, such as the 1975 ad previously mentioned. The establishment of southern cuisine as a central pillar of the regional destination image, in fact, was only just emerging at that time and was not yet a stable asset. Clearly, the focus on regional cuisine that developed during the 1970s reflected the cultural context of the decade, with its renewed interest in heritage and local traditions.[12] Even in this case, the southern tourism industry seems to have been in a phase of transition. In 1981, Alabama's tourism director Caroline Cavanaugh, upon leaving for Washington, D.C., to attend an industry meeting to promote the South along with other regional representatives, told the press, "We feel one of the big attractions of the South is its food."[13] This would turn out to be one of the main themes presented during the Washington meeting, and from Cavanaugh's words it is possible to sense that this was still an uncharted territory in the field of southern promotion. It is therefore very likely that the ensuing strategy centered on southern food, which now has become extremely popular in Deep South tourism, was born right there from the work of the Travel South group in the late 1970s and early 1980s. Interviewed in Scotland in 1982, Cavanaugh explained that it was possible to carry out gourmet tours in Alabama, something that had not appeared in the promotional material immediately preceding that date.[14] In those years the idea of food as a distinctive southern feature was also explored from a cultural point of view, culminating in John Egerton's great classic *Southern Food: At Home, on the Road, in History*, the result of his three-year journey across the eleven southern states in search of a connection between food and local culture.[15] Not surprisingly, Rick McDaniel notes a resurgence in southern regional cuisine during the late 1970s, a process that was further fostered by the arrival of television cooking shows in the 1980s.[16] This was the reaction of a regional culture that wished to explore its own distinctive traits during a time of profound change.

All of the Travel South material produced between 1977 and 1981 basically leads back to a single idea that can now be defined as a real promotional strategy, namely, to present the South as a destination suitable for everyone. This was also the case with Travel South's 1980 short promotional movie *The South*, described as "a visual interpretation of the entire spectrum of the South, both old and new," with the stated intention of "relating the romantic past of the South to exciting modern day travel and recreation opportunities."[17] However, it is a Travel South minibooklet from 1981 dedicated to honeymoon trips that best displays the new southern destination image. The brochure opens with the image of a young (white) couple on a beach, accompanied by the following text:

The South is a *performer of many moods, enough to master any scene. She's what-ever the script calls for, and that is, quite simply, whatever you want her to be.* You can have her play the city electric, up-tempo, and ablaze with life. Or you can follow her lead into a refreshing mountain wilderness. Everything necessary to make a honeymoon warm and happy is there. The cornucopia of pleasures she offers is gigantic. . . . *Nowhere is the South more vital than in her cities*—they cap-ture a South in the fast lane. Nightlife thrives after daytime's progressive beat.[18]

Here the authors go so far as to promote the "city" as the true heart of the South, something totally opposite the classic rural aesthetic. Moreover, throughout the text, the honeymoon romance is never associated with any-thing even remotely antebellum or traditional. Rather, the booklet is a clear promotional piece designed specifically for young couples from whom no particular interest in the Old South is expected, furnished with multiple ref-erences to the South as a place where all sorts of attractions could be found.

At the same time, Travel South was not responsible for the promotional ac-tivities of individual states, with each group member pursuing their own strat-egies and advertising campaigns in parallel. With more or less emphasis, each states tried to present itself as a complete, self-sufficient destination, providing every possible kind of attraction, simultaneously tied to the past and projected into the future. Within this general framework, each attempted to carve out its own space distinct from its competitors. From a promotional point of view, this was no minor issue. Most southern states offered similar attractions, with the risk of producing destination images that were difficult to distinguish one from another. South Carolina, for example, in 1979, acknowledged as competi-tors all those states that offered attractions similar to its own, i.e., beaches, his-torical sites, tennis courts, golf courses, camping, and fishing. Ranking highest among these competitors were Georgia, Florida, and North Carolina, followed by Alabama, Arkansas, Kentucky, Louisiana, Mississippi and Tennessee—in other words, the entire South.[19]

The lack of interstate coordination also led to the formation of two differ-ent interregional groups with distinct tourism-related missions, both of which existed before Travel South was established in 1965. Mississippi joined forces with Louisiana and Arkansas in a group known as Middle South, which in-cluded tourism promotion among its functions. Georgia and South Carolina, on the other hand, along with Virginia, North Carolina and Florida, formed the Coastal Plains Regional Commission (CPRC) with its own promotional tourism brand, Coastal South, which was decidedly oriented toward a sea-side and beach destination image. Middle South promotion was more about southern culture and traditional themes, as will be seen when we discuss Mississippi in detail. In both cases, however, the promotional activities of these subregions, quite limited in number, ran in parallel to those of Travel South as well as those developed independently by each individual state. Here the construction and reshaping of their promotional image became even more complex. It was a process that took place at various levels, with different actors involved, beginning with experts in the individual state tourist offices and later shifting from the regional South to the subregional macro-areas. At the same time, one should not forget local agents and private individuals involved in tourism, as well as the political establishment.

By the end of the 1970s, the results of these efforts were quite clear. The South as a tourist region already appeared quite different from the classic southern clichés described by W. Fitzhugh Brundage in the previous decade. The emphasis on modernity should not be surprising: it was, as we have seen, an old notion. What is striking, instead, marking a clear break from the previous old-fashioned promotion, is the recourse to the idea of an abundance of different attractions. The South was no longer considered only the romantic, antimodern part of the country. While this aspect partly remained, there was now room for theme parks, sports, nightlife, fashionable resorts, breathtaking modern scenery, musical tradition, and much more. It comes almost as a surprise that the USTS would choose an image of a Scarlett O'Hara look-alike and an antebellum home for its southern promotional poster. One can imagine that if the choice had been left to the discretion of Travel South the poster would have depicted a sunset over the Atlantic Ocean or the Atlanta skyline. This is not because the Lost Cause had ceased to represent an important part of the southern and American imagination tout court—far from it. However, there was clearly a desire to replace it as the main regional theme. A Travel South brochure from the mid-1970s made this clear: "Sure, these eleven states are the heart of the Old South. Everybody knows that. . . . But this is only a part of what makes these eleven states our nation's greatest vacation area. The truth is, whatever you and your family may like to do on vacation, you can find it here—in super abundance and at prices you can afford."[20]

Politics and Tourism in Alabama, Mississippi, Georgia, and South Carolina

The regional tourism promoters were able to embark on this new course also due to the changes in the political and economic situation in the South. From the second half of the 1970s, the South was going through a period of tremendous growth in its tourism industry. In the internal reports of the industry as well as in southern newspapers, there were particularly optimistic accounts of a boom in arrivals and easily earned dollars. In 1976 the South was listed as the top destination for American vacationers, followed by the Great Lakes region and the Far West.[21] Optimism increased throughout 1979 as the various figures provided a sense of relief that not even the dreaded energy crisis seemed to have shaken regional tourism. That same year also saw a significant increase in the number of international arrivals. The South was being celebrated by Travel South as the most visited area in the country; moreover, American tourists had spent $29 billion in the region, with a further $2.3 billion brought in by foreign visitors. At the same time, southern tourists spent only $21 billion in travel outside their home country. Thus, the South enjoyed a surplus of nearly $8 billion on tourism alone.[22]

However, mirroring the newfound enthusiasm for the Sunbelt South, data in newspapers and reports did not consistently capture the profound differences within the region (and perhaps intentionally avoided doing so). The South was undoubtedly an important tourist area, but few parts could rightly be considered real national destinations. Other than Texas, which, among the subdivisions of American tourist areas, falls in the category of the West, Florida was the true giant of the sector, constantly topping the national tourism charts along with California and New York. Transportation infrastructure obviously played a significant role in the competition for the tourist dollars in the South. The interstate freeway system, for example, was an important vector for tourist traffic to Florida, and states such as Georgia and South Carolina, which were better connected to the system, gained an important advantage over more isolated states such as Alabama and Mississippi. Also, Georgia and Florida were the only southern states with international airports during the 1970s, which undoubtedly benefited them greatly.

To some observers, especially within the tourism industry, this internal regional imbalance was very much apparent. In an issue of *Travel Trade Gazette Europa* dedicated to the Travel South region, it was openly stated that "the difference between the size and importance of tourism to each of the individual states is enormous. Florida, for example, has a vibrant tourism industry, while Alabama falls a long way short."[23] According to data from the U.S. Travel Data Center, by the mid-1970s, Florida led the southern states, followed by Georgia, Virginia, North Carolina, Tennessee, Louisiana, Alabama, Arkansas, South Carolina, and Mississippi.[24]

An exact assessment of the tourism industry in the individual states of the Deep South is almost impossible. For one thing, the data that would be most important—the actual number of visitors—is the most difficult to obtain, due to the extremely inaccurate nature of the information released by the state offices. What emerges from an examination of travel surveys and internal reports is a situation that is, at times, confusing to say the least. For the most part the numbers reported appear to be either inflated or calculated with a generous degree of approximation by the state offices for the obvious purpose of justifying budget requests. Alabama, for example, claimed 55 million travelers in 1978 and Georgia nearly 70 million. In the same year, the South Carolina tourist office reported 39 million visitors from out of state (all figures that, as will be seen, seem largely unrealistic for those years). For comparison, in 1977 southern California reported about 20 million tourists and Florida 30 million, and these were two of the top three tourist areas in the entire country.[25] It would therefore be inconceivable that the Deep South could even remotely reach such numbers. This issue was also closely related to a terminology problem, reflecting the poor coordination of tourism policies within the United States.

The Travel Industry Association of America's annual *Survey of State Travel Offices*, in fact, reported the number of *travelers*, a label encompassing all individuals traveling within the state, whether they were locals or people from outside the state. However, many of these were not tourists at all, but were merely passing through along the interstate highways or traveling for work. Therefore these figures should not be taken as the number of actual tourists visiting the state (who in fact were far fewer). The problem was that there was no common standard for these technical terms. Some states considered all travelers to be tourists, others took into account only visitors from outside state borders, and still others (such as Colorado) used the ambiguous term "vacationer" without specifying how this should be interpreted. Among the documents produced in those years by the tourism industry, it was common for "tourist," "traveler," and "visitor" to be used as synonyms. The issue of terminology may appear secondary, but it was recognized as particularly pressing by professionals in the field, as it generated confusion and made it difficult to conduct comparative analyses. A state tourism study commission working in Mississippi in the mid-1970s reported in 1978 that there was widespread and serious confusion about what "tourist" actually meant. The commission even went so far as to send a questionnaire to neighboring states, but had to conclude that most had no formal definition of the various key terms ("tourist," "traveler," "travel industry," "tourism industry," and others).[26] In addition to this struggle to conform to a single standard, there was also the deliberate choice to present the most optimistic and inflated data possible. It goes without saying that the smaller, less touristy states had every interest in considering as "visitors" or "tourists" even those who simply passed along their roads, perhaps stopping one night in a local motel and then moving onward. It is also evident how this confusion led local administrators to consider as part of the tourism industry a number of components that were only marginally related to it, such as bars, restaurants, and retail stores. It comes as no surprise that at some point during the 1970s, each of the four Deep South states declared tourism to be its main economic sector. While this may have been true for Georgia, it was much less so for Mississippi, South Carolina, and Alabama. The case of Mississippi provides a good example of all the inaccuracies and ambiguities within the industry. There the media and state office openly claimed that tourism was the second largest source of revenue for the state; however, the 1978 report totally debunked this statement, arguing instead that tourism was actually at the bottom of the local economy.[27] The problem was once again in the method of analysis. The report only took into account personal income as a measure of the economic impact of tourism. The Mississippi Tourist Bureau, on the other hand, also relied on tourist expenditures from out of state, tax returns, and capital investments in the industry. In 1974, Alabama governor George Wallace claimed that tourism had become his state's number one industry,[28] and that same year Governor West of South Carolina went so far as to say that "tourism has had more influence on the South Carolina economy than anything in our history."[29] Yet, depending on the method used for analysis, these claims could be strongly disputed.

Of course it goes without saying that if the number of tourists passing through the states could not be recorded with certainty, other data provided by travel bureaus, such as the total number of dollars spent by visitors or the percentage of local people employed in the tourism industry, also loses its reliability. Here we return to the confusion over what exactly is a tourism-related job and what is not. In 1983, for example, Alabama tourism director Ed Hall stated: "If you've ever worked at McDonald's, ever been employed at a motel, you are selling tourism."[30] Not everyone agreed.

Nevertheless, it is sufficient to note here how southern tourism in the mid-1970s appeared to be divided into three parts: Florida, which alone dominated the industry both regionally and nationally; an intermediate group consisting of states with a solid tourism industry such as Georgia, Virginia, and North Carolina; and finally, states such as Mississippi, Arkansas, and Alabama. This tripartition was far from irreversible. Georgia, for instance, would always maintain a privileged status, but South Carolina, which in the 1970s was still a minor and semiregional reality, would experience a boom in the following decade.

Even states less affected by large tourist flows seemed committed to strengthening their travel sectors. The less space they had within the regional tourism industry, the more pronounced were their efforts. This was true for Alabama, South Carolina, and Mississippi. The governments of these states were aware of the obvious benefits that a strong tourism sector would bring, not only economically, but also in terms of image. They were, after all, led by New South governors (with the partial exception of Alabama), often second-generation but nevertheless well set within the Sunbelt narrative of economic progress.

During the second half of the 1970s, Georgia occupied an undoubtedly advantageous economic position compared to other states in the Deep South, partly due to its tourism industry. This status, however, had only been achieved in the early years of the decade. In 1972, Thomas Doering studied the extent to which each American state's economy depended on tourism. In that year, Georgia was ranked thirtieth, below South Carolina, Arkansas, and Virginia.[31] However, as early as 1974, the local tourism industry had become a booming sector, earning the state an estimated $250 million a year.[32] This growth had much to do with the William B. Hartsfield Atlanta Airport, the largest in the South and, from 1971, a hub for international flights.[33] By 1974 it had become the second busiest in the nation behind Chicago O'Hare.[34] After airline deregulation in 1978, moreover, the Atlanta-based Delta Airlines expanded its network to compete with other companies, which resulted in the first transatlantic flights departing from Georgia in that year. Furthermore, the consequent lowering of prices, especially on longer routes, also increased incoming traffic.

This would be enough to distinguish Georgia from all the other Deep South states, at least in terms of visibility and accessibility. The state began to make significant social and economic progress during the governorships of Carl Sanders (1963–1967) and Jimmy Carter (1971–1975),[35] but it was under the leadership of George Busbee, governor from 1975 to 1983, that Georgia took its most important steps forward. A seasoned politician, Busbee represented a second-generation New South governor who nevertheless appeared critical of the Sunbelt myth, openly admitting that most of the South remained poor compared to the rest of the nation.[36] His two consecutive terms in office are widely recognized as a time of aggressive efforts at economic development, to the point that Numan Bartley speaks of a veritable economic crusade, which Busbee "pursued with almost single-minded determination," including a series of extensive trips across the United States as well as to Europe and Asia (distinguishing himself from the governors of Alabama, Mississippi, and South Carolina).[37] In 1976 Busbee was also instrumental in the establishment of the Southeast U.S./Japan Association, with the express purpose of promoting trade and tourism between the seven states of the American Southeast and Japan. Thus, by the end of the 1970s Georgia was in a unique condition. Compared to the rest of the Deep South, the state had a stronger position in the domestic and international markets, which generated investments, jobs, and a modern, cosmopolitan outlook. Large companies such as Coca-Cola and Delta Airlines were headquartered in Atlanta, and rapid innovations in television broadcasting also played their part in attracting both investments and national attention. Ted Turner's Atlanta-based TBS, for example, connected Georgia to the rest of the country via satellite cable broadcasts in 1976. Later, in June 1980, Turner further revolutionized communications when he launched the Cable News Network (CNN) in Atlanta as the world's first twenty-four-hour news channel. Investment and business promotion achieved excellent results internationally as well, since the number of international companies in the state increased from 150 in 1975 to 680 in 1982, reflecting Georgia's importance as a global economic hub.[38]

Included in Georgia's economic growth was also a new emphasis on tourism promotion by state administrators, aided and abetted by an equally aggressive campaign to draw the film and television industries to Georgia. During Busbee's two terms in office, 160 films and television shows were shot in the state.[39] The other key figure of this crusade for tourist dollars was Edwin "Ed" Spivia, director of Georgia's tourism division from 1976 and previously head of the state's film commission (created in 1972 by Governor Carter), which had succeeded in bringing major film productions to the Peach State.[40] In 1979, Spivia was also appointed head of an ad hoc international tourism committee to study new foreign marketing strategies for Georgia, with positive results.[41] In the same year, moreover, he was elected as chairman of Travel South, USA. Formerly an associate of WGST radio and the ABC network during the 1960s, Spivia was not strictly speaking a tourism-industry professional at the time of his appointment to the Georgia Tourism Division, yet his experience working with film companies and conducting public relations activities provided him with a broad knowledge of the state's natural and tourism resources. After contributing significantly to the growth of the travel industry in Georgia in the late 1970s, Spivia returned to the movie industry in 1983 as president of the Atlanta-based Filmworks USA Inc. All in all, Busbee and Spivia can legitimately be called the absolute masterminds behind the new stimulus to tourism promotion and marketing in Georgia, and one of the main reasons for the state's relative success.

Although economically disadvantaged, Mississippi entered the 1970s under the leadership of a progressive governor, Democrat William "Bill" Waller Sr. (1972–1976). The decade certainly represented a period of social and economic growth for the state, although it remained underdeveloped in many areas. During this period Mississippi attempted to adapt to the New South of the Sunbelt, but it benefited only in part from this economic miracle. As was the case with other southern states, the Magnolia State had undoubtedly changed since the end of segregation, despite the many stereotypes still in fashion. The racial issue, once the chief concern of politics, was now much less central. Here, as elsewhere, the spread of television, increased schooling, and the immigration of professional workers from other parts of the United States brought a significant change to local society. Economic growth was the major goal pursued by the moderate Sunbelt New South administrations. As Dale Krane and Stephen Shaffer point out, by the mid-1970s the state's policies were surprisingly progressive.[42] Therefore, it is not surprising that even Mississippi was committed in those years to making its tourism industry more modern and competitive. Tourism, it must be said, was still a secondary business for the state, but the newly elected governor, Democrat Cliff Finch (1976– 1980), who followed William Waller Sr., also campaigned for a complete reorganization and streamlining of the travel industry. Finch's plan was to hire more industry professionals, increase tourism's priority within the Mississippi Agriculture and Industrial Board (A&I Board), and develop new promotional strategies. The basic idea, the governor stated, was to acknowledge that "this is an industry, not a sideshow," a proclamation that attests to the amateurish, rudimentary nature of tourist promotion in Mississippi up to that point.[43]

Finch actually intended to split the A&I Board into two divisions, one dedicated exclusively to industry and the other to tourism. During his first year in office the new governor created, by executive order, a new Mississippi Tourism, Parks, and Recreation Council, charged with coordinating the activities of all state agencies responsible for tourism. The most pressing problem remained the budget allocated for tourism policies, which was lower in Mississippi than anywhere else in the entire South. Finch did not invest more money, but focused on a program of study and reorganization of existing resources.[44] The changes, however, were not insignificant.

By 1977, his administration had successfully launched a series of reform measures. The Department of Travel and Tourism (within the A&I Board) was merged with the Department of Public Affairs in order to streamline promotional efforts, while a number of new programs were initiated to increase awareness among Mississippians of the importance of tourism for the local economy. To run the newly created Tourism and Public Affairs Department, George Williams, an experienced tourism professional, was appointed. Born in 1940 in DeSoto County but raised in Arkansas, Williams had a master's degree in public recreation from Memphis State University and had spent the last four years working as a tourism specialist with the Cooperative Extension Service.[45] He also served as chairman of Travel South before Spivia was elected in 1979.

In 1977, the governor proclaimed June as "hospitality month" in an attempt to introduce locals to the attractions of their state and thus stimulate domestic tourism. Two new welcome centers were also opened along the interstates, bringing their total number in the state to four.[46] In 1979, the A&I Board became the Department of Economic Development (DED) with the express purpose of restructuring the state's economic development activities by employing experienced professionals, including those in the tourism industry.[47]

Finch's term ended in 1980, overshadowed by scandals and corruption allegations, and he was succeeded by Democrat William F. Winter (1980–1984).[48] Winter won on an economically conservative platform, oriented toward business and growth but with no direct interest in tourism. The state's image, however, was part of his concerns. A project for comprehensive reform of the state structure was summed up by Winter in the slogan "Mississippi has been fiftieth long enough," which referred to the state's position in many social and economic sectors.[49] Charles Bolton paid close attention to Winter's personality, as the new governor was a passionate historian as well as a politician with strong personal convictions about his home state. A keen observer of the relationship between his South and the region's past, Winter actively assumed a rather clear position on the heavy Confederate-nostalgic symbolism that immobilized Mississippi's historical perspective. Indeed, his idea of the South was far from an apologetic cliché of the Lost Cause. Writer Willie Morris, who had occasion to hear one of Winter's speeches during a symposium at Millsaps College in 1981, later remembered, "He [Winter] is saying things which no governor of a deep southern state has ever said. . . . This is a historic moment for Mississippi."[50]

In South Carolina, too, the 1970s began under the sign of modernization and social change, despite the persistence of certain difficulties. The Palmetto State was, in fact, still plagued by serious deficiencies in agriculture, a manufacturing sector centered solely on textiles, and a per capita income below the national average (and that of forty-six other states). Poverty remained high, especially for the African American population.[51] Nevertheless, the situation appeared to be improving rapidly with the emergence of a fresh political generation, dedicated—in full New South spirit—to addressing the social and economic issues still unresolved. Democratic governors Robert E. McNair (1965–1971) and John C. West (1971–1975) had the merits of both overcoming racial bias in politics and attracting industry and jobs to the state. James B. Edwards (1975–1979, the first Republican to become state governor since the Reconstruction) and Democratic Richard W. Riley (1979–1987) followed the same course of action. Special emphasis was placed on the recreation industry, especially after Governor McNair.[52] Developing a thriving tourism apparatus was a bipartisan effort. In his optimistic 1977 address on the condition of the state, Republican Edwards acknowledged the recent expansion of the tourism industry and hoped for even greater future growth to better "attract tourist dollars into our economy achieving economic and recreational advantages where they are needed most—here at home."[53] The goal was also to achieve a comprehensive development that left no area of South Carolina behind. Governor West stated this explicitly, throwing a dig at neighboring Georgia when he said that "we don't want any Atlanta's," meaning no "island of progress" surrounded by poverty.[54] The transition occurred relatively quickly. Virginia's Republican governor, Abner Linwood Holton (1970–1974), stressed South Carolina's move toward modernity by stating, "You're not looking at an antebellum South Carolina anymore."[55]

One element of continuity during the development of the travel industry in 1970s South Carolina was the director of the Department of Parks, Recreation, and Tourism (DPRT), Fred P. Brinkman. Another longtime professional in the field, he grew up in Missouri, and after graduating from Florida State University he began a career in the tourism industry, working until 1956 as manager of the Chamber of Commerce of Quincy, Florida, and later head of the Myrtle Beach Chamber of Commerce. He joined the DPRT as deputy director in 1967, eventually becoming the executive director in 1973.[56] Under his direction, tourism grew steadily over the 1970s. In early 1979, Brinkman affirmed that while tourism was a relatively new element in South Carolina's economy, it was "a very dynamic and growing part of the state's service industry."[57] Indeed, the relationship between the Palmetto State and the tourism industry was actually quite recent. In her book *Sombreros and Motorcycles in a Newer South*, Nicole King traces a brief but accurate history of the origins of the travel industry in South Carolina. Despite some initial attempts during the 1920s and 1930s (mainly involving Charleston), the real acknowledgment of its tourism potential occurred only in 1945, when the first nationwide advertising program was launched. However, it was not until 1967, under Governor McNair, that South Carolina took on a more modern and competitive approach to the promotion of tourism.[58] For the Palmetto State, the 1970s represented a moment of transition in the process of establishing tourism as an important pillar in the state's economy. By the mid-1970s, tourism was already a profitable business, but it was only near the end of the 1980s that it became the state's main industry.[59] In 1979, Director Brinkman drew optimistic conclusions from the past decade as he looked toward a future that appeared to be all about international tourism: "For many years South Carolina was a regional vacation destination, but over the 1970s we grew into a vacation area of national importance. We will add 'international' to that designation during the 1980s."[60]

Serious economic problems, combined with equally serious problems of image, meant that the tourism industry in Alabama had less fertile ground in which to grow. In addition, the state's political elite had little real interest in promotional policies until at least the mid-1980s.[61] From a recreation-industry standpoint, even in Alabama the decade of the 1970s lay partway between the end of World War II, when southern states first began to establish state offices responsible for promoting tourism, and the 1980s, when the first major successes in this sector were achieved. Interestingly, George Wallace's political career as governor (1963–1987) opened and closed with an acknowledgment of the development of tourism. In his infamous 1963 inaugural address, following his well-known declaration "segregation now, segregation tomorrow, segregation forever," Wallace went on to say that "we [Alabama] have the favorable climate, streams, woodlands, beaches, and natural beauty to make us a recreational mecca in the booming tourist and vacation industry."[62] Twenty years later, in his 1983 program, the aging governor boasted, among other alleged successes of his previous terms, that he had made tourism a billion-dollar-a-year business in Alabama.[63] This was an exaggeration. Although the decade of the 1970s had indeed begun with a tourism boom seemingly destined to last, this growth turned out to be short lived, with the state not only hit hard by two energy crises (that of 1973 and especially that of 1979) but also struggling to presenting itself positively and effectively to the tourist market.[64]

The image of Alabama in the 1970s cannot help but be immediately associated with that of Governor George Wallace, a true icon, for better or worse, on both a national and international level. Initially a vocal defender of the segregationist status quo and then, in the latter part of his life, a paradoxical champion of equality and civil rights, Wallace influenced Alabama's politics and image for over twenty years. Holding the office of governor four times between 1963 and 1987, including the brief gubernatorial term of his first wife, Lurleen, from 1967 to 1968, Wallace is unique in the political landscape of the South and of the United States both for the exceptional length of his tenure on the scene and for his ability to influence political discourse. Someone referred to this long period as the "Wallace freeze,"[65] a dormancy of the political scene and public discourse that prevented and delayed the development of a truly modern and progressive Alabama capable of leaving behind the unbecoming segregationist past of the fifties and sixties.

It was only during his third term (1975–1979) that the governor began a policy of gradual rapprochement with Alabama's Black society, appointing some

African Americans to his cabinet and toning down his aggressive rhetoric. It was the beginning of a reconciliation that would culminate in a public apology during his reelection campaign in 1982. It must be said that Wallace was also aware of the need to project a less static and negative image of the state. A 1976 memorandum studying opportunities to win the African American vote for Wallace's nomination at the National Democratic Convention declared: "We intend to demonstrate Alabama is a moving state that does not deny rights and opportunities by showing progress during the Wallace administrations."[66]

Historians, however, generally agree that the Wallace era was negative for Alabama, not only in terms of its image, but also in terms of its economy.[67] Beginning in 1970, a fairly aggressive policy to attract industry and generate newfound strength in local business brought about a brief period of economic growth that, however, ended quite soon. In 1977 the state government loudly promoted, in an excess of confidence, the alleged miracles of Alabama's economic boom of the past six years. The following year saw the beginning of a strong downward trend that would continue throughout the 1980s.[68]

Wallace's long tenure in power was shortly interrupted by the interregnum of Forrest Hood "Fob" James. A former Republican, James won mainly because of a constitutional ban that prevented Wallace from running for a third consecutive term. In the absence of the favored candidate, the newcomer James gained the support of Wallace himself. In other words, his election should not be seen as a real break with the Wallace era. From a political point of view James showed himself extremely unprepared and confused in his choice of objectives to pursue, proving incapable of obtaining support among the political forces of the state.[69] J. Wayne Flint, in his monograph on twentieth-century Alabama, goes so far as to dismiss him as "one of the most inept governors in memory."[70] James also aggravated Alabama's already bad image with a series of gaffes and inappropriate comments, mostly due to his religious fundamentalism, and was widely ridiculed by the national media.[71]

In terms of tourism, however, James must be credited with initiating an international promotional campaign in 1980 and 1981 aimed primarily at Canada, the United Kingdom, and Latin America. During James's time in office, Alabama even attended a convention of tourism representatives in New Zealand and began working with the Japan National Tourism Organization.[72] It was the first time Alabama advertised itself as a tourist destination outside of North America. This international market debut was not accidental, since it coincided with another milestone: in 1981, for the first time, the number of tourists entering the United States surpassed that of outbound visitors. Canada was the country that generated the greatest flow of tourists to the United States, about 50 percent, and was obviously the primary target of many state promotional efforts. Along with Mexicans, Canadians were also the visitors who spent the most money in the country during their vacations, making Canada and Mexico favorable market areas for every state interested in tourism development.[73] At the Alabama Governor's Conference on Tourism in May 1981, Fob James showed his confidence in Alabama's tourism prospects by declaring that the state was moving rapidly toward a service economy.[74] In addition, Governor James should also be credited for his appointment of the vigorous Caroline Cavanaugh to head the state travel bureau. She replaced Doug Benton, a trusted Wallace loyalist for whom, apparently, promoting Alabama sometimes coincided with promoting George Wallace himself.[75] "Of course," Benton said to the press, "we're selling George Wallace all the time."[76] Like her counterparts in Mississippi and South Carolina, Cavanaugh had a rich resume as a tourism and publicity professional. Born in Greenville, Alabama, she had lived in forty-eight of the fifty states before being appointed by the governor to head the Alabama Bureau of Publicity and Information. From 1973 until her appointment she served as vice president of the Andalusia Area Chamber of Commerce. In February 1979 moreover, while still running Alabama's travel division she also became vice chairman of Travel South USA, when Georgia's Ed Spivia was elected governor. Although the previous travel bureau Director, Doug Benton, was also a professional in the field to some degree, the choice of someone from outside Wallace's inner circle undoubtedly allowed the Bureau to work more independently. The new professional approach to tourism is reflected also in the new agency chosen to produce Alabama's ads, Steiner-Bressler Advertising of Birmingham.[77] The agency was chosen precisely because of their "innovative and creative approach to state travel advertising," as Cavanaugh explained.[78] The previous agency—Luckie and Forney, which had handled the election campaigns of Senator Howell Heflin (1978) and Governor Wallace himself (in 1970 and 1974)—was also probably too involved in politics.[79] The year 1979 actually marked the first time in Alabama history that the state's tourist advertising agency was chosen after extensive interviews with representatives of different firms rather than by direct appointment. This is significant, as it reflects the new, efficient, and studious approach that was being devoted to tourism promotion in those years.

Eventually, however, after some alleged expense report irregularities in 1982, Cavanaugh lost her spending authority in the travel division. In 1983 she left her role when Governor James's term expired, becoming director of marketing and public relations for the Brookwood Medical Center in Birmingham.[80]

In conclusion, for Georgia, Mississippi, and South Carolina, the 1970s represented a time of rapid political, economic, and even social change, in which the local political elite recognized the vital role of tourism in sustaining growth. The case of Alabama, still under Wallace's influence, was unique. Yet even in the so-called Heart of Dixie, the late 1970s were a major turning point, precisely because of the need to adapt to a new type of promotion capable of reaching out to Europe and Latin America and of shaking off the worst of Wallace's legacy. From the mid-1970s, the governor tried to distance himself from his own previous excesses. For all four states, then, it was a period in which rethinking, reorganizing, and updating the local destination image was not only useful, but almost essential. What is more, all four state offices were led by professionals well connected within the regional tourism environment. Three of the four tourism directors served at the top of the Travel South board during the 1970s. And all of them, with the partial exception of Ed Spivia, had professional backgrounds related to advertising and tourism.

State Travel Offices

As mentioned above, southern states began founding state offices for tourism in the wake of World War II. This had become a necessity if they wanted to be part of the growing travel industry. By the 1970s, the South had larger and better-funded travel offices than many other American regions, which shows that it was definitely on a path to expand services and improve its image.

Although industry professionals constantly complained of operating under financial constraints, the situation was generally positive for the Deep South. In 1977 and 1978 the average national budget for state travel offices was $1,271,000, a figure exceeded by all former Confederate states except Mississippi. In fact, in the whole, the South was the region with the highest budgets for its tourist offices.[81] In every southern state, the number of staff employed in tourist offices was also higher than the average of twenty-five.

Despite annual variations, the budget situation for the period between 1977 and 1981 appears quite similar. The Deep South, more specifically, was an area of mostly medium-sized state travel offices edged by states (Texas, Tennessee, and Florida) with very large budgets. On the one hand, this data can be misleading, since the relationship between office budgets and the actual growth in the tourism industry is not direct. California, for example, had no travel office despite being an extremely tourist-oriented state, with far more visitors than any state in the former Confederacy. On the other hand, it is clear that southern states showed a greater interest in this sector than the western area of the United States. At least for the purpose of this work, the actual results of their efforts are not important; what is important is to note that they were investing significant amounts of money to promote themselves and improve their image.

Another gauge of southern states' focus on tourism is their relationship to international advertising. By this measure, the second half of the 1970s represented a clear turning point for the southern (and American) tourist industry. Overseas promotion was indeed marked by significant changes between 1976 and 1981. By the mid-1970s, in fact, few dollars were being spent in this area, and the target countries for advertising campaigns were virtually limited to Canada alone.[82] The United States had its own government office in charge of foreign promotion, the USTS, but its results were rather mediocre. Moreover, not all regions and states were adequately represented in official national advertisements, thus causing an internal imbalance. Therefore, the burden of overseas promotion fell mostly on individual state offices that could hardly afford effective international campaigns.

In 1977, only nine states in the entire country claimed to have paid for ads or conducted promotional activities in a foreign country other than Canada. Merely two of these were in the South. One was Florida, of course, whose ads and advertisements reached Germany, the United Kingdom, Mexico, France, and Japan, while the other, interestingly enough, was Mississippi, which claimed to have placed ads in Germany and the United Kingdom.[83] Nevertheless, an abrupt and important change occurred in the following years. Not only was there a general increase in the budgets available for overseas promotion, but also a surge in the number of states that looked beyond Canada in their choice of promotional targets, rising from eight in 1977 to twelve in 1979 and then finally to fifteen in 1981. By that time Georgia, Tennessee, Kentucky, Alabama, and Louisiana also reported paying for promotional activities abroad, especially in Europe.[84]

The risk, however, is to interpret this period of general growth in overly optimistic terms for the states of the Deep South. They were still impaired by serious image problems and a local tourism industry in many cases ill-equipped to keep up with the demands and expectations of the political elite. The main issue that concerned southern state travel offices was evidently the lack of a coordinated promotional effort involving all the various local tourism sectors. Within each state there were, in fact, numerous agencies, citizen groups, counties, and local chambers of commerce conducting their own tourism-related microactivities. State offices did not have the means bring all these players together in one concerted scheme. Local communities also failed to recognize tourism as a viable economic sector. Even Governor George Busbee, in the March 1978 issue of *Amenities*, the official magazine of the Georgia Hospitality and Travel Association, admitted to readers: "You and I . . . are among a small minority of Georgians who recognize Georgia tourism as an industry."[85] The following year an internal report by the Alabama tourism office echoed this statement: "The public needs to better understand the role of recreation and tourism and its contributions to the state's social and economic structure."[86] The same concept was also expressed by professionals in South Carolina.[87]

This same issue plagued U.S. tourism in general and was addressed by the USTS, which specified, in a 1977 report, that one of the main problems in the American economy was "the lack of understanding of the importance of tourism in the overall economic development plan at the state and local level."[88] Likewise, documents produced by the state offices of Georgia, Mississippi, Alabama, and South Carolina at that time show how tourism had only recently started becoming "modern." Beyond the lack of local awareness, there was a whole series of problems affecting the industry, especially the deep gap between political expectations and the real domestic situation.

The goal of state tourism offices was obviously to provide advertising coverage in key market areas. Given the tight economy, the competition between states, and the energy crisis, it goes without saying that the states needed to identify precise regions in which to invest their resources. A large part of the offices' activities revolved around determining which areas could guarantee the most visitors. It would have been unimaginable for states in the Deep South to run advertisement campaigns across the whole country. The costs would have been prohibitive and brought only minimal economic returns. Only destinations such as Florida, California, and New York could possibly venture into a promotional program of that magnitude. The less touristic states had to streamline their efforts, as they still do today. It has already been illustrated how tourism in the South was driven primarily by southerners traveling within the region. The aforementioned 1979 Travel South report showed that about 60 percent of visitors to the South were local.[89] One might assume, then, that Deep South states chose to focus on promotion designed specifically for other southern states. Yet this is only partly true. The promotional activity of the Deep South tourism offices actually had a substantial reach that extended to the Midwest and parts of the Northeast.

Once again, George Busbee's Georgia was on top of the charts, as the Peach State's ads covered a wider market than her other three sister states. In 1975 the focus was still on the Canadian and midwestern markets, but in 1977 the aim was to strengthen promotional efforts in neighboring southern states, in Ohio, in the West and Midwest (Texas, Oklahoma, Indiana, Missouri, and Kansas), and in Canada.[90] The following year, Ed Spivia announced that the Mid-Atlantic area would also see advertisement coverage.[91] By 1978, Georgia had ads in eighty-three publications, including newspapers and magazines.[92] Milt Folds of the state Department of Industry and Trade claimed that the 1978 campaign was the largest Georgia had ever undertaken, reaching a wide audience in fourteen metropolitan markets and employing print advertising, television commercials, and billboards.[93] Later, the energy crisis forced Georgia's Tourism Division to reconsider its strategies. Because of high gasoline prices, advertisements were concentrated mainly in neighboring states. The 1980 plan mentions television, radio commercials, and eight-page ads placed in newspapers in seventeen southeastern areas, all in states bordering Georgia.[94]

The situation in South Carolina was somewhat similar. Here, the target markets for advertising were the Mid-Atlantic, the East, the Northeast, and the central United States as well as the Canadian regions of Ontario and Quebec.[95] In 1976 and 1977, there were ads in forty-one magazines, for a total of 121 black-and-white and nineteen color advertisements.[96] In 1978 and 1979, however, the total number of publications dropped to twenty-five, slightly more than Mississippi but less than Georgia.[97] The 1979 energy crisis also affected the extent of the Palmetto State's promotional campaign. In 1980 *Business and Economic Dimensions* noted that, just as in Georgia, "South Carolina's marketing efforts have shifted from a national to a regional coverage in the recent past."[98] The range covered by the ads had actually shrunk to areas within five hundred miles of its coastline, namely Georgia, North Carolina, Maryland, Virginia, and West Virginia. The results seemed to confirm a new trend. In July 1979, at the height of the energy crisis, the director of the South Carolina tourist office reported that the state was experiencing an increase in visitors from neighboring states, while those from Ohio and other northern states had notably declined.[99]

Alabama identified its primary out-of-state target in a slightly more circumscribed area between the East North Central, East South Central, and West South Central. This included eleven states, four of which were in its immediate proximity (Arkansas, Tennessee, Kentucky, and Mississippi), as well as Texas, Oklahoma, Wisconsin, Illinois, Michigan, Indiana, and Ohio. In 1978, the state's ads appeared in twenty-five publications, the same figure as South Carolina.[100]

More limited, on the other hand, was the promotion for Mississippi. In 1977 the state placed forty ads in twenty-two newspapers and twenty magazines; the following year that number changed to twenty-five newspapers and fourteen magazines, and they began incorporating television and radio spots.[101] Mississippi's promotion campaign centered on the following states, in order of importance: Louisiana, Texas, Florida, Illinois, Missouri, Indiana, Michigan, Arkansas, and Alabama.[102]

Yet, despite all the considerable promotional efforts, the vast majority of visitors to the Deep South came from the surrounding areas. In Mississippi, for example, most tourists hailed from the four adjacent states of Louisiana,

Tennessee, Alabama, and Arkansas.[103] The situation was similar in Alabama, where, between 1977 and 1981, the majority of visitors came from other areas of the South—over 70 percent, with most traveling from the two neighboring states of Georgia and Florida.[104] The same pattern is observed in South Carolina, where North Carolina, Georgia, and Florida appear to be the three states that generated the most tourists.[105] There is no precise data, however, as to where visitors to Georgia came from. In 1978 Ed Spivia released a list of the states that produced the most inquiries for information about local tourist attractions. These included Florida, New York, California, Ohio, and Illinois.[106] Compared to Alabama, Mississippi, and South Carolina, there was unquestionably a more widespread interest in the Peach State, an interest that also stemmed from the election of Jimmy Carter to the U.S. presidency.

Reputation, Competition, and Florida: The Challenges of the Deep South Tourism Industry

Alabama, Mississippi, Georgia, and South Carolina were cooperating at various levels to attract visitors both from across their borders and from abroad. At the same time, however, they were also in constant competition with one another, each seeing its neighboring states as a potential pool of visitors to attract to their own destinations. This competitive state of affairs caused problems for promotional strategy, as each state had to distinguish itself from its direct competitors. Southern tourism professionals understood best what were the most pressing issues. These can be broken down into two macro areas: problems related to the image and reputation of individual states and structural problems in the local tourism system.

In terms of image problems, Alabama and Mississippi faced the greatest challenges. At the Governor's Conference on Tourism in 1979, a roundtable of experts drew up a list of obstacles that were slowing Alabama's tourism promotion. They discussed inadequate funding, the need for more coordinated promotional efforts, and the "Alabama bad image, created largely by media headquartered on east and west coasts."[107] A research survey conducted that same year by publicist Mac Patrick showed that the two images most often associated with Alabama by outsiders were racism and southern dialect, and he urged that the state be promoted in a more favorable light.[108]

During that conference, Cy Steiner, a member of the advertising agency that handled the Alabama materials, took a more positive view of the matter: "We have another particular problem—the image of Alabama. We take billboards and we put them around the South and we run our spots around the South. I don't think the people in Georgia, Tennessee or Mississippi are going to be really worried about what our image is. They know that it is not as bad as everyone believes. They have about the same problem we have."[109] In other words, this was an issue for the entire South, not just for Alabama. According to Steiner, tourism would not be overly affected, since most of the state's visitors came from within the southern borders, a region that largely shared its problematic image. However, data from Mississippi seemed to challenge this notion. A 1973 survey carried out on around two hundred frequent travelers from eight other southern states showed that 30 percent had a negative opinion of Mississippi. The two most cited causes were a vague "it did not appeal to me" and a more alarming "racial situation."[110] It is also interesting to note that the 1979 Tourism Conference in Alabama considered media based on the East and West Coasts to be primarily responsible for this poor perception of the state. Even though the South at that time was in the midst of a process of rapprochement with the rest of the country, the persecution complex typical of old southern culture was still strong[111]—yet another indication that the spread of the redneck chic, the election of Jimmy Carter, and the long-debated southernization of America had by no means solved the problem of perception, which was actually very deep-rooted within American culture. As for Alabama, a 1981 BBC interview with Caroline Cavanaugh, director of the state tourism office, provides significant insight. One of Cavanaugh's main concerns was to defend the state from its own reputation: "And that's another point I'd like to go over. Is that we are a very safe state, and you will find that our people there are treated equally. You will not find that there is a lot ignoring or overlooking a person because of his race or his background. Which is not what the news media and the television ad all usually projects."[112] And again, on another occasion in England: "You know most people say, oh Alabama, you know, they have a negative opinion but that's because of television and things like that."[113] In domestic advertisements, these kinds of messages had already disappeared from the promotional discourse. Of course, the Deep South was aware of its image problems, but by the early 1980s these were not being addressed so blatantly. When promotion was intended for an overseas audience, by contrast, there was clearly a greater need to reassure the public that Alabama was no longer the same state that had appeared on television twenty years earlier in reports showing beatings of civil rights protesters. Attitudes toward Confederate nostalgia, however, were different, at times even ambiguous. During another interview in Scotland in 1982, for example, Cavanaugh, this time referring to the Civil War, spoke of the "War of Northern Aggression," an extremely pro-Confederate term for the conflict that was used only in the South. The other Alabama speaker in the studio, Bill Armistead, likewise used the same definition shortly afterward. This was likely not accidental but rather a specific linguistic choice, since tourism officers in general are usually quite careful with their words—so much so that they sometimes have to apologize for material that offers less-than-amicable messages to visitors, even if it is produced outside of their government offices.[114] In 1979, for example, Ed Spivia had to publicly apologize to a northern tourist who had been offended by a Georgia postcard that read "Every yankee tourist is worth a bale of cotton. Greetings from Dixie," explaining that it was material produced by a third party and not subject to state regulation.[115] A term like "War of Northern Aggression" would, in fact, have been impossible to use in official domestic promotion. Overseas, things were different. The fact that this was said in Scotland suggests a precise decision to employ unusual and extremely "southern-sounding" terminology, meant to arouse public curiosity and generate fascination by exploiting a regional animosity that by that time was mostly fictional. The more folkloristic Confederate representations had already been limited in promotional material designed for circulation within the United States. Beyond national borders there were other standards. This was not only due to the fact that outside the United States there was some confusion as to what exactly the Confederacy and its symbols represented, but also because most of the world knew the South only from those southern images circulated by *Gone with the Wind* and similar pop-culture phenomena. It is easy, therefore, to imagine that Cavanaugh and Armistead were purposely using a term that sounded like something out of Margaret Mitchell's novel. This would also help explain why a 1979 article in a French travel magazine announced the publication of the first Travel South booklet as "le manuel des confédéres," specifying that it was available only in English, i.e., the "langue du general Lee."[116]

This image of the South abroad is also demonstrated by travel articles about the region published in other countries. For instance, a series of articles written in England in 1981 and 1982 to introduce Alabama to the British emphasized the exotic and un-"Americanized" character of the region. In particular, a somewhat ironic piece published in the *Evening Times* illustrated the relationship between the past and memory in the South: "All that Southern charm still abounds a century after the 'war of northern aggression' (it never was a civil war in the eyes of the Johnnie Rebs) . . . Selma, where historic freedom march took place 16 years ago. That, for southerners, is too recent to be of historical importance."[117] The mythical image of the South was everywhere: "Did you see *Gone with the Wind* over Christmas? Then you are ripe for a holiday in Alabama."[118] Likewise, various Canadian articles glorified the usual aspects of the old romantic South and its antebellum homes.[119]

Mississippi was in an even worse situation than Alabama in terms of image. In 1975, a report about the state's tourism situation admitted that "we have a serious perception or image problem."[120] This is also evidenced by the fact that over the years, Mississippi, unlike Alabama, produced a variety of promotional materials for the domestic market explicitly designed to counter the state's poor reputation. During Governor William Waller's tenure (1972–1976), the new state slogan was "Mississippi, the state of change," a change that was to be seen both in social and economic terms. During those same years, the state launched the Re-Think Mississippi promotional campaign, featuring three advertisements titled *Miss-understood, Miss-informed,* and *Miss-impression.*[121] Published in national newspapers and magazines, the ads featured such slogans as "We're out to ruin our image" or "Apparently they think it's nothing but gators and swamp,"[122] a promotional campaign designed specifically to counter the Magnolia State's negative reputation (and not just on racial issues). One such ad also appeared in the magazine *Black Enterprise* in 1976.[123] By the late 1970s, this strategy seemed to be abandoned, without having achieved any real success. In 1980, a memorandum from George Williams, the state tourism director, conceded that "the image of the state can be vastly enhanced."[124] The idea was to rely on a nationwide advertising agency that could make Mississippi more visible on the American market. The efforts of the small state office and its advertising agency alone were not deemed sufficient. The image problem remained unresolved, and still in 1981, the director of the Department of Economic Development, William Hackett, openly stated that "Mississippi's biggest problem is that of image."[125]

South Carolina was not exempt from image problems either. However, unlike Alabama and Mississippi, its challenge was not a matter of countering a bad reputation, but rather of carving out a distinct image to exploit for promotional purposes, distinguishing itself from its direct competitors. The DPRT, the state department in charge of tourism, had actually conducted a market survey on this very subject in the late 1970s and had alarmingly concluded that potential visitors "had no image at all of South Carolina."[126] One of the goals of the 1979–1980 promotional campaign was precisely to build a recognizable and viable image that would make South Carolina more easily marketable. This was a problem that also affected, at a local level, a number of cities across the state. Dennis Judd reports the case of a national survey conducted by the state capital, Columbia, at the end of the 1980s. Much to the disappointment of the city's tourism industry, it turned out that most respondents had never even heard of Columbia; many confused it with the South American country.[127] The same problem was shared with the Coastal Plains Regional Commission (CPRC), the interstate group of which both the Palmetto State and Georgia were members. In 1980, the CPRC recognized the need to find a clearly identifiable image for its overly generic tourism promotion of the area.[128] South Carolina's two main tourism themes, beaches and Charleston, were not considered so incisive and established as to reassure the state's tourism sector. Developing a competitive image for the foreign market posed another dilemma: how to get Europeans interested in the state. In 1980, the USTS had officially answered this question, advising South Carolina to take advantage of the South's major ace in the hole: "We [USTS] suggested that South Carolina identify themselves in relationship to the whole of the U.S. and also that they associate their area with Margaret Mitchell's classic *Gone with The Wind*. State officials were most appreciative."[129] Once again, it was the national tourist board that suggested exploiting the classic southern theme. It is equally important to note that, despite this advice, South Carolina did not produce any promotional pieces using *Gone with the Wind* or Old South imagery in the following years.

The situation in Georgia, the state of newly elected President Carter, was quite different. In 1976, state tourism director Ed Spivia expressed great optimism about recent results.[130] This same optimism was echoed by Governor Busbee when he announced the record set during the first six months of 1977, when the tourism industry grossed more than $2 billion, seeing a 40 percent increase in the number of visitors to the state's nine welcome centers.[131] In December 1977, during an industry meeting, Spivia illustrated the incredible progress made by the state: "Georgia ranks number 2 in tourism, although it ranks number 9 in the budget allocated for promotion, among the South. On a national level, Georgia ranks number 7 and number 9 transversely, in tourism."[132] No doubt this was an outstanding achievement.

Part of this optimism could also be explained by Jimmy Carter's election to the presidency, a form of free large-scale publicity that gave the state an advantage over its direct competitors. Busbee admitted this during the December 1977 Tourism Conference: "I believe we are going to see something called 'the Georgia fascination' emerge. I believe we are going to see hundreds of thousands of tourists, initially drawn by the presidential spotlight, completely enchanted with the state itself . . . . Thanks to the Carter Presidency, the world, and particularly the traveling public, is having a 'Love affair' with Georgia."[133] In 1977, optimism about tourism growth was so high that no issues of any kind were being raised at industry meetings. Tourism was growing, and with it Georgia's media exposure. In another speech in late 1977, Busbee asserted that growth could be even more remarkable: "Our only true—negative—at this point is the simple fact that we're not yet doing enough."[134] No other state of the Deep South was witnessing such a positive trend. Alabama and Mississippi, in the second half of the 1970s, still suffered from their tarnished reputations, while Georgia, thanks in part to Carter's election, enjoyed high visibility and aroused curiosity in large sectors of the American public.

Upon closer examination, however, it is evident that there were various problems in the Peach State and that not everything was going as well as it seemed. For example, only a few specific parts of Georgia were influenced by tourism, while the rest of the state remained almost entirely excluded, especially those areas farthest from Atlanta. South Carolina had the same problem, as tourism was mostly concentrated in the area of the Grand Strand and Charleston. Following Carter's election, the Georgia tourism industry realized, not without some concern, that the area around the president's hometown, Plains, was completely underdeveloped in terms of tourism. A local attitude and image problem was also noted in the area implementation strategy report: "Attitudinal Changes: . . . Improved images and southern hospitality will go a long way to promote tourism as a major industry in Plains Country. The attitudes of the people are key to successful local promotions, events and an expanded interest in the area."[135] The goals to be achieved included to "dispel negative images, and connotation existing in the area and sometimes assumed by passing travelers." Another problem was that "the area's less sophisticated populace" had a negative impact on passing visitors.[136] In short, even Georgia had its own set of image-related problems. This was another symptom of the uneven growth of the Sunbelt South. Beyond the Atlanta metropolitan area, the Peach State looked very much like the rest of the Deep South, or at least the tourism industry feared it might.

Image and reputation, however, were not the only factors that influenced local tourism in the South. Unsurprisingly, a substantial problem was being next to a giant like Florida, which attracted millions of visitors each year. All four Deep South states complained that they needed to find a way to "hold" within their state borders the thousands of tourists who passed through on their trips to Florida. This need sometimes turned into a precise promotional plan. In 1981 South Carolina produced advertisements aimed specifically at retaining northern visitors traveling to Florida.[137] Even in Georgia, despite the generally positive situation, Ed Spivia announced in 1978 that the main goal to be achieved was "[to] make Georgia a vacation/destination area, not just a pass-through."[138] In spring 1980, a promotional campaign was also launched with the heading "Tourist End Destination," a clear sign that this phenomenon had not yet been reversed.[139]

Becoming a final destination, a destination in its own right and not just a stop along the way, was obviously a problem linked to the quantity and quality of attractions offered to tourists. From the documentation produced by the respective tourist offices it is clear that another key issue for the four states was precisely the scarcity of major attractions, especially in Alabama and Mississippi. Caroline Cavanaugh, director of the Alabama Bureau of Publicity and Information, complained about this in 1979 and concluded that "what Alabama needs most is a super attraction on the scale of Disney World and Six Flags . . . a family playground."[140] Mississippi had the same problem. Robert Robinson, director of the A&I Board, appeared in January 1976 before the U.S. Congress to testify about Mississippi's economic growth programs. On that occasion he declared that Mississippi "does not attract a large number of tourists each year primarily because we do not have a destination tourist attraction. . . . For the past three years efforts have been made to find a major tourist attraction in Mississippi."[141]

In this matter, Georgia was surely the most advantaged of the four. Not only was its capital city, Atlanta, a tourist destination in its own right, but there were also two very popular attractions in the state, the Six Flags Over Georgia amusement park and Stone Mountain Park. Even South Carolina, on a smaller scale, had a few arrows in its quiver; though less visited than Georgia, the state coastal area, the so-called Grand Strand, and the city of Charleston were two attractions that set Carolina apart from its direct southern competitors. The beautiful local beaches, in particular, were considered by state tourism officials to be its main asset: "In South Carolina, the ocean beaches are the greatest single attraction."[142] Both states, moreover, were on the route leading from the North to Florida and could therefore manage to keep a number of those visitors within their borders. But neither Atlanta nor South Carolina's natural and historic beauty were enough to compete against the true giants of the tourism industry.

Here, however, there appears a first but substantial distinction between these states: on the one hand, Alabama and Mississippi, united by serious image problems and a dearth of real attractions to sell on the national market; on the other, states like Georgia and South Carolina, which, despite some difficulties, seemed to be more in line with the general advancement of southern tourism during the 1970s.

Jimmy Carter: A True Southern Attraction?

"Who hasn't heard of Plains?" rhetorically asked the 1978 official brochure on Plains Country, the subregion that was President Jimmy Carter's hometown.[143] The town itself is a small cluster of houses in southwestern Georgia with little to offer. During the 1977–1981 presidential term, it attracted numerous visitors in proportion to its size, but it was far from being the main tourist attraction of the state. It was visited by about 900 to 1200 tourists a day during 1976, numbers that might seem impressive, but in fact were not relative to other destinations.[144] Once travelers had photographed the Carter family farm, there was little or nothing to do and see. In most cases, they left immediately for Florida or other destinations outside of Georgia. As early as November 1976, Spivia complained to the press: "One of the problems is that so many people are going into Plains . . . but then heading back to the interstate and on to Florida."[145] However, it is clear that the tourism bureau hoped to make the small town a base from which to develop a more steady flow for tourism, not just for passing through. In 1976, the CPRC awarded $75,000 to Georgia to study Plains's potential as a tourist center. In 1977, Georgia built its tenth welcome center right on the outskirts of the town,[146] and that same year Spivia was commissioned to develop the infrastructure needed to accommodate tourists arriving there.[147] Georgia clearly hoped to make Plains a solid tourist base in the southern part of the state.

Spivia also believed it was possible to promote tours of the area, which could include, in addition to Plains, Roosevelt's Little White House (in Warm Springs), Callaway Gardens, and Westville, a nineteenth-century reenactment museum. This tour idea was eventually realized with the cooperation of Alabama and Tennessee. A 1978 brochure invited visitors to "take the Presidential Route," an itinerary of Deep South locations associated with prominent American presidents. These included Jimmy Carter, Franklin Delano Roosevelt, Andrew Jackson, and James Polk, as well as former Confederate president Jefferson Davis.[148] A large billboard along the interstate showed their portraits in cartoon form (figure 1). Mooresville, Alabama, where Andrew Johnson lived while studying to become a tailor, was also later added to the tour.

Another Presidential Route brochure described Davis's decision to rebel against the federal government as follows(without, of course, ever mentioning slavery): "Jefferson Davis—wealthy plantation owner, statesman, Army soldier—*became the champion of the constitutional rights of a state to choose and maintain its own institutions*."[149] Here we are in the midst of Lost Cause rhetoric while at the same time in a promotional context designed to capitalize on the election of the new progressive southern president Jimmy Carter. Once again, old and new interact in a South that is no longer quite the same as before, but not yet entirely different. After all, celebrating the former Confederate president in official state or national promotional materials had become much less problematic, thanks to a congressional pardon signed in October 1978 by Jimmy Carter himself, restoring full citizenship to Davis. Despite the promotional hype, however, Plains tourist fever waned rapidly. The *Atlanta Constitution* spoke of 229,000 visitors in 1977, but lower numbers were estimated for the following year.[150] The Carter mystique was already ebbing,

Figure 1. A roadside billboard advertising the Presidential Route. From left to right: Andrew Jackson, Jefferson Davis, FDR, and Jimmy Carter. President James Polk's portrait is missing, because he was evidently not considered easily identifiable by the public. Georgia Archives.

and it was soon recognized that Plains would never become a Monticello or a Mount Vernon. Hugh Carter, cousin of the president and owner of one of the local stores, told the press in 1980 that the flow of tourists was now at a minimum.[151]

Although Plains had limited success as a tourist destination, it probably had a greater effect on American culture. It became, in some ways, the quintessential small southern town, whose inhabitants seemed somewhat naïve and backward, but also honest, straightforward, and genuine. Georgia's official booklet *This Way to Fun*, indeed, introduced it as "the most famous small town in America."[152] To put it another way, Plains was a place where you could have imagined seeing the Duke brothers' Dodge whizzing by. This was somewhat acknowledged in the advertisements. The Presidential Route tour brochure, for example, stated that "the fascinating feature of Plains is the people who live there." All in all, a late-1970s take on the classic, rustic, nostalgic charm of small-town America.

The gas station run by Jimmy Carter's brother Billy also became an iconic site, pulling in as many tourists as the president's home. José Blanco dedicated an article to this phenomenon in which he claimed that "the station was, and still is, a piece of 1970s popular culture and for many a symbol of Americana at its best."[153] Billy became the "redneck ambassador" of the United States. The popularity of his gas station, however, also showed how weak Jimmy Carter's personal draw was for tourists. What people really wanted to experience was the rustic flavor of a small southern town.

The election of Jimmy Carter and the figure of the president himself hardly ever appeared in the tourist advertising of the period. The brochures and booklets always mentioned Plains, of course, but only one ad from Georgia directly referenced the election of the new president. It was a very simple, general ad, only produced in 1977, dedicated to the state of Georgia in its entirety. Its slogan read "What made news last year, makes a great vacation this year,"[154] with obvious reference to the 1976 election. The text cited the state's most important attractions such as Atlanta, Stone Mountain Park, Six Flags, the Golden Isles, Plains, Andersonville, and Roosevelt's Little White House. Yet what really separated Georgia from the rest of the South was underlined in one particular phrase: "The Georgia you've seen on TV. Already a part of history." Georgia was in the national spotlight, while the rest of the Deep South was much less so. It marked a total turnaround in the relationship with the media. In Alabama, as late as 1982, Caroline Cavanaugh still had to point out that her state was no longer the one seen on television in the 1960s.

Another vague attempt to use Carter's image occurred in 1978, on the official brochure for Plains Country. Here, the new president was blatantly used as a link between an old South and a new one. In this area, tourists could find "a town built like an 1850 rural village. A city graced by fountains and Southern mansions. One place depicts the history of Civil War days. Another had made history as the home of the 39th President of the United States."[155] It should not come as a surprise, however, that tourism advertising of the period did not consistently mention Carter. The Tourism Division indeed had purposely chosen not to go overboard in exploiting the Carter (and peanut) theme, rightly feeling that these topics would soon disappear from people's radar.[156]

Although scarcely exploited in the official material, the president nevertheless remained an important symbol of reunification between the South and the rest of the nation in popular perception and in some tourist sites. An interesting case involves the historic site of Andersonville, the Confederate prison camp where thousands of Union soldiers died from starvation. The camp commander, Swiss-born captain Heinrich Wirz, was one of the few Confederate officers who was not romanticized by southern popular culture, and one of the very few to be hanged for war crimes in 1865. No myth of courage and chivalry could be built around Andersonville in the years following the conflict. The camp remained a divisive site, despite attempts to convert it into something different in the early 1970s. In 1971, when Andersonville came under the jurisdiction of the National Park Service, an attempt was made to designate it an "American" memorial site, dedicating it to all American soldiers taken prisoner in every war.[157]

By then, the camp cemetery already housed the remains of those who had fallen in more recent conflicts: World Wars I and II, Korea, and Vietnam. This effectively made the site a place of American memory tout court. This effort to apply a patriotic interpretation to Andersonville occurred, not surprisingly, during the last phase of the Vietnam War, when the need to heal internal rifts in the nation was greater than ever. This project, however, appears to have been only half successful, at least until Carter's election. In the common perception, Andersonville remained above all a symbol of Confederate war crimes and, more generally, a grim reminder of the less seemly aspects of the Civil War. An Iowa newspaper wrote in 1976 that "today [Andersonville] it's a symbol of the fratricidal division that Carter's candidacy for President began to heal."[158]

After Carter's election, visits to Andersonville increased by 200 percent, a staggering number. Between October and December 1975, 18,736 tourists had visited the site. The following year, in the same time frame, there were 41,472. In addition, the time spent by visitors at the site also rose dramatically, by 100 percent.[159] The influx of visitors was so great that the eponymous town of Andersonville, just outside the camp, actively worked to convert itself back into a tourist destination through small-town charm.[160] This growth in visitors is actually not as surprising as it would seem in some reports of the time. Since Andersonville is close to Plains (both are in Sumter County), it is clear that many of the visitors who went to see the president's home also stopped to visit the Confederate prison camp. Yet Carter effectively altered the perception of the site. He was the sign that times had changed.

One 1976 statement by a visitor center official in the small town of Andersonville is explicative of this shift in perception:

> In the last few years and especially since Jimmy Carter began running for the presidency, more and more people have been coming here to learn the truth. . . . The South has been defensive about itself and its history for a long time. Now the people here no longer pretend there was no such thing as Andersonville prison. . . . You can see the scars healing in a place like this. We're getting 200,000 people a year through here, because of Jimmy Carter. They come from the North and the South. And we're all looking at our history a little more squarely now.[161]

Carter's election contributed to making Andersonville a place of catharsis, well suited to help overcome North-South partisanship, Lost Cause mythology, and a fictionalized Civil War narrative. It was now "a place that Americans can go and vow that such will never happen again."[162] After all, battlefields, sites of massacres, murders, or catastrophes (places of so-called dark tourism or thanatourism) can easily become memorials that consolidate national sentiment and the identity of a community.[163]

By the end of 1976 (the year of the bicentennial celebration as well as of Carter's victory), Andersonville had become a site of American memory, as demonstrated also by the long list of institutional or semi-institutional figures who visited the camp that year, especially from Georgia, such as Congressman Jack Brinkley, Senator Herman Talmadge, Carter's mother Lillian, and his daughter Amy, as well as an unspecified number of journalists and media correspondents.[164]

There were also protests. Not everyone was willing to accept this "American" view of Andersonville, since no single memory of the past can satisfy everyone. In 1980, for example, local chapters of the United Daughters of the Confederacy (UDC) held a commemoration in honor of Captain Wirz, whom they claimed had been unjustly tried and portrayed as a vicious monster.[165] By then, however, UDC and other similar groups had lost much of their influence on local society and past memory, especially regarding state-sponsored sites.

Another example of Carter symbolizing national reunion comes from Alabama, although this case is quite different from Andersonville. The White House of the Confederacy in Montgomery was the first presidential residence of Jefferson Davis and his wife, Varina. It recorded around two hundred thousand visitors in 1975, a remarkable figure even if not supported by precise data.[166] By comparison, Plains, Georgia, attracted only a few thousand more in 1977. The renovation and public reopening of the White House took place in 1976, that is, precisely during the height of the national bicentennial celebrations and just two years before the official pardon of Davis. The initiative had not been planned in the context of the festivities, but was somehow also connected to a wider discourse that simply concerned American history tout court. The local associations that paid for and supervised the works conceived the reopening of the Confederate White House not only as a moment of celebration of southern history, but also as a way to integrate that celebratory discourse into an official national narrative. They tried to do so by capitalizing on Carter's election. The president-elect himself was invited to the inaugural ribbon-cutting ceremony, though local leaders admitted that they did not expect him to show up.[167] The desire to tie the historical site to the figure of the first president from the Deep South was evident. It was an attempt to legitimize the Lost Cause and the extremely sectarian interpretation of the past proposed by the White House of the Confederacy, while local elites also argued that it was a site of *American* history. The most iconic moment, in this sense, occurred when Jefferson Davis's great-grandson spoke on the inaugural day, stating that the Confederate president's "faith in the United States was very evident, and I think he would have been proud here today to see that faith renewed."[168] The viewpoint was opposite from that of Andersonville, but the aim similar. In Georgia, it was the nation that sought a connection to the newly elected president to make inroads into the southern narrative, while in Alabama it was the classic South that attempted to use Carter to rejoin the national narrative (at least in part).

In short, Carter's election was not a watershed moment for southern tourism. It benefitted Georgia to some extent, but did nothing to address the Peach State's status as a transient destination, nor did it increase visitor numbers in a steady way. The other Deep South states gained even less from the election, remaining estranged from any sort of Carter mystique. At the same time, Jimmy Carter himself began to be perceived as a problem rather than a resource for the American tourism industry, including by southern tourism professionals. In 1978, the Carter administration planned to permanently shut down the USTS due to its poor performance. Much of the tourism industry protested this decision, including Travel South and all of its member states. Although not very effective, the USTS was the only source of promotional assistance for many states, especially in overseas promotion, which relied on the foreign offices of the USTS.[169] Ronald Reagan eventually closed the USTS in 1981, replacing it with the new, albeit less autonomous, U.S. Travel and Tourism Administration (USTTA). This agency was eventually suppressed in 1996, with its functions transferred to individual states and the private sector, aligning with the proposal of the Carter administration years earlier.[170] Thus, while Carter was hardly ever perceived as a trusted ally by the southern tourism industry, his presence did have an undeniable symbolic value that indirectly benefited a South that was trying to rebrand itself (figure 2).

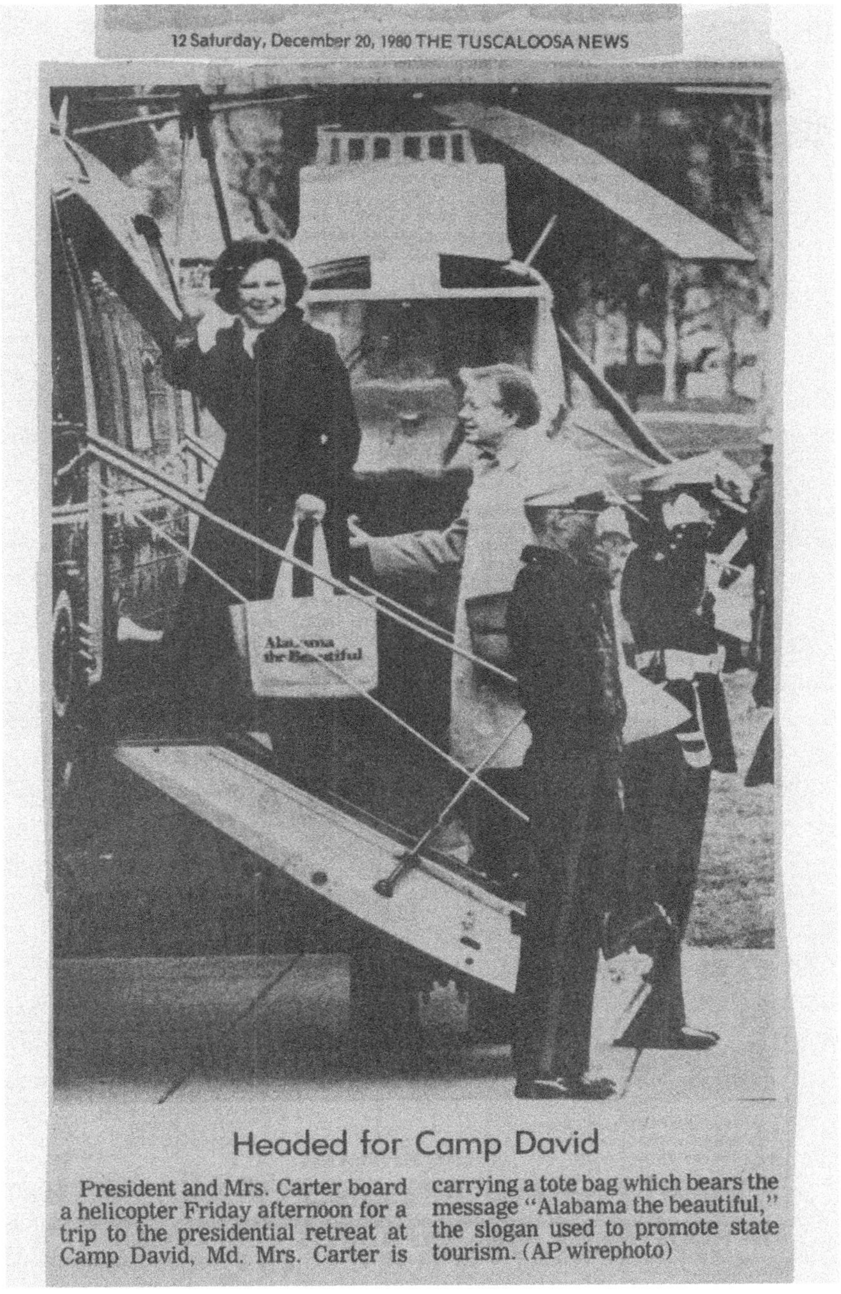
12 Saturday, December 20, 1980 THE TUSCALOOSA NEWS

Headed for Camp David

President and Mrs. Carter board a helicopter Friday afternoon for a trip to the presidential retreat at Camp David, Md. Mrs. Carter is carrying a tote bag which bears the message "Alabama the beautiful," the slogan used to promote state tourism. (AP wirephoto)

Figure 2. President Jimmy Carter and his wife, Rosalynn, board a helicopter for a trip to Camp David in 1980, as the first lady carries a promotional bag produced by the Alabama tourism bureau, with the slogan "Alabama the Beautiful." *Tuscaloosa News*, December 20, 1980, Alabama Department of Archives and History.

CHAPTER 3

Alabama and Mississippi

One key detail, all too easy overlooked among the complexities of tourism promotion, is the main slogan produced by a state travel office for an advertising campaign. Often a single sentence can say something about the overall design of the marketing strategy.[1] Alabama's chief tourism theme in 1977 was "Alabama Has It All,"[2] a slogan that had been in use since 1971 or 1972, appearing in advertisements as well as various promotional newspaper articles.[3]

The idea behind this catchphrase was the wealth of attractions available to visitors. This is a common concept, regularly employed in tourism promotion. Because it is such a simple and straightforward formula, it is not particularly surprising to find several examples in older ads. What is remarkable, if anything, is how minimally it was used, especially in the case of Alabama. Although it was customary to list a number of attractions in an ad, the earliest example in which the overwhelming abundance of attractions is explicitly used as the basis for the promotional message can probably be found in a 1964 advertisement.[4] From the mid-1970s, with the Alabama Has It All campaign, this concept became predominant, immediately conveyed by the slogan and further reinforced by a visual apparatus. The idea of an abundance of attractions also entailed more publications and promotional articles to cover every possible market niche. A new series of tour brochures produced in 1975 promised to "offer visitors . . . unlimited options on what to see, to do and enjoy. There will be fly-drive plans, city package tours, hunting-fishing-sports tours, sightseeing tours, beach packages, and all sorts of combination packages."[5]

This identification of the state with a wealth of things to see is a strategy often based on the idea of an entire world in miniature.[6] It was no coincidence that in 1979 the Alabama Bureau of Publicity and Information decided to change the state's slogan to "Alabama the Beautiful." The state was now promoted directly as a "Mini-USA," a concentration of everything the United States had to offer.[7] Cy Steiner of Steiner/Bressler Advertising directly referred to this concept in 1979 during the annual Conference on Tourism: "Every state has some of the same things to offer. People come to see historical places, mountains, white sand beaches, antebellum homes, etc. What we really have to sell in Alabama is an idea . . . . What we have in Alabama is America in microcosm. Basically what we have is America the Beautiful right here in Alabama. The Campaign theme for the state is 'Alabama the Beautiful.'"[8] It is an interesting choice for a slogan, if only because it seemed to avoid in any way presenting the state as southern rather than American. Alabama was beautiful *precisely because* it represented a smaller version of America. In other words, Alabama was part of the United States and ideally embodied the beauty the country as a whole had to offer. Not surprisingly, the new slogan was adopted just as the state entered the international tourist market in 1980. Since the United States was experiencing a favorable moment in tourist arrivals from abroad, it must have seemed natural for the travel bureau's advertising professionals to try to capitalize on this momentum, placing Alabama in a less regional and more national framework.

This new slogan, however, would almost immediately come under severe criticism. Because the new catchphrase did not entirely replace the previous one, the result was that in 1979 Alabama ads were using two different slogans at the same time.[9] This may not seem like a serious issue, but it was just the kind of dilemma regarding immediate brand recognition that was so important to the admen of the time. Others criticized its lack of impact and excessive vagueness. Above all, the new slogan was attacked for resembling too closely the national promotional ad *America the Beautiful*.[10] Again, there was concern over the possibility of confusing the public, although it is clear that this similarity between the national and state slogans was exactly what the Steiner/Bressler Advertising aimed to exploit with the new wave of international arrivals.

In spite of all the criticism, the slogan remained in place, and it was not until 1983 that it was changed to "Alabama the Beautiful: The Way To Go," the new addition implying that the state tourist office had realized that Alabama was, and remained, a transitory destination, thus using this very notion to revise its promotional material.[11]

Mississippi, on the other hand, employed a different strategy. Tourist slogans for the Magnolia State seemed far more designed to call to mind the idea of a destination deeply anchored to its southern regional identity. In the mid-1970s, Mississippi used "Mississippi: America South," switching in 1978 to "Mississippi: It's Like Coming Home," a slogan that played on the classic theme of southern hospitality but also referred to the supposedly old-fashioned (and slow-paced) southern lifestyle, even using the image of an old rocking chair as the official campaign symbol.[12] What was missing here was a direct reference to the idea of a wealth of attractions. Mississippi used this solution more cautiously than other states, probably because there were very few real attractions within its borders. It was not until later, in 1982, that the Magnolia State would choose to aim directly at "abundance," with the campaign slogan "All the things you're missing . . . are yours in Mississippi."[13]

Clearly, the bombastic rhetoric listing the cornucopia of attractions did not necessarily reflect reality. Actually, both Alabama and Mississippi had a scarcity of real tourist attractions. In addition, many visitors were not traveling to these states to experience anything specific, but simply for business or to visit relatives (and it is debatable whether or not this type of visitor can even be considered a tourist). A study conducted by Auburn University in Alabama in the late 1970s recorded, albeit with some degree of approximation, that among the activities carried out by travel parties in the state, "visiting friends and relatives" ranked first (24.8 percent in 1977, 25.34 percent in 1978).[14] The first actual tourist activity was "visiting historical sites" (between 19 and 22 percent).[15] Mobile and Huntsville, with their respective seaside location and NASA Center, emerged as the two destinations most often mentioned by travelers passing through Alabama. According to Caroline Cavanaugh, these were also the two destinations in the state preferred by foreign tourists (excluding Canadians); Japanese tourists were most interested in the Port of Mobile and German tourists in the NASA Center.[16] More precise visitor numbers are difficult to obtain. A list of the top ten travel/tourist attractions compiled in 1979 showed that in the past year the only attraction with over 500,000 visits was GreeneTrack, a dog track and casino in Eutaw. GreeneTrack was followed by a zoo and a car track in the rankings for top destinations. The top historic attraction, Tannehill Ironworks Historical State Park, was seventh overall, with 192,959 visitors.[17] A less official list, reported in 1977 by the *Montgomery Advertiser*, showed a similar situation, with a true historical attraction ranking fourth, the Colonial Fort Condé.[18] Still in 1981 the top three most visited attractions were a state park and two dog tracks.[19] From 1977 to 1981 the approximate number of visitors to Alabama's national historic sites—Horseshoe Bend National Military Park, Russell Cave National Monument, Tuskegee Institute National Historic Site—were well under 100,000 a year. In 1981 a major increase was recorded for these three attractions, especially the Tuskegee Institute, one of the most important sites for African American culture in the state of Alabama, which reached about 32,000 visitors that year.[20] These were low numbers compared to other attractions, but it is still significant that they experienced an increase during this period. This was not just the result of a growth in Black heritage tourism, but rather the consequence of a precise strategy devised by the local tourism industry. By 1977, plans had begun for the development of the city of Tuskegee, which, it was hoped, would be transformed into a major tourist destination by capitalizing on the Institute's fame. The goal was to reach 150,000 tourists a year by 1985. The matter was delicate, however, in part because of the town's tense community relations.[21]

In Mississippi, a 1975/1976 questionnaire issued by the state tourism director George Williams provides a more accurate picture. He compiled a list of reasons why tourists visited the state, with relaxation, scenic tourism, and recreational activities appearing at the fore. There is no mention of historical tourism, while "to see a specific attraction" ranked last.[22] The greatest problem for the Magnolia State, apart from its image, was a lack of attractions, something that both the public and private tourism sectors lamented. George Tribble, marketing manager for Delta Airlines, further troubled members of the Mississippi Tourism Commission by judging that not a single attraction in the state had the characteristics to achieve national relevance.[23] To overcome this situation, the state launched a preliminary inquiry into the possibility of opening a theme park in Mississippi, which could be tied to the state's tourist promotion, like Disneyworld in Orlando, Florida. The Commission strongly advised against it, as there were no conditions to implement such a project. Nevertheless, three theme parks were planned: Flintstones Park, Dixieland USA, and an unspecified reconstruction of an old town in the Columbus-West Point area.[24] After all, in Travel South's five-year plan drafted in 1974, theme parks were also mentioned as a possible means of increasing the South's promotional reach, so it is not surprising that Williams sought to pursue that target in his own state. However, none of these parks opened in the end. In 1974 the Mississippi legislature set up a commission with the purpose of analyzing the tourism situation in the state and to suggest possible ways to promote its development. The work lasted three years, and the results were well below the state tourism officials' expectations. Already in 1975, a first preliminary report painted a chaotic picture.[25] There was no reliable list of state attractions, nor was the commission able to create one. Information gathered was vague and often outdated. The report gives a significant, albeit nonspecific, idea of the type of tourist attractions in Mississippi. By that date there were only 102 sites in the whole state that were considered "tourist facilities." Among these the vast majority were actually natural sites such as parks and lakes; only five museums and ten antebellum home pilgrimages were included in the report. The three most visited attractions in 1974 and 1975 were artificial lakes and nature reserves, while the only site of historical value among those listed was Vicksburg National Military Park. This ranked fourth with more than 1.5 million visitors—not a small number but still much lower than other attractions topping the list.[26] A much lower volume of visitors went to Beauvoir, the house near Biloxi, Mississippi, where Jefferson Davis lived from 1877 until his death in 1889. However, this was a place of symbolic importance to the Lost Cause. It was here that, in 1980, the Sons of Confederate Veterans (scv) placed the tomb of the "unknown Confederate soldier." (Mississippi actually considered both scv and another neo-Confederate group, the Order of the Stars and Bars, to be "local historical societies."[27]) Beauvoir recorded just over 66,000 visitors in 1975. By 1977 these numbers had risen to about 74,000, decreasing again in the following years.[28]

All in all, these figures clearly show a style of tourism that tended decidedly toward general amusement and recreational activities, distancing itself from the stereotyped Deep South image where the only entertainment offered to travelers was to participate in a fictional narrative of the past. Is it therefore possible to conclude that historical and cultural tourism was of little relevance to the South? Not exactly. Data from travel bureaus include all visitors, regardless of where they came from. It is very likely that many of those visiting lakes and natural parks were state residents, whereas most of the visitors to historic attractions were from out of state, as it is usually the outsider who wants to "experience" the culture and history of a specific destination. In addition, cultural and historical attractions related to the antebellum South, although less visited than other attractions, were the only specific feature of tourism in Alabama and Mississippi, standing out in the popular imagination and, by the mid-1970s, probably appearing more economically significant than they actually were for both states. This situation must also be considered from the point of view of southern tourism professionals. The fact that the state and private tourism sector in Mississippi felt that they did not have attractions large enough to succeed in the national marketplace shows that antebellum homes were not considered sufficiently relevant. Something else was needed. While historical and cultural attractions had their own importance, as an integral part of the destination image that states offered to foreigners and out-of-state travelers, they certainly did not provide the greatest economic return. This undoubtedly contributed to the proliferation of images and themes that differed from the traditional ones.

Here, in the heart of the Deep South, two parallel narratives coexisted in the late 1970s. On the one hand, there was a more modern and up-to-date tourist narrative that focused on the recent innovations that had taken place in the region over the past two decades; on the other, numerous traces of the older, classic southern destination image could still be found. Indeed, tourist advertising in both Alabama and especially Mississippi still abounded with promotional material centered on the romantic antebellum South, the ads appearing to have changed little, if at all, from the previous decades. A good example can be found in two Mississippi advertisements for antebellum home tours dating February 1955 and March 1978.[29]

There were virtually no differences between these two ads, both containing a textual part listing the locations where the events will be held and a visual part consisting of the classic southern belle in costume in front of an antebellum home. The only notable change is the disappearance of the Confederate battle flag from the 1978 ad, as this symbol had already become less central in the state-sponsored southern iconography of the period. The general attitude of the ads, however, remained unchanged, with the old plantation South still being celebrated: "Enjoy the treasures of the antebellum past in every section of the state. Tour magnificent mansions and stately homes filled with rare antiques, silver, crystal and china. Concerts, pageants, balls and other cultural events add to the charm of Mississippi's Pilgrimages."[30] An even more celebrative tone is found in a 1981 Alabama radio commercial for antebellum homes. The script appears to be a genuine summary of all the rhetoric and mythology of the Old White South: "It was a time worth remembering. Southern belles in crinolined skirts. Air heavy with magnolia. White fields of cotton as far as the eye could see. That era is gone . . . but the magnificent mansions that cotton built live on . . . these elegant reminders of a bygone way of life are preserved. They take you back to yesterday."[31]

In Mississippi, antebellum homes and their mythical aura were still so prominent in the local imagery that the state tourism bureau produced guides dedicated exclusively to home tours.[32] It would be almost impossible to quantify the number of people who took part in Mississippi antebellum home pilgrimages, although this figure would be of interest. A document related to the city of Columbus, in Lowndes County, mentions "thousands of visitors" on local pilgrimages, but it is still an approximation that official travel office records do not chronicle.[33] A narrative extolling the Old South frequently appeared in the ads produced by Alabama and Mississippi at the time, both in promotional materials designed for circulation in neighboring states (such as radio commercials) and in advertisements aimed at the northern or western markets. Even the states' main tourist brochures contained much of this old-fashioned appeal. In the *Alabama Has It All* booklet, for example, the section entitled "Yesterday" is dedicated to antebellum homes: "The Old South is gone. But there are over 2000 places where you can walk through a doorway and into the best of those times—elegant, stately, ornate. They're Alabama's fabulous antebellum homes. . . . You'll see why our ancestors went to war to save the Old South."[34] The text conveys the idea that the Confederate soldiers, both rich and poor, had fought exclusively to defend the beauty of aristocratic homes and gardens from northern aggression. At the same time, though, the official brochures and advertisements produced by the Alabama and Mississippi state travel offices also highlighted new elements that were shaping the South's tourist image—an example of the profound changes taking place in regional promotion. These new developments, in sharp contrast to the traditional southern promotional narrative, included both radical new themes, such as Black history, and new communication strategies, such as image fragmentation and niche targeting.

By the mid-1970s Alabama's main promotional publication was the official pamphlet *Alabama Has It All*, produced for the Bureau of Publicity and Information by the Lucky and Forney advertising firm. The first release of the booklet dates back to 1975, and the bureau had already produced various versions by 1979.[35] The front cover of a smaller-format edition of the booklet immediately catches the eye: a photo collage including an African American child, an image rarely used in southern tourist material at the time.[36] Interestingly, an identical photo of the same child, pictured fishing with his father, later reappeared in a 1981 issue of the African American magazine *Ebony*, in an article that dealt with fishing tourism and particularly discussed Alabama.[37] The presence of African Americans in Alabama's sports tourism imagery had important significance. Hunting and fishing had been central themes for southern tourism since the late 1800s. By establishing itself as a sportsman's destination between Reconstruction and the early 1920s, the South effectively made hunting and fishing an authentic southern experience in the eyes of outsiders. This also had huge repercussions for interracial relationships in the region and for Black access to hunting and fishing. As these activities became central to the tourism industry, the local white elite often restricted African American access to hunting and fishing areas, reserving them for whites only.[38] By the 1970s, however, even these very popular outdoor activities, constantly advertised by state offices, had changed from the traditional promotional style of the first phase and begun to show a more inclusive façade. Indeed, the very approach to fishing tourism in Alabama highlights the new professional tack of state advertising. In 1979, Caroline Cavanaugh responded to some questions from the local press by pointing out that one of the problems with advertising under previous administrations had been the "shotgun effect," or the excessive generality of their promotional targets. She brought up the state's promotion of fishing areas as an example, remarking that Alabama should have been more careful to focus specifically on bass-fishing groups and deep-sea-fishing groups, which were abundant in the Deep South. She called this latter method a "rifle-shot" approach, which meant identifying a well-defined target and focusing on it.[39] Therefore, Cavanaugh's bureau likely intended the photo of the African American father and son—as well as the article in *Ebony*—as one such rifle shot, i.e., a promotional message aimed at the specific target of Black fishing enthusiasts in the state.

Beyond the choice of subject, it is important simply to note the use of a photo *collage* as the principal image on the booklet cover. One cannot overstate how crucial pictures and illustrations are in the world of advertising, and in tourism advertising in particular.[40] Images, the subject matter portrayed, the way in which they are organized and arranged within the brochure—none of this ever merely presents what is "out there."[41] Rather, they "subliminally guide tourists via mediated discourse and an agglomeration of producer interpretations."[42] Therefore, in modern advertising a collage of photos is more than just a list of possible attractions; it is a way to imprint the very idea of abundance and wealth of entertainment into the reader's mind.

The text from the 1975/1976 *Alabama Has It All* booklet is of special interest for understanding the overall scheme behind state promotion.[43] The work divides the state into three equal parts, North, Central, and South Alabama, with roughly the same variety of attractions in each area, so much so that it is difficult to make thematic distinctions among the three, despite the booklet's vague attempt to market them, respectively, as the outdoor green area, the history buff area, and the generic leisure area. While history is a recurring subject, the reader is assured that there is much more to do and see: "But don't get the idea that all of Alabama is history. Not by a long shot."

This promotional strategy of dividing the various states into tourist regions is typical of the 1970s. To emphasize their abundance, the tourist bureaus of Georgia, South Carolina, Mississippi, and Alabama all created different subregions, promoting each as equally bountiful but at the same time unique in some way, with a specific theme carved out for each.[44] Alabama had three regions, Mississippi five, and South Carolina ten, while Georgia was divided into three regions until 1978 when it increased the number to seven. During this period, the images of Alabama's tourist regions were the least clear or defined.

Dividing the territory into various areas and assigning one or more specific themes to each subregion also served an additional function: it prevented the image of the state from remaining limited to a single definition or representation in the reader's mind. For example, the 1975/1976 *Alabama Has It All* stated: "South Alabama is the closest to the Deep South portrayed in the movies, books and songs." This meant that the familiar images of the Deep South shared in the American imagination did exist (because the public wanted them to), but at the same time not *all* of the state was actually like that. Conveying a message of cultural uniformity would have been counterproductive for a state that felt the weight of its reputation for backwardness.

It is also interesting to note the booklet's emphasis on Native American culture and the history of local tribes (Cherokee and Chickasaw). What was lacking was any reference to African American history or culture. Of the prominent historical figures in the state mentioned, only two African Americans are included: W. C. Handy, called the Father of the Blues, "a very special black child born in a log cabin in Florence in 1874," and George Washington Carver, a "quiet, gentle man who was born in slavery" and would later become professor at the Tuskegee Institute and one of the most prominent Black scientists of the twentieth century. There is no other reference to other Black figures or heritage, while Natives are mentioned at least a dozen times and placed in the overall context of local state culture. It should be pointed out, however, that Black figures had already been used in Alabama's official promotion. As early as 1973, an *Alabama Has It All* ad invited people to visit the W. C. Handy Museum in Florence, even though the musician was not described in the text or visually shown as a Black man.[45]

Another version of the booklet produced around 1977 provides other interesting data. In the section titled "Historical Attractions," the text argues that Alabama's history did not end with the Civil War: "If you think Alabama's historical attractions bring alive the War between the States, you're right. But if you think that's all the history you'll find here, you're wrong."[46] An entire section of the booklet called "Leap into Tomorrow" is devoted to the state's modern, cutting-edge technology. Here were photos showing the U.S. Space and Rocket Center—the most important Alabama attraction of its kind—and the U.S. Army Aviation Museum. "Leap into Tomorrow" is followed by a section titled "Or Back to Yesterday," devoted mostly to antebellum homes. There is a clear attempt to present Alabama as equally linked to its past and projected into the future, despite the disproportionately high number of historical attractions.

The state's next official promotional booklet was *Alabama the Beautiful*, published in 1979. In a 1981 version found in the Alabama Archives, the cover appears straightforward and simple: a pond among blooming camellias, the state flower.[47] The brochure opens immediately with a different approach than the one taken by its predecessor *Alabama Has It All*. While natural beauty is the first image presented to readers, the very first page features "a beautiful black woman with a laughing child," "a magnolia-skinned southern belle with music in her voice," "graceful mansions that cotton built," and "cannons that stand as a proud reminder of a valiant heritage." This was a clear attempt to make the state's image more inclusive without abandoning the classic layout altogether: a southern belle next to a Black woman, both still in the shadow of a heritage valiantly defended by Confederate cannons. A more ambiguous symbolic element is also present. The figure of the white girl is shown alone with the typical attributes of purity, whereas the Black woman is with a child. This difference in the appearance of the two figures seems to echo the myth of the Black matriarch: the African American woman described first and foremost as a mother and especially as a single mother.[48] Nevertheless, the inclusion of a Black woman in the opening of the booklet is of great importance, since the cliché of the southern belle is for the first time enriched or complemented by a Black element.

The most obvious novelty, however, appears in the "History/Culture" section, which opens: "Alabama the Beautiful is part of the history of the Civil War. And the history of Civil Rights. The beautifully restored church where Martin Luther King shared his vision of brotherhood stands almost within the shadow of the First Capitol of the Confederacy." For one thing, "Civil War" has now become the only term used to designate the conflict, with the "War between the States" disappearing from all publications in the Alabama the Beautiful campaign. This was clearly no accident, and in fact, it seems to have been a matter of debate within the bureau. The choice of specific terms in these publications was never casual. A preliminary draft for *Alabama the Beautiful*, archived in Caroline Cavanaugh's office files, contained the term "Civil War" in the opening lines. Cavanaugh deleted it, adding a comment: "Why not change this phrase to something like—Cannons are a proud reminder of a valiant heritage? This way, the term 'Civil War' will be avoided. Many Alabamians maintain that the proper terminology is 'War Between the States.'"[49] In other words, Cavanaugh was not only proposing to remove from the first page of the state's main tourist booklet a term that was not particularly popular among the inhabitants of the state (who were evidently considered the most likely readers of the text), but also to rephrase the entire sentence to avoid direct mention of the war. This would suggest that the traditional southern definition of the conflict was by that time no longer acceptable for a publication of this type, at least in an Alabama struggling with its image.

However, despite Cavanaugh's remarks, the term "Civil War" did appear in the booklet. Why was her note ignored? Was it because the advertising agency in charge of editing the brochure advised naming the war directly—perhaps for marketing purposes, to better imprint itself in the minds of Civil War enthusiasts? As mentioned earlier, all of the ads produced by the bureau between 1980 and 1981 for the Alabama the Beautiful campaign call the conflict the "Civil War," never the "War between the States."[50] It is difficult to see this as a coincidence rather than a conscious change in the linguistic register of the bureau's promotional material.

To return to the "History/Culture" section of the booklet, the symbolic contrast between Dexter Avenue Baptist Church (Martin Luther King Jr.'s pastoral home and a key center in the organization of the Montgomery bus boycott) and Jefferson Davis's Confederate White House certainly should not be overlooked, especially when compared to material produced just a few years earlier. The previous brochure, *Alabama Has It All*, presented a white-centric image of the state, with only two brief references to Black figures in the entire, lengthy text: W. C. Handy and Washington Carver. In the 1975/1976 brochure, Alabama's historical attractions were implicitly traced back to one major event in particular: "Central Alabama is a history buff's dream. It is literally the Cradle of the Confederacy." A few years later, however, Alabama would present itself as a place of dialogue between white and Black heritage, integrating the civil rights era into the official state narrative, even if in contrast with its Confederate past. In these years, politics were marked by the same attitude. In his 1979 inaugural address, Governor Fob James stated: "I believe if Robert E. Lee and Martin Luther King Jr. were here today, their cry to us, their prayer to God—would call for 'The politics of unselfishness'—a people together."[51] There was plenty of room for these thematic contrasts in a South that had experienced a profound change in its symbols and myths. The new South stood side by side with the old, not removing it from its place of honor in the popular consciousness (and thus from the advertising narrative). This was another symptom of the rise of the previously mentioned "myth of the biracial South."

With *Alabama the Beautiful*, the state's official material saw a substantial increase of images involving African American society. There was now a full-page photo of Dexter Avenue Baptist Church with the entire congregation and choir posing for the camera, another of the Tuskegee Institute Chapel, and a third of the Booker T. Washington National Monument. All of this appears as a great leap forward, with images that evoke not merely the presence of Black people in the state but African American heritage. These were not simply generic photos; they portrayed events and experiences that were central to Alabama's (and America's) Black population.

The juxtaposition of two contrasting themes, such as "the Confederacy" and "Civil Rights," still recurs in the Alabama booklet to this day (and, more generally, in the official brochures of all Deep South states). For example, immediately after the only mention of Jefferson Davis in Alabama's 2018 state guide, the text refers to Martin Luther King Jr.; the same phenomenon can be seen in the 2018 Mississippi booklet.[52]

It is worth noting that the bureau also used the same photograph of the Dexter Avenue Baptist Church employed in the 1979–1981 booklet to produce a single full-color advertisement targeted explicitly at Black heritage tourism, a first for Alabama and for the entire Deep South. The text openly claims that "no other state in the union is as rich in Black history as Alabama the Beautiful."[53] The fact that the state had begun to focus on Black tourism can also be seen in another ad published for the first time in the African American magazine *Ebony* in 1981.[54]

W. C. Handy, one of the Black Alabamans cursorily mentioned in the *Alabama Has It All* booklets, now became the main protagonist of a radio commercial also produced in 1981, which was branded "Alabama the Beautiful." Dedicated to the state's museums, the commercial opened with the following lines: "A small black child sat in front of the log cabin, listening . . . in his head . . . to a new kind of music. The blues . . . fathered by W. C. Handy."[55] While the script was similar to a previous one produced in 1973, what was new was that the commercial made a direct reference to a museum dedicated to an historical Black figure. The 1973 ad had similarly opened with the W. C. Handy Museum, but it never referred to Handy's skin color; he was simply "the man who played the Blues."[56] In the 1975 booklet, he was actually recognized as a Black man.

Likewise, Black heritage claimed a space in the audiovisual promotional material produced by the bureau. There is no record of the exact number of promotional films made in those years, but by March 1980 there must have been at least seventeen, a remarkable figure for a low-tourism state like Alabama.[57] We know the titles of some of these movies: the evocative *More than Cottonfields*,[58] *Alabama . . . Has It All*,[59] and *Travelin' Alabama*,[60] as well as older films titled *How Ya Comin', Alabama?*,[61] *Alabama Holiday*, and *Alabama beyond the Interstate*.[62]

In 1980, the tourism division was about to release another promotional film specifically focusing on Alabama's historical attractions. Once again, the main attractions presented were antebellum homes. The preliminary script contained hints about the images that would appear in the various sections of the film. It was specified to lay particular "emphasis on old homes."[63] Images of pilgrimages to Tuscaloosa, Eutaw, Greensboro, and various other cities were also used. Finally, in 1981, a new twenty-minute film on *Alabama the Beautiful* went into production.[64] Antebellum homes were now no longer the focus, although the narrative style continued to be particularly emphatic when describing them. African American history now occupied more space, with the addition of the Dexter Avenue Baptist Church ("where Dr. M. L. King began his civil rights crusade") and the African Extravaganza event in Selma.[65] George Washington Carver's home museum also received more attention than in the previous commercial: "You'll feel the presence of the man who founded the school because he was determined that blacks have a better quality of life."

Therefore, by the early 1980s, Alabama's tourist image was no longer exclusively white, and even though Black culture and heritage still played a small part in the overall picture, it was nonetheless acknowledged. Prior to the Alabama the Beautiful campaign, there are few recorded examples of an attempt to establish this recognition. In a booklet produced by the Alabama Historical Commission in cooperation with the tourist office around 1977, focused on the state's historical landmarks, Governor George Wallace's opening lines read: "The War Between the States is a war close to the memories of many citizens whose fathers or grandfathers fought in it to preserve the only way of life they knew—or whose fathers of grandfathers were freed as a result of it."[66] The traditional southern designation of the conflict was maintained, but the state's Black population was granted a voice in the memory of the war, which is significant and obviously a manifestation of the governor's attempt to reach out to Alabama's Black society. Other than this, the only attention given to Black Alabama prior to the launch of the 1979 campaign was in the cursory mention of Handy and Carver in the early 1970s.

Something similar is also found in Mississippi's promotional material, albeit not as markedly. The only Magnolia State guidebook produced in those years was the 1978 *Mississippi: It's Like Coming Home*,[67] which remained in use until 1982 when it was replaced by *All the Things You're Missing . . . Are Yours in Mississippi*.[68] As early as 1973 the state Agricultural and Industrial Board had begun planning a comprehensive state travel guide, which was not completed until 1978.[69] During this lengthy period of planning and debate, a careful review was carried out of the role of tourism in Mississippi's economy, as discussed in chapter two.

The 1978 booklet opens with a classic summary of local attractions: natural beauty, landscapes, historical sites, antebellum homes. The chapter on the state history begins remarkably with the statement that "Mississippi is history. . . . Mississippi isn't living in the past—the past is living in Mississippi." History, or the past, is a central element of the booklet, but the text is particularly careful to emphasize that this past was not exclusively related to old plantations or the Confederacy.

Indeed, the state's history is evoked through "Indians and other travelers," "places founded by Spanish and French explorers and settlers," "elaborate mansions and giant plantations," going as far back as the dawn of time: "The past began millions of years ago in Mississippi." Great attention is also given to the local Native tribes: the Choctaw, the Chickasaw, and the Natchez. The classic antebellum period was an "elegant era in a state and time devoted to King Cotton," but it seems to be just one among the many and varied historical phases of the state, and not even the most significant. The Civil War is always referred to as the "Civil War," never as the "War between the States," but as in Alabama it still appeared as a mythical event without cause or effect. Slavery is never mentioned, despite the emphasis on Mississippi's wealth during the reign of King Cotton: "King Cotton's reign was firmly established. Mississippi became one of the nation's wealthiest states. This is the era when most of Mississippi's grand mansions were built . . . but flush times could not last forever, and on January 9, 1861, Mississippi became the second state to secede from the Union. It would be the last to reenter." The language and style are essentially neutral and merely descriptive, though a few more colorful choices feature from time to time. For example: "Nathan Bedford Forrest and other Rebels harried the Yankees before and after the fall of Vicksburg." Some reminiscences of Lost Cause ideology can also be found in such passages as the following: "Armed conflicts alone did not defeat the Confederacy: blockaded ports and the economic slowdown choked the South." Here appears one of the myths dear to Confederate partisans, namely that of a South never truly defeated on the battlefield but brought to its knees as a result of the North's economic stranglehold.[70]

The "Cultural" chapter features other important elements. The text opens with a curious statement: "In a world that sometimes obscures traditional human values, Mississippi artists and their art stand out as seers and celebrators of the human condition in its many forms," which is a clear take on Mississippi's friendly new image as well as an inclusion of minorities in the general discourse. This sentence may seem far-fetched in a late-1970s Mississippi guidebook, but it was actually in full compliance with the state policy of image rehabilitation that had been pursued for years. The text mentions a number of Black artists—Margaret Walker, Muddy Waters, Bo Diddley, B. B. King, and Dorothy Moore—and there is even room for a large photo of African American actors performing at the Jackson Opera House.

The narrative includes references to antebellum homes and pilgrimages, but there is no segment dedicated to this type of attraction. A page in the "Festivals & Events" section dealt with house tours and the "genteel South" in general, but it was only listed as one of the many activities or themes on offer. In fact, as the text carefully states, "Whatever your interests, Mississippi has an activity you'll enjoy." The Magnolia State did not give up on the idea of an abundance of activities and attractions, despite limits in its tourism industry.

The next guidebook, *All the Things You're Missing*, produced in 1982, featured some new elements, although the overall structure remained largely unchanged. The booklet opens by declaring that antebellum homes and pilgrimages are "romantic journeys through time [and] offer an experience you will never forget with the fragrance of wisteria."[71] However, unlike the previous booklet, this one includes a photo of an African American couple enjoying themselves. As far as we know, it is the first instance of a photo in a Mississippi promotional piece in which Blacks are actually portrayed as tourists and not as locals or entertainers. The vacationing couple, as a photographic subject, was usually white. Symbolically, this photo of Black tourists is an important element, as it implies that the A&I Board had finally recognized the possibility that African Americans might also read the booklet and choose Mississippi as their vacation destination.

The Delta Blues Museum, inaugurated in 1979, was also included among the various attractions in the new booklet. The relationship between blues music culture and Mississippi tourism is complex and requires a brief digression. Stephen A. King's seminal study on the subject investigated the apparent delay with which the Magnolia State recognized and exploited the appeal of blues and its legendary performers. Certainly Governor William Waller's declaration in November 1975 that blues was officially a local Black heritage art form had important symbolic value,[72] but blues tourism did not begin until the late 1970s, and until the mid-1990s it was a phenomenon exclusively centered in and around the Clarksdale and Greenville areas.[73] The reasons behind its eventual emergence included the birth of the Mississippi Delta Blues Festival in 1978; the founding of the Delta Blues Museum in Clarksdale in 1979; the renovation and restoration of the "street where the Blues was born," Beale Street in Memphis, Tennessee; the reevaluation of the blues as an object of cultural study by William Ferris; and the founding of Malaco Records, an independent label based in Jackson, Mississippi, that experienced a boom in sales between 1976 and 1985. The combination of these elements generated a new-found interest in the genre.

In its early days Mississippi blues tourism was quite limited. What contributed to its rise to fame was the fact that it clearly functioned as a pocket of African American resistance in the state's overwhelmingly white tourism industry. It is no coincidence that the Delta Blues Festival initially had an aspect of preservation within the local African American culture.[74] It was not long before the national press took notice of the festival and its symbolic importance. The *Washington Post* published an article describing the event in an idyllic way, emphasizing the absence of any racial animosity.[75] (Clearly the press was keeping an eye on the event expecting trouble.) The importance of these attractions during this period, however, should not be overstated. Early on, the Delta Blues Festival attracted almost exclusively locals from the Greenville area. Similarly, in its first years, the Delta Blues Museum struggled to remain open due to low visitor numbers (between thirty and forty per month in 1979 according to King).[76] The museum received no public funding, either state or federal, and managed to survive only through private donations. Therefore, in the second half of the 1970s, blues tourism was hardly a real attraction for Mississippi, let alone an alternative to the perennial antebellum theme. While a segment of the tourism industry acknowledged blues as an artistic expression intimately linked to local Black culture, it was not formally designated as a Black heritage asset, nor deemed especially lucrative for promoting Mississippi. In 1978, the booklet *It's Like Coming Home* did not even mention the blues, and it highlighted some Black bluesmen only to emphasize the influence their music had on the Mississippi-born King of Rock, Elvis Presley.

The Elvis image, however, was another missed opportunity for Mississippi's tourism industry in the late 1970s. When the King died in 1977, his small hometown of Tupelo, Mississippi, began the process of conversion into a tourist destination bound to the memory of its most famous son. Sure enough, the town had already been for years a pilgrimage destination for Elvis enthusiasts, but after 1977 the volume of business increased. Within a year of Elvis's death, there was a Presley Heights neighborhood in Tupelo, as well as a Presley Drive leading up to Presley Park. There was of course also a Presley Supermarket and an Elvis Presley Heights Restaurant. The King's birthplace, meanwhile, had become a town memorial. Townspeople themselves had partly assumed the role of tourism agents. For example, due to the lack of an official Elvis Museum in town, a Mrs. Boyd had opened a private one inside her home, consisting of a series of newspaper clippings and photos of the artist. Mr. McMillian, the owner of the Elvis Presley Heights Restaurant, on the other hand, took tourists on an informal tour of Elvis's childhood sites.[77] Yet Tupelo always remained a secondary destination for Elvis enthusiasts, who concentrated on Graceland, the artist's residence in Memphis, Tennessee. This is also because, as Michael Bertrand points out, Tupelo's local administrators were slow and half-hearted in pursuing the memorialization of Elvis in the cityscape, due mostly to the citizens' skepticism of making Tupelo a go-to place for outside visitors.[78] As such, most of the initiatives were amateurish, taken up by small private parties.

The state tourism department also did not particularly emphasize the Elvis image. In the early 1980s, an "Elvis pilgrimage" in Tupelo was advertised, and the department was working on a promotional film titled *This Is Elvis*. But otherwise, the artist's name occurs little in promotional material produced between 1978 and 1981.[79] One of the reasons was obviously the lack of other attractions in the area of Tupelo. In compiling a list of places of interest in that part of the state, the department could mention only Rowan Oak, William Faulkner's house in Oxford; an Antebellum Pilgrimage also in Oxford; Holly Springs and Panola County (without even specifying what kind of attraction was marketable in these two destinations); and the Jacinto Courthouse in Jacinto.[80] Tupelo was thus a minor destination, in a region not particularly rich in attractions, within a state suffering from dearth of attractions generally.

In short, the local music scene and the blues had not yet become key assets for Mississippi's tourism industry. Nevertheless, only a few years later, the new state guide *Rich in Memories: Mississippi* (1985) would open with the following lines: "Mississippi is . . . an oldster sitting around the town square. Last home of Jefferson Davis. Greenville, home of the Blues."[81] A juxtaposition (the Confederate president named alongside a reference to Black culture) that recalls the case already seen in the Alabama booklet (Confederacy and civil rights). From then on, Mississippi's tourist image would increasingly rely on its musical tradition, which now appears as the dominant aspect in the overall picture.

It must be said that the Alabama promotional material also shows little attention to the local music theme, which began to be exploited more strongly only in the early 1980s. Music also started to appear more prominently in promotional texts; in 1980 for example a Travel South ad announced that "Alabama has it all, from bluegrass music festivals and historic Indian theatre . . . to the space wonders at Huntsville."[82] As noted earlier, as early as 1973 and 1975 Alabama produced advertisements featuring W. C. Handy, but aside from that one legendary artist, music had no place in the state's image. Then, by the early 1980s things began to change, though Alabama was associated mostly with the country genre rather than blues. Indeed, the state administration used white musicians with a more traditionally southern appeal to promote Alabama. The state had been holding an official Hank Williams Memorial Celebration since 1973, for example, yet nothing of the sort existed for W. C. Handy, although the Black bluesman was named in some advertisements.[83] From the beginning of the new decade, musicians associated with the new southern country rock genre were also directly involved in tourism promotion. In 1981, for example, Governor Fob James designated three days in May as "Alabama the Beautiful Country Weekend" to celebrate a ballad recently produced by the country frock band Alabama that would be played on radio stations around the state.[84] The previous year, a memorandum from Caroline Cavanaugh stated that there had been the idea to appoint the band as "Alabama Ambassador" after they performed at the annual Alabama Conference on Tourism in April 1980.[85] Also in 1981, the tourist bureau approached Glen Wood of the Boutwell-Wood Recording Studio to produce a song called "Alabama the Beautiful" to be used as an advertising jingle. This gained so much popularity that officials considered making it the state's official anthem.[86] The lyrics of the song were basically an advertising script that listed the scenic beauty of the state, including its landscapes and storied architecture: "Your marbled mansions with mirrored halls, echo days gone by."[87] Not surprisingly, the state administration chose to identify the state of Alabama with the southern rock genre, which had become fashionable during the 1970s, partly because of its power to convey a sense of national purpose and patriotism. Other southern destinations such as Nashville, Tennessee, after all, had recently prospered by exploiting that same imaginary. By the early 1980s, however, in terms of musical identity, Alabama, Mississippi, Georgia, and South Carolina all lagged behind much more important southern destinations. Tourism in New Orleans, for example, had been related to jazz music since at least the 1940s, and Nashville, which started promoting itself as a music tourism destination only in 1970s, had far more visibility and success than any music-related destination in Mississippi, Alabama, Georgia, or South Carolina.[88] The problem was not just the inherent weakness of the tourism industry in some of these states, but also the fact that they could not really boast a deep identification with the most famous musicians born there. Elvis was associated mostly with Memphis, where he lived and died. W. C. Handy, though born in Alabama, was also claimed as an icon by Memphis, because it was there that the Black artist achieved his success.

Both Alabama and Mississippi, however, by the end of the 1970s were on the verge of a major step, namely the production of a state-sponsored Black heritage tourist booklet. In 1983, the Alabama tourism bureau published the country's first state travel guide dedicated exclusively to African American culture, *Alabama's Black Heritage: A Tour of Historic Sites*, produced during George Wallace's last gubernatorial term under the direction of Ed Hall, who replaced Caroline Cavanaugh as director of the tourism bureau that same year.[89] The guidebook listed eighty-two sites and buildings related to African American culture in the Camellia State. It was a first for Alabama, which was also the first state in the country to produce such a guide. A year later, work began at the Mississippi Department of Economic Development to prepare a similar guide dedicated exclusively to Black culture. It was the first time the state had to reflect on and inventory possible Black cultural tourist attractions: "A search is under way to identify black people, places, things and events of significance to the state's heritage for a Mississippi tour guide about blacks."[90] Alvin Benson, one of the men behind this groundbreaking idea, told the *Clarion-Ledger* that there was a particular need for this new tourist guide, because "we have a lot of people visiting our state who are interested in a portion of the state's black history."[91] It is difficult to say if Benson was making this claim based on actual data. There is a high possibility that the entire operation was designed primarily to keep up with Alabama, although it can also be seen as an attempt to revive the state's image. However, while state governments in the Deep South were indeed beginning to accept and recognize Black heritage by the early 1980s, they still viewed it as a phenomenon separate from general tourism. Alabama and Mississippi did not simply add a thematic chapter within their guidebooks; instead, they directly created new specific booklets focused solely on that market segment. In other words, Black tourism was intended as a separate sector, distinct from the rest of the tourism industry.

While the broadening of the two states' overall image to include Black heritage, in however limited a way, seems to have begun in the late 1970s and early 1980s, the inclusion of Native American culture and imagery within the tourist narrative is an entirely different story. As briefly mentioned above, the booklets produced by Alabama and Mississippi put a strong and obvious emphasis on local Native American history and tradition. The stereotypical, somewhat caricatured images that for so long had dominated white America's perception Natives (that is, the iconic Indian warrior, the sensual squaw, and so on) were already a thing of the past. In the booklets, the representation of Native culture was not particularly gauche. A page and a half of *Alabama Has It All* (1975/1976) are dedicated exclusively to the appeal of local Indian culture, and *Alabama the Beautiful* even opens with a large two-page photo dedicated to a Native culture festival, a scene from the Creek Nation's Powwow celebrations. In *Mississippi: It's Like Coming Home*, the Native theme is even more present, and the booklet goes to great lengths to draw for an entire chapter a full historical picture of the state's past, incorporating Native culture. Again, the photo choice in the Mississippi guidebook shows both historical sites and contemporary representations of local tribes and their traditions. In short, there is not the same taboo toward Native peoples that was reserved for Black society. The culture and past of Native Americans are seamlessly incorporated into the history of the two states. For African American culture, this only happened later, and at a much slower pace.

Denise Bates describes this gap between the southern recognition of Native and African American identity. By granting Native people a place within southern society—more or less paternalistically—southern states attempted to redeem themselves from their tarnished image and reputation as the most racist and violent region in the entire country. It is no coincidence that between the 1970s and 1980s, when this need to improve the South's image became more pressing, there was a substantial integration of Native elements in southern tourism literature.[92]

A series of events also celebrated this ideal rapprochement between Native and American culture in the Deep South. In 1980, the Deep South International Indian Job Fair was held in Huntsville, Alabama, and in 1981 some local tribesmen were invited to participate in a public event dedicated to celebrating the state's heritage. Finally, in 1982, the first week of autumn was declared Indian Heritage Week in Alabama.[93] In 1978, Margie Tyler of the Mississippi Department of Tourism organized a fashion show with replicas of clothing worn by key female figures in Mississippi history. There was the wedding dress of Varina Davis, wife of Confederate president Jefferson Davis, as well as dresses from other Mississippi first ladies, but the show also included a traditional Choctaw costume made by Choctaw women from a local reservation near Philadelphia, Mississippi.[94] Moreover, 1981 was the year in which the Choctaw Heritage Council succeeded in founding a Choctaw Museum of the Southern Indian in Mississippi, inspired by a similar museum in North Carolina dedicated to the Cherokee Nation.

Slightly overshadowed in Alabama's promotion was the theme of modernity. This idea was not new in southern promotional material; during the previous thirty years Alabama had already relied on the image of a destination where old and new coexisted. As early as 1940 a state advertisement claimed to offer a "striking contrast—historic mementos of cultures which flourished under six different flags, amid scenes which symbolize the resurgent New South."[95] However, both the 1976 booklet and the one that followed did not linger too much on this theme. There were, of course, the usual references to a state that was now "in the future," but these did not go much further than that. Even the photographic sections of the brochures did not feature any distinctive images suggesting a modern destination. The only real attraction along these lines (apart from some generic references to Birmingham's nightlife and fashionable hotels) was, obviously, the Space and Rocket Center in Huntsville, hailed as "a big piece of the future." Visitors could "visit the past and explore the future in the same day," as a Huntsville brochure stated.[96] This was the big innovation in Alabama's ads during the 1970s: in the previous promotional activities the emphasis was on *modernity*, but now it was the *future* that was brought to the forefront.

Another subsidiary brochure titled *Alabama: From the Stone Age to the Space Age* also demonstrates this trend, explicitly exploiting the theme of bridging the gap between the past and the future.[97] This publication, however, was more than just a tourism promotional piece, as it focused primarily on illustrating the state's potential economic resources with the clear purpose of attracting investment and business rather than just visitors. Again the Alabama section of a 1977 Travel South promotional insert asserted: "Alabama is one of the few places on earth that manages to revere its past without closing its eyes to the future."[98] If modernity is, in some way, linked to more or less tangible characteristics—such as efficient infrastructure and up-to-date accommodations—the idea of the future is deeper and less defined. For a state that was lagging behind in terms of infrastructure and tourist accommodations, it was easier to take advantage of Huntsville's NASA facilities and present itself as a place where the future could be experienced rather than overemphasize modernity.

As for Mississippi, things were somewhat different; the state placed much more emphasis on modernity. This is most likely because its tourism rhetoric was still closely connected to an older form of promotion, where descriptions of economic and industrial potential accompanied tourist attractions. In several passages the booklet *Mississippi: It's Like Coming Home* offered messages more focused on presenting a state that was at long last modern and in line with the rest of the country than on promoting tourism. The opening introduction, for instance, reads: "Tour a NASA project, and watch as things grow— cities as well as crops. Look everywhere for new thinking in agriculture and industry, the arts and sciences." And again: "In recent years Mississippi has not only balanced agriculture with industry but has also combined the two fields. Smaller operations like processing plants for locally-grown crops are found throughout the state." The text remarks that "Mississippi awaits you with both the old and the new." In these examples it is easy to see strong traces of Mississippi's post–World War II industrial tourism promotion as described by Burt Buchanan.[99] Significantly, the state felt the need to remind its potential visitors that it was not as backward as some might believe. This was followed by a brief but detailed illustration of the five tourism areas into which the state was divided, each with a short descriptive text to match: the Hills, Delta, Plains, Heartland, and Gulf Coast.[100] What is notable is that the five subregions appear incredibly similar to one another. The most recurring theme is once again a constant tension between old and new. The Hills region, for example, is described as follows: "A progressive industrial center, the land of Faulkner also boasts Indian mounds, Civil War battle sites, Elvis Presley's birthplace, lovely old homes." In the Heartland tourists could find "the best of the old preserved, with emphasis on the new," while in the Plains region "today antebellum mansions stand near jet airports, and scattered throughout the area are thriving towns, large and small industries and numerous family farms." The pattern is repeated for every other subregion. Conversely, very few attractions were actually related to the idea of modernity, to the point that the "new" elements mentioned in the guide are not supported by any references to any specific site. Still, it is evident how the Mississippi tourism division felt it necessary to include these formulas as a reassurance about the state's situation. After all, only a few years earlier, the Magnolia State had launched its Re-think Mississippi promotional campaign (mentioned in chapter 2) with a similar goal:

to convince readers that Mississippi was no longer the state they had come to know from the grim media reports of the 1950s and 1960s.

However, unlike Alabama, Mississippi advertisements produced between the 1940s and 1960s do not seem to have been particularly interested in tackling the subject of progress or modernity; it seems to be a more recent theme.[101] Only a few well-defined topics appeared in newspaper advertisements published in the previous decades: outdoor sports, historic battlefields, and antebellum homes. In Mississippi even the Native American theme seems more recent than in Alabama, with the earliest example possibly found in a 1969 ad.[102]

The second half of the 1970s presents some novel elements in the way promotional materials addressed the Civil War and the Confederacy. It must be said that the general approach continued to be celebratory and at times even pro-Confederate, but new features were gradually emerging. In the 1976 booklet, for instance, Alabama emphasizes that the war was a marketable part of the state's history: "Central Alabama is a history buff's dream. It is literally the Cradle of the Confederacy," a phrase that almost takes for granted that the history of the Confederacy is the only one that might interest visitors. Somewhat paradoxically, however, the Civil War is only mentioned a few times in the guide, and very few related historical sites are actually featured. This is also the case in the other state promotional pieces. When covering Sturdivant Hall and Gorgas Home (two antebellum homes), the guide provides a large full-page image of the Confederate flag with President Jefferson Davis's portrait. While there is no reluctance to present images that directly relate to the secession and its protagonists, there is an actual physical lack of attractions connected to the Confederacy and the Civil War in general within the state's borders. Caroline Cavanaugh, the director of the tourist bureau, admitted the problem in 1981, commenting on the new booklet release: "There is not a battlefield from this period [Civil War] in the state; no large Confederate forces ever faced opposing Union forces on land within Alabama in the 1860s."[103] This shows that the Civil War theme was still extremely popular, and that there was a tendency to exploit it even more than the real state landscape would allow. Although there were no battlefields in Alabama, one of the first brochures produced with the Alabama the Beautiful logo confidently assured that travelers could visit "Civil War battlegrounds that almost seem to echo with the distant sound of cannons firing."[104]

In fact, one of the most important battlefield parks in the U.S. is located in Mississippi: the Vicksburg National Military Park, site of the 1863 siege. By the mid-1970s it had welcomed over 1.5 million visitors, thus undoubtedly representing a huge asset for the state's tourism industry.[105] However, there are traces in the department's archival papers that show the management of the state tourist office's caution about overemphasizing the Civil War legacy within its promotional strategy. In a letter dated 1978, director George Williams enclosed an article from a Canadian newspaper titled "Why the Whole Town of Vicksburg Still Lives for the Civil War."[106] This piece was in no way critical of the city of Vicksburg's emphasis on the war; on the contrary, it celebrated the meticulousness and accuracy of the historical reconstructions in the Military Park. Yet the tourism division director wrote that "this article is certainly not one to be proud of" and "I have received several reports of too much concentration on the Civil War on the sales pitch."[107] Apparently, the emphasis on the Civil War within the state's promotional materials had become problematic and was beginning to be reconsidered. The same year, Williams also complained about the ongoing clandestine sale of Confederate memorabilia to park visitors.[108]

In short, in terms of the Civil War, Mississippi's situation was opposite to that of Alabama. For the latter, where the tourism industry had no strong and direct contact with the Civil War, the bureau was forced to resort to any expedient in order to insert that theme into its overall image; in Mississippi, by contrast, because the Civil War was much more central to the local tourist landscape, the focus was set on *not* overemphasizing that aspect. Even so, the ultimate goal was the same in both cases: to make the local destination image more varied and less narrow.

The Mississippi Tourism Department seems to have had an ambiguous relationship with promotional materials specifically related to the Civil War. By the mid-1970s, much of the advertising supervised and produced directly by the tourism office appeared quite cautious in presenting this theme. To be sure, there was no shortage of references, even celebratory ones, to President Davis and the Confederate soldiers, but this was only a small part of a much larger picture. One cannot rule out that the idea of a city (Vicksburg) so "obsessed" with the Civil War would be cause for embarrassment, given that Mississippi in those years was careful to present itself as a more modern and friendly destination than it once was. Perhaps, while commenting on that Canadian newspaper article, George Williams had in mind another article that had appeared in the *New York Times* the previous year: "Vicksburg is obsessed with its past. A onetime Vicksburger, whose family still lives there, told me 'I grew up with history, playing in the National Cemetery and Military Park, soaking in the Civil War, and, in the schools at least, constantly reliving the past.'"[109] This was another fairly positive piece, but the whole thing could also be interpreted as a warning for professionals in the state tourism sector. Too much obsession with the past was no longer the right key to access the tourist market. This sense of embarrassment toward an excessive attachment to the conflict could very well have been amplified by the recent celebrations for the bicentennial of the United States (between April 1975 and July 1976). This was an event that by its very nature celebrated national unity, and the Magnolia State took it very seriously, promoting itself with slogans such as "Mississippi was the 14th Colony."[110]

What remained quite evident in the overall image of both states, however, was the antebellum theme. In their promotional materials, both Alabama and Mississippi almost always focused on conjuring this image through antebellum homes, plantations, and southern belles in costume. Mississippi in particular exploited the theme much more than anywhere else in the South. This in a sense forced the state's tourism bureau to concentrate on this aspect, especially when there was a need to distinguish Mississippi ads from the rest of the South.

In advertisements produced for the tristate Middle South association (along with Arkansas and Louisiana), it is clear that the Magnolia State was carving out its own space through the exploitation of the antebellum theme. A 1980 Middle South insert in *National Geographic* specified that Arkansas had "mountains, rivers, lakes," Louisiana "a gumbo-rich heritage," and Mississippi "Old South elegance."[111] The same concept was also expressed in two other Middle South pieces from 1977 and 1980.[112]

There is no doubt that when Mississippi had to put its image in direct competition with other southern states, the less distinguishable aspects gave way to already established themes that could differentiate the state from its competitors. In "Come South for the Winter," a Middle South ad published in Canada in 1979, the thematic division between the three states was evident, and nothing was said about Mississippi except that it "offers sunny deep-sea fishing, antebellum homes, and the Civil War history."[113]

Nineteenth-century mansions and houses could be found all over the former Confederacy, but no state was as strongly associated with them as Mississippi, where the tradition of house tours or pilgrimages dated back to the 1930s. However, archive records reveal a more complex situation than one might have thought. A 1977 report by Historic Columbus of Columbus, Mississippi, states that "each state of the Union has a symbol to distinguish it from others. On all maps, Mississippi can be identified by an antebellum home or a magnolia. *If the State is known throughout the country for its homes, then this is what the State Tourism Department earnestly needs to focus upon.*"[114] The precise context is unclear, but what is plain is that an internal debate was taking place in the Mississippi tourism industry: on the one hand, local agencies such as the Columbus Association (a town with twenty-one antebellum homes in 1977), who wanted state advertising to focus more on this theme; on the other, George Williams's tourism department, which evidently intended to carry out a promotional activity less obsessively centered on such places.

This contention between local operators and the state office is critically important. The new elements and features that appear in the promotional materials of the two states are mostly related to the advertising produced by the official state tourist boards of Alabama and Mississippi. Below this level was a vast galaxy of local players (cities, counties, single attractions, hotels, motels, resorts, and many others) that produced their own advertising (usually small brochures or very simple ads with limited circulation) over which the state tourism division had little or no control. Locally produced brochures specifically dedicated to antebellum homes, for instance, were promotional pieces in which the language and overall tone appeared much more celebratory than in that of state-sponsored material. When not directly managed by the state, even individual attractions had the freedom to offer interpretive plans and narratives of the past or local culture. This was the case of the brochure produced for the Rosemont Plantation near Woodville, Wilkinson County, Mississippi, where Jefferson Davis spent his early years. The text describes Davis as "U.S. Congressman, U.S. Secretary of War, President of the CSA, Author, Mississippian and American Patriot."[115] It may seem somewhat ludicrous to attribute the status of patriot to the president of the Confederacy, but we are once again presented with a classic theme dear to the Lost Cause ideology: Confederate heroes are seen as the quintessential embodiment of the true American spirit. By the end of the 1970s, such an image seems to have been possible only outside the state tourism division, which was already careful to avoid this kind of rhetoric.

Something similar though not directly related to actual tourism promotion occurred in November 1976 in Montgomery, Alabama. The day the White House of the Confederacy reopened to the public, the great-great-grandson of Jefferson Davis took the floor, proclaiming: "His [Davis's] faith in the United States was very evident, and I think he would have been proud here today to see that faith renewed."[116]

The emphasis on the classic antebellum setting was by no means exclusive to Mississippi (or Alabama) promoters. In cases where advertising for the Magnolia State originated elsewhere, the overall picture stayed the same. Such was the case with promotional material from the Delta Queen Company, an Ohio-based agency that promoted Mississippi River tours. Their 1977 brochure states that Natchez "is the Romantic Deep South scent of magnolias . . . [and] many antebellum mansions," while Vicksburg "is the hospitable southern city steeped in Civil War history."[117] A similar pamphlet produced in 1979 asserts that the Natchez Pilgrimage "also includes the color and excitement of a confederate pageant. A glimpse of time gone but not forgotten."[118] And another text, trying to attract visitors to a plantation, declares that "you can even pick cotton in a working plantation!"[119]

In plantation homes, visitors could have more or less sugarcoated experiences. In Leflore County, Mississippi, Florewood River Plantation had been in operation since 1974. It was a sort of living history site based on a real antebellum cotton plantation, complete with costumed reenactors. The historical narrative given at Florewood was superficial and distorted, and it had deliberate omissions about the more controversial aspects of the southern past. In a 1978 interview, the park's public relations Director offered a clear statement of intent about Florewood's "historic mission": "Antebellum life will be depicted at the festival in the clothing worn by hostesses, the food, music, and decor. . . . Artisans will also be working in the plantation slave quarter, but the harsher less creative aspects of slavery will not be portrayed. . . . There's no reason to, this is a fun time."[120] In other words, it was a classic embellished celebration of the old antebellum South. However, thanks largely to newspapers, it turned out that the debate over the slave quarters in Florewood generated some level of media attention, even reaching Mississippi Governor William Waller. A letter to the editor of a Mississippi newspaper, the *Greenwood Commonwealth*, sheds some light on the matter. When the state-sponsored plantation opened in 1974, it included no mention of slavery and no slave cabins, though these would be added later. Governor Waller himself declared that "slave quarters are a negative fact of history."[121] The problem was actually somewhat deeper, as there was a widespread fear that showing "real history" (in this case the actual living conditions of slaves) would damage Mississippi's already tarnished image. The letter to the *Greenwood Commonwealth* strongly criticized this decision, suggesting that it was the absence of slave quarters that would discredit the state. If Waller's concern was the image of Mississippi, the letter ironically pointed out, then it would also be necessary to dismantle all the statues of Confederate generals and soldiers, lest some naïve tourist be shocked to discover why they had fought.[122] What the author of the letter probably did not know was that Florewood's original plan actually included slave quarters, but the NAACP and local Black leaders contacted Governor Waller to protest this plan and ask not to reenact this page in American history. There were, in fact, two conflicting opinions in the local African American community on the subject. Some believed that it would be instructive and ultimately useful to show what slavery had actually been like. Others, however, protested the degrading image that a costume reenactment would give to the African

American experience in the slaveholding South.[123] This anecdote illustrates, if nothing else, the existence of a situation in Mississippi in which the African American voice, though obviously still limited, was beginning to be heard even in matters relating to the organization of sites of historical importance within the local landscape, at least when it came to state-run installations or attractions, such as Florewood. Things were less immovable than they might have appeared. The Black mayor of the small town of Fayette, Mississippi, for instance, told reporters that he believed the Florewood Plantation was supposed to show the daily life of slaves, but he would have preferred that the site had been built in the Natchez area (where a famous pilgrimage of antebellum homes took place) because showing "the struggle for slavery from the beginnings to 1975 would be ideal, from an economic and historical standpoint"— an attempt, in other words, to renegotiate the local historical narrative in a nonviolent or overtly critical manner.[124]

It also seems that by the end of the 1970s the blatant historical falsification offered by certain attractions was much less accepted. Some traces of criticism of an overtly embellished portrayal of the past can even be found in major southern newspapers. In a 1978 article from a popular southern style supplement, the author describes his recent participation in a Natchez pilgrimage: "In order to absorb the experience, one must put on one's historical blinders and remember that what is shown is not an accurate portrayal of what pre–Civil War years held for everyone. The whole slavery matter is ignored. No slave quarters are shown. . . . Inside the homes, the furnishings are elegant and tasteful, but not necessarily period pieces."[125]

Another aspect to keep in mind when looking at the promotional material produced in those years concerns the space that the classic antebellum South occupied in the overall picture. As was also the case for the Travel South USA promotion, Alabama and Mississippi tried to convey the message of multifaceted destinations, suitable for everyone and full of different and varied attractions. This is also why the partitioning into subregions was adopted, as well as a similar process of associating distinct themes with certain cities or towns. An example of this latter is evident in a small-format black-and-white booklet produced in 1979 in Alabama, *Alabama the Beautiful 52 Weeks a Year*.[126] Huntsville was "The Rocket City," Montgomery "The First Confederate Capital," Mobile "The Gulf Coast," Tuskegee was "Booker T. Washington's Homeland," and so on. This tendency to associate a city with a precise image, even if obviously simplistic or outright false, was already an established trend at both the regional and national level. In his essay on tourism in New Orleans, J. Mark Souther notes how this new marketing idea developed precisely between the 1970s and 1980s, evidently in conjunction with the emergence of new, more specific and sectorial types of tourism.[127] This also led to the association of given places with certain attractions. In some cases the antebellum theme could become the prerogative of specific areas or cities rather than the entire state. In Alabama, for example, Demopolis was the "Land of Antebellum Plantations," according to the *Alabama the Beautiful 52 Weeks a Year* booklet. Even more remarkably, Georgia condensed its whole antebellum charm into a special tourist region called "Classic South."

In the 1970s, paper advertisement also changed. Whereas earlier advertising broadly invited readers to visit the state by listing a variety of sites or places, specific ads were now being produced and aimed at target audiences. The Alabama the Beautiful campaign featured ads focused on scenic landscapes, golf, fishing, lakes, beach tourism, hiking, hunting, "romantic getaways" for couples, antebellum homes, and of course Black heritage.[128] This also entailed a reorganization of the antebellum theme in the broader general framework. The less specific ads had become so crowded with places, names, and themes that it is hard to tell which image is the main one. Also, the photos chosen to support the text were very careful to give an idea of the large number of attractions available. The decision to make the ad a veritable collage of many different photos is clearly due to the idea of what Ted Ownby called the "variety trope," the abundance of different attractions and the corresponding "world in miniature."[129] The technique of employing a wide range of photos to emphasize the appeal of a place was certainly not something new to the advertising industry. Tourism ads had already been implementing this strategy for decades. The fundamental novelty, however, can be seen in the symbolic function of these photos. Traditionally, photos in old advertisements of this type represented specific attractions, clearly identifiable through text. Advertising collages during the 1970s, on the other hand, used photos whose main purpose was to call to mind certain types of activities or broader themes, such as leisure at the beach, nature, sports, and entertainment.

It was not until the mid-1960s that the new way of structuring advertisements through a large number of evocative rather than descriptive photos seems to have become widespread in the tourism industry of the South. By the 1970s, this type of promotional message had been perfected, assembling a large number of small photos. It was the visual hallmark of the variety trope.

Another major issue to consider is international promotion. The two states do not seem to have produced any real advertising specifically aimed at foreign countries. In the second half of the 1970s, Mississippi and especially Alabama began timidly to approach the international tourism market, although the bulk of this promotional activity was carried out by Travel South, USA.

Individual states must have found it incredibly difficult to reach an international audience on their own. Notably, a few interesting exceptions are preserved in the records of the Alabama Bureau of Publicity and Information. The first is a small article about the state in English, German, Spanish, and French, clearly intended for publication in some unspecified magazine. It was titled "Alabama Is a Mini-U.S.A." and published in 1980.[130] The text openly exploits the theme of Alabama as a small version of the United States: "If you had to choose one state that best represents the 48 contiguous American states, it would have to be Alabama." When the target of the piece was a foreign country, it became convenient to place the state within a national rather than regional discourse, that is, associate the state with the entire United States and not just the South. In those years the USTS advised South Carolina to pursue the same strategy and promote itself abroad as an American destination.[131] It is unclear, however, whether "Alabama as a Mini-U.S." was a similar USTS proposal or an independent idea of the state bureau. The article presents a remarkable summary of local attractions: "So many domestic and foreign travelers have visited the big American cities, but they haven't seen America. In Alabama they can experience the rural roots that account for the strong American character. They can learn about America's Black heritage. They can witness the charm of the Old South or the progressive lifestyle of the South's new industrial age."[132] Black heritage once again figures as an integral part of the state's image, a new theme that from the 1980s onward appears constantly in the material designed to circulate within the United States and, as is evident here, also abroad. Another advertisement was published in 1981, "Alabama La Hermosa," which was nothing more than a Spanish translation of "Alabama the Beautiful" and intended for circulation in Latin America. The images offered by the ad are once again an assortment of various themes: water sports, fishing, antebellum homes, a rock concert, a smiling family posing in front of the World War II battleship the USS *Alabama*.

More interesting is a folder in the Alabama archives vaguely labeled "Belgian" and actually ascribable to SABENA, the former Belgian national airline. The folder contained only a few photos and excerpts from a 1978 publication made available to passengers on SABENA aircrafts, covering Atlanta as well as other southern states and destinations.[133] Since June 1978 the company had been operating nonstop flights from Brussels to Atlanta, the main southern port of entry to the United States. Clearly all of the southern states were interested in attracting European travelers arriving in Georgia. What is remarkable is that these photos are completely different from those normally used in domestic promotion. In particular, two photos show laughing African American youngsters unloading watermelons from a pickup truck in what appears as an unconventional rural setting (figure 3). The general approach of the ar-

Figure 3. Some photos related to a promotional piece on Alabama for the Belgian airline SABENA's magazine *Sabena Revue*—Atlanta, 1978. Alabama Department of Archives and History.

ticle was clearly to show a rural, folksy Alabama, evidently because it was considered more interesting for a European audience. Other photos of local people are clearly chosen specifically to evoke very rustic, almost redneck imagery (figure 4).

While no trace remains of ads intended for the British market, even though Alabama began advertisement campaigns in the United Kingdom from 1981, a few promotional scripts intended for England have been preserved. Here the state advertises everything the South has to offer: "all . . . that is associated with the American South: plantations, cotton, gracious mansions, river

Figure 4. Photos of local Alabamians from the 1978 issue of *Sabena Revue*. Alabama Department of Archives and History.

boats, the Civil War, etc."[134] It is not surprising that this emphasis on southern identity was used overseas rather than for the domestic market. There is no mention of Black heritage, and it is stated that "even today Alabama still flies the Confederate flag from the white dome of its State Capitol—below the U.S. and State flags." Indeed, the Confederate mystique appears much more prominently here than in the material intended for circulation in the United States. Another 1981–1982 promotional script for the United Kingdom entitled "Alabama—A Culinary Delight" includes a series of recipes, obviously designed specifically to intrigue non-southerners and that played on Confederate and Civil War references: "Yankee Rebel Fruitcake, Confederate Date Cake, and Oysters Johnny Reb, are colorful reminders of the past."[135] However, aside from these elements, there were few differences with the material designed for domestic use. Once again, many and varied attractions were presented, with special attention to gastronomic tourism, which, by contrast, had rarely been addressed in promotion within the United States.[136]

If Mississippi directly produced any foreign advertising in those years, there remains no evidence. Even in Canada, where both states claimed promotional interests, all advertising activity was carried out through Travel South and, in the case of Mississippi, through Middle South as well.

In conclusion, Alabama and Mississippi show clear signs of a marked change in their promotional image, an adjustment that seems to have taken place between the 1970s and early 1980s. The most obvious dimension of this change was, of course, the introduction of Black heritage tourism. Governor Wallace's Alabama was the forerunner of this new course in state advertising, followed shortly after by Mississippi. The reason for this choice was twofold: on the one hand, there was a clear desire to carve out a piece of this new and expanding market, while on the other there was a continuing attempt to make the image of the two states more friendly and inclusive. The same idea was also behind the inclusion of Native Americans in the promotional material— no longer mere stereotypes in costume, but more or less an integral part of the local society and history.

The other novelty, so to speak, concerned the number of themes presented in promotional materials. The antebellum South, with its homes, its plantations, and, more generally, its Lost Cause, undoubtedly remained important in the overall picture, but it was no longer the cornerstone of the two states' tourist image. These attractions were cited quite often, but other activities, such as fishing, hiking, elegant accommodations, or beaches, were also regularly mentioned, making the final result less monothematic. Clearly, this was a deliberate choice to portray a more modern and up-to-date Alabama and Mississippi to the American public. The exotic, rustic, and antimodern South that had dominated the American imagination for more than half a century was now too limited for the local tourism sector. The shift in emphasis was also part a new marketing strategy that increasingly resorted to compartmentalization and thematic subdivisions among various areas or cities. Thus antebellum homes became a specialization of certain areas (Natchez or Columbus in Mississippi, Demopolis in Alabama) rather than of the entire state.

It is worth noting once again that this did not mean that the Lost Cause had ceased to attract visitors, nor that its appeal was somehow fading among the general public. On the contrary, it is evident that all of the symbolic and imaginative paraphernalia of the Old South had, in reality, a much greater weight than is apparent from the study of advertisements and tourist booklets. However, it is precisely this discrepancy between the image proposed by the tourist offices and the reality of local tourism that is of particular importance, since it shows how, in the mid-1970s, state agencies with economic-promotional competencies had embarked on a new path that moved away from the conventional one still in place only a decade earlier.

CHAPTER 4

Georgia and South Carolina

Relative to Alabama and Mississippi, Georgia and South Carolina present some significant differences when it comes to the tourism industry. Firstly, their perceived image was not marred by the same aura of social backwardness as its sister states. Georgia in particular was unique in the American context of the late 1970s, as it provided the nation with its first Deep South president since the Reconstruction, suddenly making it the center of interest for the media and the American public, albeit for a short period of time.

The self-proclaimed Peach State was also one of the real tourism mammoths of the region, in a considerably weaker position than Florida but still far surpassing Alabama, Mississippi, and South Carolina. South Carolina, on the other hand, represented a singular case study in the southern panorama. Here, in fact, tourism promotion appeared quite different than in the other three states. By the 1970s the Lost Cause and the classic South had almost completely disappeared from its overall destination image, which was instead geared toward a very emphatic promotion of beach vacations, seaside tourism, and coastal resorts. The obvious goal was to emulate Florida's image rather than that of other Deep South states.

Once again, the promotional slogans of Georgia and South Carolina say something about their respective advertising strategies and the position tourism occupied in the economy of each state. In 1977 Georgia used "For a Good Time or a Lifetime" as its catch phrase, later changing to "Georgia . . . This Way to Fun."[1] Both are generic slogans that did not help distinguish Georgia from the other states, as they referred to vague concepts common in the advertising industry. Moreover, "This Way to Fun" is a slogan that immediately conjures up the idea of a transient destination, as indeed Georgia was, focused on attracting tourists on their way to Florida. South Carolina, on the other hand, changed its slogan three times between 1977 and 1981, a clear sign of special attention to promotional policies and the desire to establish a precise destination image. In 1977 to 1978 the Palmetto State had no slogan at all, the only case in the entire United States aside from neighboring North Carolina. Shortly afterward it presented two generic ones: "You Couldn't Have Seen All of Me" and "See More of S.C.," both clearly aimed at conveying the variety trope, the idea of a state with multiple attractions. The following year the slogan was changed to "Come See S.C."[2] During the late 1970s both states resorted to the strategy of dividing their territory into different tourist subregions, associated with better defined and more structured themes than those used by Alabama and Mississippi.

As South Carolina promotion professionals admitted, Georgia had been the first to fully embrace this strategy in recent times, and they had followed suit.[3] In 1977, Ed Spivia's Georgia Tourism Division launched a plan to create seven new tourist areas, each with a distinct promotional theme and body of advertising material, supervised by a regional coordinator. Previously Georgia had promoted only three different regions, all based on purely geographic traits: Mountain, Piedmont, and Coastal Plain. The Tourism Division had clearly aimed to sell Georgia as a large, single whole where you could find everything almost everywhere. This is indicated by the deliberate vagueness with which the promotional images of these three former subregions were designed. In an official presentation held in 1976, Spivia introduced the three main slogans and themes for the Mountain, Piedmont, and Coastal Plains advertisements: respectively, "Serenity Crowned by a Frill of Color," "A Whirl of Excitement Wherever You Go," and "Poetry Etched in a Morning Sky,"[4] all generic images of beauty and variety, without any specific ideas to support the promotional structure of each area. The new subdivision took place in 1978; promotional activities changed accordingly, with the creation of new brochures, booklets, thematic routes, and tours. This new approach fully reflected the aggressive take on tourism by the Busbee-Spivia duo. Only a year earlier, Governor George Busbee had openly complained that up to that point "our advertising approach has been on a general basis and hasn't had a specific hard-sell approach."[5] The working relationship between the tourism office and the state administration was also reconsidered. The plan called for the appointment of seven regional directors, one for each area, who would respond directly to Spivia and the Tourism Division. These new regions, unlike the previous ones, now presented a reasonably clear and identifiable thematic image, although some were more immediately recognizable than others.[6] For example the Big A, corresponding to the Atlanta area, is easily promoted with references to attractions of big city life, while the Northeast Mountains have an advertisement focused on outdoor activities and environmental tourism; the Colonial Coast is supposedly the destination centered on historical tourism of the Revolutionary War period. Other regions, however, appear more difficult to associate with a specific theme, such as Heart of Georgia, which is explicitly presented as an area where some of the same attractions that characterized the other six regions could be found, while Plains Country appears to have been a subregion developed around the hometown of newly elected President Jimmy Carter and a vague idea of rural charm. The Plains Country description refers to the myth of a slow-paced rural southern lifestyle: "Plains Country is where rural Georgians take life easy, ignore the hectic pace of the big city in favor of wide open spaces, and in some cases, deliberately stop time."[7]

Once again, the picture that emerges is that of a state with numerous features and attractions, at times close to the more traditional aspects of the southern image and other times decidedly launched toward new modern horizons. Clear references are also made to classic promotional trends. A good example of this can be seen in the thematic region called "Classic South" where all of the state's antebellum charms are concentrated. Both the city of Savannah and Atlanta are excluded from this area, since they are presented as the state's modern, future-oriented destinations, despite the never-ending myth of Scarlett O'Hara.[8]

South Carolina, on the other hand, was divided into ten subregions, the highest number of any state in the Deep South, even though it was the smallest in terms of territorial extent. Unlike Georgia, and probably contrary to the wishes of the state DPRT itself, the regions of South Carolina often appear more tied to geographic elements than to specific thematic themes, perhaps the result of a less thoughtful subdivision. The regions were the Grand Strand, Historic Charleston, Lowcountry and Resort Islands, Santee Cooper Country, Swamp Fox Country, Capital City, Thoroughbred Country, Old Ninety Six, Old Catawba Nation, and Upcountry Carolina. These ten regions were used as tourist areas for the first time in a booklet produced in 1980, and the names were a combination of already established designations and new ones assigned just for the occasion.

Georgia and South Carolina not only had a more favorable image than Alabama and Mississippi; they also had more attractions on which to capitalize in their advertising, as well as more visitors. A 1978 travel report provides interesting information on Georgia's attractions. During the first six months of the year, state parks were the most popular destinations, with over 6 million visitors. These were followed by recreational areas, generic attractions together with national monuments.[9] Only 113,776 visits were recorded to historic sites during that six-month period. Since about 21.8 million tourists were registered in the Peach State at that time, state-monitored historical sites accounted for just 0.5 percent of the total number of visits.[10] It is true that national monuments can sometimes be counted as historic sites, but with these included in the total, historical tourism continued to lag far behind its recreational counterparts.

Better data is available for 1977, as the *Atlanta Constitution* published a list of the ten most-visited attractions in the state according to numbers released by the Tourism Division. In first place were the state parks with about 14 million visitors in 1976. These were followed by Stone Mountain Park with 4 million visitors, Jekyll Island with 2.7 million, and Chattahoochee National Forest and Oconee National Forest with 2 million visitors each. The other attractions record much lower figures.[11] These figures are significantly higher than those recorded by attractions in Alabama, Mississippi, and even South Carolina, making Georgia a real tourism giant compared to its sister states. One of the most visited nonnatural attractions in the region was Six Flags Over Georgia, an amusement park founded in 1967, located not far from Atlanta and unique in the Deep South. A 1977 letter to Ed Spivia from the park's marketing director told of more than 2 million visitors in the last 150 days, including at least a million from out of state.[12]

South Carolina lacked Georgia's natural landscape appeal, but this was made up by a greater emphasis on beach tourism. According to the tourism office, beaches were the most popular attraction for the state, registering about 6 million visitors in 1975;[13] likewise, coastal areas in general recorded about one-third of all visitors to the state in 1977.[14] State parks also topped visitor numbers, with around 11 million paying admissions in 1979.[15]

Georgia's first relevant tourist booklet in the second half of the 1970s was *This Is Georgia: Georgia Days*, in circulation from at least 1973 until 1978.[16] The booklet was a large and very simple brochure, divided into the three tourist regions in which Georgia was partitioned until 1978, namely Mountains, Piedmont, and Coastal Plain. Camping sites, annual events, golf courses, lakes, hunting areas, historic sites, colleges and universities, snow skiing, welcome centers, and tours were listed for each city in every region. The booklet is simple and schematic, much more so than its equivalents in Alabama and Mississippi. The text is reduced to a brief description of each of the three regions, with emphatic tones and an ad-like structure. There was no section devoted exclusively to Georgia as a whole, nor was there one on its history or culture. The idea of associating every area with a particular image had not yet been implemented. All three tourist regions were presented as equally rich in history, nature, and entertainment. The text reassured readers that each area was a "region of plenty" or a "kaleidoscope of activity." Only on a very subtle level were there some implicit distinctions. Thus, for example, Mountains was somehow the area suitable for tourists looking to relax in the wilderness. Piedmont instead was the region where most of Georgia's antebellum heritage was concentrated: "History and a gracious way of life reside in white-columned mansions and graceful gardens. This area takes pride in the number of historic homes that have survived the ravages of time and stand as reminders of a bygone era."

Contrary to what one might believe based on the state's more modern appeal, 1970s Georgia devoted just as much space to the antebellum classic South as both Alabama and Mississippi—if not more. This is quite evident in the booklet produced in 1979 titled *Georgia: This Way to Fun*.[17] There are significant differences from the previous material, mainly due to the presence of the seven newly established tourist regions, which profoundly influenced the promotional strategy. The actual names of these new areas are an effective summary of what they stood for. Pioneer Territory is described mainly through references to Native American culture and the heroic deeds of pioneers. The Northeast Mountains were similar to the previously illustrated Mountains, associated with the theme of adventure, the outdoors, and natural beauty. The most interesting of these regions, however, is Classic South. As mentioned earlier, this was designed as a region dedicated solely to the Old South theme. All thirty-four lines of text in the presentation focus on that one image. The tone is even more emphatic than the one used in Mississippi and presents a true compendium of southern nostalgia: "In the Classic South, chances are that nothing will ever destroy what the Civil War could not, including a fierce pride in all that was left behind. What kind of pride is this that characterizes a people devoted to an era not their own? . . . Beauty is a part of it, and elegance too. . . . Respect for the events of the past has inspired monuments to the Confederacy." The cultural implications contained in this short text are quite relevant. The booklet seems to suggest that not only Georgians, but all southerners were still devoted to the myth of the Old South. More importantly, the relationship between southern nostalgia and the Confederacy is openly acknowledged. The Classic South here seems to be composed of two elements: a longing for a regional legacy and a celebration of the Confederacy. The same was true also for other southern tourism advertising of this period. The 1975 booklet *Mississippi: Your Guide to Travel* described the Natchez pilgrimage as "ante-bellum magic," and the image chosen to illustrate the event was an actor in Confederate uniform—hardly an "antebellum," or literally "prewar," figure.[18] It was likely an unintentional overlapping of images, whereby the few years that the Confederacy actually existed were made to represent the entire southern past, particularly the antebellum era. The same occurred in the Georgia brochure dedicated to the Classic South region (each of the seven areas had its own exclusive material), which invited visitors to "rambling antebellum mansions," "boulevards lined with blossoming trees," and "the Southern sun flickering on well-kept gardens."[19] The photo on the brochure cover immediately established a strong thematic link between the antebellum South and the Confederacy: a phantomlike girl in nineteenth-century period dress descending a staircase while a similar ghostly gentleman soldier in Confederate uniform gallantly reaches up to offer her his hand (figure 5).

Travel Tips

In Georgia's Classic South

Rambling antebellum mansions. Boulevards lined with blossoming trees. The Southern sun flickering on well-kept gardens. The Classic South is an ideal setting for a relaxing, much-welcomed vacation.

Figure 5. Front cover of the *Classic South* brochure, 1979–1980. The photo and brief description clearly show how the antebellum South was the main promotional theme adopted for this region. Georgia Archives.

This optical effect that makes the two costumed figures resemble spectral apparitions underlines the aura of romanticism and nostalgia for a lost time (and Cause) that always accompanies the antebellum theme. This idea resurfaces at least one other time, in the July 1978 issue of *Outdoors in Georgia*. Here the Classic South region is introduced by a very positive mention of Confederate ghosts: "In Madison, Georgia real and imaginary Confederate ancestors live like friendly ghosts among people too proud to let them pass away. Kept alive by tales of their simple heroics and complicated misadventures, these memorable figures serve as special guardians of the cherished tradition of the Classic South."[20] This double reference, textual and visual, to ghosts suggests the existence of an actual trope: Confederate spirits as guardians of the classic South and its traditions, another explicit overlapping of the southern Confederate past with the entire heritage of the region. Notably, antebellum homes were mentioned in the opening text of four out of seven brochures dedicated to the new subregions, making them the most frequently named attraction, a clear sign of their importance in the overall tourism landscape of Georgia. This theme had already been widely exploited by the state during the 1970s. In 1974, during the Georgia, So Much, So Near promotional campaign, the official booklet was divided into thematic sections, two of which were entirely devoted to antebellum homes.[21] Again, in the This Way to Fun campaign (launched after 1978), a large brochure called *Historic Homes* was produced, dedicated exclusively to the antebellum homes and virtually identical to an earlier publication released in 1970–1971.[22] Georgia had a very important reason for this nostalgia toward the Old South and the antebellum myth: Atlanta, the state capital, was the city associated by definition with Scarlett O'Hara and the work of Margaret Mitchell in general. It is difficult to realize how deep and almost obsessive the worldwide passion was for *Gone with the Wind*, both the bestselling book and the Oscar-winning film—a fascination that has never fully waned and still continues to attract several thousand visitors to Georgia every year.

It goes without saying that *Gone with the Wind* was not, by any means, the only film to draw visitors to the state. *Deliverance* (1972), for example, proved to be another real advertisement for the state's scenic landscapes.[23] As late as 1977 a Georgia travel article played on the film's popularity: "If you can do anything Burt Reynolds can do, okay, ride the foamy waters of the Chattooga River."[24] At that point, Georgia had actually appeared on the big and small screen far more than any other state of the Deep South. Its connection to cinema was so strong that it was the only state among the four examined to produce advertisements citing the names of famous actors with the express purpose of attracting film productions.[25] Still to this day, no other movie has ever come close to *Gone with the Wind* in drawing visitors to a destination, in this case Georgia and Atlanta in particular. The tourist-promotional image of the city was paradoxically structured around two apparently irreconcilable opposites: on the one hand the idea of modernity, cosmopolitanism, the New South, and progress, and on the other antebellum nostalgia. Margaret Mitchell's novel was undoubtedly the city's most iconic cultural product, the one that (mostly white) tourists wanted to find when they arrived in Georgia. A 1979 Atlanta travel guide had to specify: "Sorry folks, but Tara, Scarlett O'Hara's plantation, doesn't exist. Don't blame the Yankees."[26] An unofficial 1980s ad advertised the opening of the Scarlett and Rhett Show, an entire gallery of movie memorabilia: "Atlanta and her thousands of guests will be able to visit what half the world thought we had anyway: a commemoration to *Gone with the Wind*."[27]

The popularity of *Gone with the Wind* was so widespread that it escaped any oversimplified presentation. Even Black tourists were not entirely immune to the power of its narrative. Their view of the story, however, was sometimes the exact opposite of the traditional white perspective. In 1972, a group of forty-six Black women from Ohio traveled South in search of their roots. The itinerary included several cotton plantations, antebellum homes, and other Civil War–era buildings. In short, they were visiting the same attractions through which the white South celebrated itself. They chose to visit southern plantations to see and understand how their ancestors had lived and suffered, with one woman informing a local reporter that "a lot of us had seen the movie Gone With the Wind, and we decided we would go down South and see what it was all about."[28] This was another demonstration of the awakening of Black cultural tourism and its power to reappropriate narratives traditionally intended to exclude Blacks.

Atlanta's attachment to Scarlett O'Hara has never really waned. Jennifer Dickey acknowledged how, prior to the 1996 Olympics, the premiere of the 1939 movie *Gone with the Wind* was still celebrated as one of the city's most significant events.[29] In popular imagination, the film symbolized the city itself. Not surprisingly, during the 1960s, even Delta Airlines promoted Atlanta with a poster featuring Vivien Leigh as Scarlett.[30] In 1974 the Western International hotel chain advertised its Atlanta establishments with a highly symbolic ad depicting Scarlett O'Hara in front of a Confederate battle flag.[31] The November/December 1979 issue of the Atlanta Historical Society newsletter announced, "The city's most remembered image-maker was unveiled for all the world to see at a gala premiere on December 15, 1939, at the late great Loew's Grand Theatre. In recognition of the fortieth anniversary of the premiere of

'Gone With the Wind,' the Society will present a special holiday exhibit focusing on the impact and continuing popularity of the film."[32]

The myth of Scarlett O'Hara was so far reaching that sometimes it was even exploited to promote an image diametrically opposite to the classic old-fashioned one. Thus, for example, in the July 1978 issue of *Outdoors in Georgia*: "Scarlett O'Hara would hardly recognize her Atlanta. But she'd like it. Atlanta in the late seventies is much like the *GONE WITH THE WIND* heroine herself—vibrant, courageous, in command of all in her purview."[33] This relationship between the city and the book/film, however, was not always acknowledged without reserve. By the 1970s, Atlanta's economic and political elite in particular often saw it as a source of embarrassment, since they sought to portray Georgia's state capital as a mix between "an international city" and "a city too busy to hate."[34] Atlanta, then, experienced a moment of contrast between the desire to move into the future and the nostalgic celebration of its mythical past. It is interesting to note that in all of the official promotional material produced by the Tourism Division during the late 1970s, the Gone with the Wind theme was virtually never exploited, despite its great success with the public. Not even the Classic South region used the novel or the movie in its ads, while Atlanta was promoted exclusively as the great modern, cosmopolitan destination. Thus, for example, in *This Way to Fun* it was pointed out that "the Big A . . . Atlanta and environs boldly dominates the impressive New South." Neither of the state's official booklets, *Georgia Days* and *This Way to Fun*, ever mentions the title of the novel or the name of its main protagonist. In fact, according to the Tourism Division's plan, Atlanta and its surroundings were to be the region in contrast to the antebellum South, as though they represented two antithetical sides of the same coin: the old/traditional and the new/modern. This was clearly stated in the short description of the two regions prepared by the division for the new campaign's ads: "CLASSIC SOUTH: Antebellum plantations and homes bring Georgia's past to life," and "THE BIG 'A': Atlanta's all you've read about—dining, nightlife, major league sports and family fun."[35]

It was mostly local and private players in the city's tourism industry—rather than official state tourism promoters—who made use of the imagery associated with Margaret Mitchell's novel. This was something of a paradox: as much as Atlanta tried to capitalize on its progressive, metropolitan New South appeal, most tourists traveled to the city to experience the romance of the Old South.[36]

The figure of Scarlett O'Hara was actually of great relevance to the entire South and not just to Georgia. She was the model for the trope of the girl in nineteenth-century dress—the southern belle, a recurring character in Deep

South promotional material and one appreciated by American culture in general, becoming a symbol of the Old South and, to some extent, of the Lost Cause. From Atlanta, Scarlett had moved by association to represent Georgia as well as the South as a whole. Although the novel's popularity was not openly exploited as a thematic image in the various state publications, the state was not embarrassed to capitalize on it in other media. In 1981, for example, during Georgia Week, Ed Spivia's Tourism Division sent three agents to Toronto, Canada, to promote the state while dressed as Rhett Butler, Scarlett O'Hara, and Confederate General Robert E. Lee, the latter in full military uniform.[37]

This type of promotion was not just reserved for foreign countries; the Tourism Division also intended to send the three actors (which included General Lee) to a convention in Savannah, Georgia.[38] As Avrahm and Dougherty point out in discussing advertising in Texas, a narrative produced by promotional material is as appropriate for locals as it is for foreigners. Therefore, just as the fictional image of Texas "is suitable also for Texans," so the myth of *Gone with the Wind* and the Lost Cause in general were also suitable for Georgians.[39] As Celestine Sibley recalls, the citizens of Atlanta were the first real fans of Mitchell's book.[40] This also suggests that there may have been professional reasons behind the Division's choice not to associate Atlanta with Scarlett or the antebellum era. Was there even a need to? After all, the general public had already interiorized that piece of the Atlanta destination image, leaving room for advertisers to increase the capital's appeal by associating it with new and different themes such as sports, modernity, and nightlife, an especially convenient strategy as it truly differentiated Georgia from the rest of the Deep South, setting the stage for a credibly modern, cosmopolitan destination.

Another factor that contributed to the complex nature of the self-proclaimed "city too busy to hate" was Atlanta's role as a center of Black tourism since the early twentieth century.[41] The Martin Luther King Jr. National Historic Site became one of the main locations for Black heritage tours and a true pilgrimage destination for many African Americans. The figure of Dr. King himself was obviously a powerful catalyst. Not surprisingly, Atlanta was one of the few southern travel destinations recommended to *Black Enterprise* readers in 1974;[42] this suggestion would be repeated in the 1980 summer season, alongside Virginia, Florida, and New Orleans.[43] Of course, Black tourism was dedicated not only to retracing the memory of the civil rights movement, but also to enjoying the leisure activities and varied entertainment that the city had to offer, which sometimes included the celebrity of actors or television series. The importance of television for tourism destination images went far beyond the racial divide. A Black tour organized in 1980 by the Gray

Line company and advertised in the *Atlanta Constitution*, for instance, was promoted as "the fascinating tour that traces the events and places in the life of Dr. Martin Luther King Jr.," but further promising to show the "resplendent black residential areas that you've seen in magazines and on television."[44] These tours were completely independent of the state Tourism Division, prepared, advertised, and sold directly by travel agencies, particularly Black travel agencies, which began appearing across the country in the 1970s. While state promotion still appeared white-centric, underneath it there was already a well-developed network of associations and travel operators who grasped the ever-growing demand for Black tourism. An Atlanta "black heritage tour" organized by TourGals is attested in 1977,[45] while another, the "Negro Heritage Tour," is documented in Savannah in the same years.[46] No such tours existed in Alabama and Mississippi at that time.

Atlanta was not, however, the only tourist destination tied to a particular narrative and image of the past. Indeed, perhaps the best-known and most monumental altar to southern memory was located just a few miles from the city. This was Stone Mountain, the so-called "Mount Rushmore of the South" with its giant portraits of the three major heroes of the Confederate pantheon, Robert E. Lee, Thomas "Stonewall" Jackson, and Jefferson Davis, carved into the rock. Along with Six Flags, it was one of the most visited places in the state, registering approximately 4 million visitors in 1977.[47]

The monument was unveiled in 1970, but its conception and realization had been long and tumultuous. As early as 1915, the Atlanta chapter of the United Daughters of the Confederacy proposed building a memorial on Stone Mountain and commissioned the sculptor Gutzon Borglum, a northerner of Danish origin, to carve it. Borglum however stepped away from the project in 1924 and devoted himself to another project that brought him far more fame: the carving of Mount Rushmore. As for the Stone Mountain memorial, it took another fifty-five years to be completed, after several interruptions due to World War I, the Great Depression, and World War II. For all intents and purposes, it was not until the 1950s that interest was rekindled in completing the monument, which by then had obviously become also a powerful symbol of massive resistance to the civil rights movement. In 1958, at Governor Marvin Griffin's urging, the state of Georgia purchased Stone Mountain for a new state park. Works then resumed in 1964, and the sculpture was officially unveiled in 1970. While construction was still underway, another project was initiated, tying the new park to the romantic Old South and *Gone with the Wind*. A replica of an antebellum plantation was opened in the park in 1963, and African American actress Butterfly McQueen, the well-known slave Prissy from the *Gone with the Wind* film was hired to live inside the antebellum home, where she remained until 1965. In 1968 she eventually threatened a lawsuit and prevented the park from using her photograph to continue promoting the plantation. However, by then, the association between the park's plantation and Scarlett's Tara was already well established, with great profit for the local tourism industry.[48]

Thus, in contrast to places like the White House of the Confederacy in Alabama or the Jefferson Davis mansion Beauvoir in Mississippi, Stone Mountain presented itself as something between an amusement center and a public park. Encircling the mountain itself was, in fact, Stone Mountain Park, which since the late 1960s had housed amusements of various kinds and pavilions that could be rented for special occasions, such as parties, receptions, and weddings. School and scout groups, as well as trade delegations from other countries, made field trips or regular visits to the park. Indeed, in some promotional literature, the three carved busts appear as secondary in the overall context of the general recreational activities, while in others the stone images are not shown at all. This is especially apparent in promotional material from the late 1970s. In the booklet *This Way to Fun*, for example, the section naming the mountain no longer featured a photo of the park as it had in the previous edition. On the same page there was instead a large format photo of a family of Black visitors in front of MLK's grave in Atlanta.[49] A 1980 article on Stone Mountain Park in *Travel/Holiday* magazine briefly mentioned the Confederate stone images only toward the end, after profusely extolling the scenic beauty and the amusements of the park.[50] Even Mrs. Busbee, Georgia's first lady, noted this dual nature of Stone Mountain Park in her welcome address at the governor's 1977 annual tourism conference, when she remarked that the site could very well just be a place to spend time with family: "The figures on the face of Mount Rushmore, South Dakota, are an impressive lesson in history, but believe me, that's quite a trip to make for a single family, especially if not all of them are history buffs . . . *Why not go to Stone Mountain instead? The trip's a dream now that Georgia interstates are completed, and for those not interested in history, there's a world of family fun for everyone.*"[51]

Of course, the purely southern-Confederate aspect of the site was clearly evident, literally carved in stone, but it was also mitigated and decontextualized by its proximity to a park frequented by families. Certainly, the mountain itself had a history that made it anything but a neutral location. The second chapter of the Ku Klux Klan had been founded there at the turn of the century, and Klan meetings were often held there until at least the 1960s. Martin Luther King had pointed out the symbolic supremacist role of the mountain when, during his famous "I Have a Dream" speech, he proclaimed, "Let freedom ring from Stone Mountain of Georgia."

Robyn Autry devotes a lengthy analysis to this blend of symbolic messages associated with Stone Mountain. She noted how after the 1954 *Brown v. Board of Education* Supreme Court decision the dominant culture of the white South was deeply committed to safeguarding its heritage by working a disassociation between the Confederacy and the Civil War, thus preserving it from the stigma of slavery and racism.[52] This included the development of the mountain and park as family recreational areas. The celebrations for the inauguration of the sculpture, in 1970, had the clear purpose of reaffirming the unity between North and South, whether real or fictitious, which was necessary in that turbulent period of protests and social upheaval. The opening speech by U.S. vice president Spiro Agnew at the inauguration ceremony, arriving at the last moment in place of President Nixon, appears as a programmatic manifesto of everything that the new Stone Mountain Park represented, namely overcoming the North-South divide and the problematic aspects of southern history: "As we have shed our blood on opposite sides, we now face and admire one another. . . . This new South rejects the old grievances and the old political appeals to the worst in all. The new South embraces the future."[53] By masking the pro-Confederate and overtly racist discourse of its origins under a thick layer of generic American state-park appeal, the dominant white culture intended to "lessen the 'moral burden' of the past."[54] Beneath the surface, however, there remained (and still remains today) a subversive, countercultural, and divisive symbolic subtext, waiting to reemerge. Even mainstream media often broke through the veil that separated the neutral image of Stone Mountain from its deeply symbolic burden. As late as 1981, the *Atlanta Constitution* called the park a "monumental tribute to the indomitable spirit of the Confederacy."[55] Seen from the perspective of mainstream American culture, Stone Mountain was yet another counterpublic historical space in which it was acceptable to celebrate a past as well as a set of beliefs considered outdated and unacceptable by a majority of citizens. This was possible precisely because the most equivocal message evoked by the mountain happened to be decontextualized within a family park.

In the 1970s, Stone Mountain was a popular attraction for Americans of all backgrounds. Its softened image worked well to convey the idea of a South where the past was still revered but without the former bitterness, sometimes in a more light-hearted way. "Even a Yankee can be moved when gazing at it," a Pittsburgh newspaper travel report stated.[56] Another New Jersey article hailed the park as "the true symbol of the Old South."[57] The site was also visited by many African Americans and was not considered inappropriate by most Blacks. In 1973, *Black Enterprise* actually went so far as to invite readers to visit the park and enjoy its attractions.[58]

The Lost Cause mystique at Stone Mountain did not, however, end with the carving of the portraits. At the end of the 1970s the park still included the replica of an antebellum plantation opened in 1963, replicas of Confederate locomotives in service during the war, and two ships for lake cruises, the *Robert E. Lee* and the *Scarlett O'Hara*, as well as an educational installation on General William Sherman's infamous march to the sea titled "War in Georgia."[59]

In short, from a symbolic point of view the site still appeared in the late 1970s much more southern than "American," visibly focused on evoking an idea of a South that was anything but modern (the plantation, the Civil War, the Confederate aura). There remained only a few discordant references to the park's desire to be a bridge of reunification between the North and the South. Consider, for instance, the following passage from the 1980 official brochure: "Georgia's Stone Mountain Park was created *to honor the Southern way of life and ideas which helped form the American lifestyle.*"[60] The text clearly states that much of the American tradition is due to the South, thus bridging the sectional gap while maintaining a strong southern bias. In 1983, the park would add a laser show that projected a gigantic image of Martin Luther King Jr. onto the mountain directly above the Confederate heroes—a very strong symbolic gesture that nevertheless did not really take anything away from the implicit celebration of the Old South.[61]

This desire to diminish, but not eliminate, the most controversial aspect of Stone Mountain was clearly due to commercial interests, that is, the choice not to alienate any segment of the public. Mixing different experiences and messages while at the same time emptying them of meaning is another aspect of the "commodification of culture," often associated with heritage tourism, a process that can generate what is known as "tourist kitsch."[62] It is no coincidence that a *New York Times* tourist report described Stone Mountain as "the very epitome of kitsch."[63]

The simplification and trivialization that characterize tourist kitsch are another manifestation of the variety trope, that is, the constant search for different themes and images. Indeed, by the 1970s, Stone Mountain had several different images: it was a place of American memory, a place of southern memory, a place of recreation, and even a place of countermemory. The tourism industry intentionally contributed to the establishment of all these images. Its purpose was once again the same: to provide a bit of everything for everyone.

Something similar to what happened at Stone Mountain occurred at another historic tourist site in Georgia. This was Liberty Hall near Crawfordville in the northeastern part of the state, home of Alexander Hamilton Stephens, vice president of the Confederacy. According to the *Atlanta Constitution*, the park surrounding the house (which also included a campsite, pond, and picnic area) recorded 289,414 visitors in 1978.[64] It was a higher number than that registered in Plains during the same period, although surely not all of these visitors actually visited Stephens's house, which was only one of the park's attractions. It was also a much higher number than that recorded in the same year at Beauvoir, Jefferson Davis's home in Mississippi (71,327 visitors).[65] This in no way signifies that Stephens enjoyed a more widespread fame or devotion than that reserved for the Confederate president; rather it suggests that Mississippi had generally fewer visitors than Georgia and that the presence of a park around Liberty Hall was responsible for attracting large crowds evidently more interested in a relaxing day outside than in visiting the Confederate statesman's home. Besides, Alexander Stephens was always far less celebrated by the Lost Cause than Lee, Jackson, and the Virginia elite of the Confederacy in general. Stephens's Cornerstone speech, which posits the maintenance of slavery as the root cause of the insurrection, has always been ill-matched to one of the Lost Cause's central tenets, namely that the South seceded on the point of a constitutional principle regarding states' rights. In hardly any respect can Lost Cause zealots think of Stephens as a "Confederate hero." His bad relationship with Jefferson Davis and his belief that the South should have remained loyal to the Union place him on the fringes of southern mythology, thus preventing Lost Cause–related tourism from flourishing at his home. Furthermore, Stephens returned to national politics after the war, being elected to the U.S. Senate in 1866 (although he was not accepted by the Republican-controlled Senate) and then again in 1873, remaining in his seat until 1882, when he became governor of Georgia before dying the following year. This, too, helped make him a mere southern political figure involved in the Confederacy rather than an actual symbol of the Confederacy like Davis, Lee, or Jackson. His figure, being of little importance to the Lost Cause, was also of little relevance as a symbol of reunion between North and South in the second half of the twentieth century.

In fact, while the former owner of Liberty Hall was celebrated with particular enthusiasm in the promotional material, there is no sense of any attempt, unlike at Stone Mountain or Andersonville, to present Stephens or his mansion as a bridge between the North and the South: "Though small, thin and lame, Stephens was one of *the South's greatest statesmen*, serving *as Georgia* governor and senator as well as Jefferson Davis's second in command."[66] The 1978–1979 brochure is actually very similar to an earlier version from the mid-1950s. Gone, however, was the former description of the southern vice president as "*trusted friend of the Negroes* . . . beloved by all who knew him."[67] Such a blatant historical misrepresentation would have been impossible in the late 1970s.

Following the official definition adopted by the state government, neither Liberty Hall Park nor Stone Mountain Park were considered historical attractions but rather simply "recreational areas." Even the plantation inside the park was seen as a generic attraction like any other amusement park.[68] In the same way, the Atlanta Cyclorama, an imposing oil painting of the Battle for Atlanta completed in 1885 and one of the most cherished tourist sites in the city, was considered simply an "attraction." It is at this exact site that the very complexity of the South can be seen, also reflected by the recreational industry, especially in terms of the inclusion of the African American perspective in the mainstream of the southern tourism landscape.

The circular painting, depicting the 1864 Civil War battle in Atlanta, was actually created by German artists hired by the American Panorama Company of Milwaukee, Wisconsin. The painting debuted in Minneapolis in 1886 and became a traveling exhibition in the North before being housed in Indianapolis. At that time, the painting portrayed the battle from a northern perspective, as it was conceived and designed for a northern audience. However, when American Panorama went bankrupt, the painting was purchased by Georgia businessman Paul M. Atkinson, who brought it to Atlanta in February 1892 (after a stint in Nashville and Chattanooga). Only at this point did Atkinson have the painting modified to transform it into a celebration of the Confederacy, making it suitable for a southern audience. Atkinson hired artists to change the color of the uniforms from blue to gray, or to totally change the meaning of some of the scenes depicted. By the end of the nineteenth century, the Cyclorama had gone from a Union victory to a depiction of a Confederate triumph—which was perhaps a bit paradoxical, since the rebels were defeated in the Battle of Atlanta. More financial problems followed soon, and eventually the painting was donated to the city of Atlanta in 1898 and put on display in Grant Park, first in a wooden structure and then in a new stone one. The painting was further retouched and modified with the addition of new scenes and a voiceover soundtrack in the late 1930s. By then, Governor William Hartsfield openly tried to detach the Cyclorama from the excesses of the Lost Cause to support his vision of a modern Atlanta well integrated in the New South.[69] Thus, by the time mass tourism developed after World War II, the painting had also a reconciliatory meaning for North and South, not only because of the alterations that occurred in the 1930s, but also because of the partial healing of the sectional divide that had taken place in the meantime. By the 1970s, Cyclorama was a beloved attraction for Americans both from the North and from the South, as it portrayed the heroism of Confederate and Union soldiers joined together by a single national resolve, an example of a singular kind of American heroism.

At the end of the 1970s, Cyclorama was registering about three hundred thousand visitors a year (more than those visiting the Plains area and all historical attractions combined), at least half of whom were from outside of Georgia.[70] When the deteriorating condition of the building that housed the painting placed the site in jeopardy during the late 1970s, it fell to the administration of Maynard Jackson, Atlanta's Black mayor, to take action in order to safeguard it. A small debate ensued, illustrative of the conflicting relationships that can exist between a historical attraction, collective memory, and the narrative of the past. The irony of a Black mayor being called upon to preserve the painting was pointed out at the time, and it was believed by some that he would rather see the work destroyed, given that the canvass depicted the Civil War, an event largely intended for white history.[71] This very notion demonstrates something about the imagery associated with the commemoration and narrative of the Civil War. To assume that a person of color was uninterested in the remembrance of the war was to exclude him a priori from the community affected by that event and thus from its memory. In short, the Cyclorama, by the late 1970s, appeared as yet another site of shared white memory. This implicit exclusion of Blacks was the culmination of the process of national reunification that historically, since the late nineteenth century, could only occur by excluding slavery from the collective commemoration of white America.[72] In response to these voices, Maynard Jackson himself explained that the celebration of the Civil War was also, and above all, about Blacks. He stated to the press that "the Cyclorama depicts the Battle of Atlanta, a battle that the right side won [the Union]. It was a battle that helped to free my ancestors, and I'll make sure that that depiction is saved."[73] Jackson's approach fits within the broad context of the symbolic reappropriation of the southern landscape that Black America had been pursuing since the late 1960s, even through tourism. Those who criticized Mayor Jackson were well aware that Cyclorama was far from neutral in its narration of the past. Even in 1978, during the Confederate Memorial Day holiday, the Cyclorama hosted a group of United Daughters of the Confederacy, one of the most active memorial associations committed to promoting the Lost Cause. During the 1950s, the Daughters had led schoolchildren on visits, illustrating the southern version of the Civil War.[74] However, by the late 1970s, the Cyclorama approach to the past was about to change rapidly, a change in some way anticipated by Mayor Jackson's position. It is no coincidence that the narrative offered to visitors quickly took on a different form, as evidenced by the texts featured in the Cyclorama tour guides.

The following is a very clear example. A detail of the painting shows an African American holding a horse by the bridle in front of a wounded Confederate officer lying on the ground. Until the late 1970s this scene was described to visitors as representing the loyal slave protecting his master, but in the early 1980s, the same scene was described as an allegory of emancipation, a slave overthrowing his Confederate master and about to escape.[75]

The growth of Black cultural tourism was obviously behind many of these changes. Although official promotion did not mention it, Black tourism existed and was widespread in Georgia and throughout the Deep South. By the mid-1970s Black tourists had reclaimed a number of historical and cultural sites from which they had previously been excluded, such as the Cyclorama. A similar case can be seen at Fort Sumter in South Carolina, the sea fort in Charleston Harbor where the Civil War actually began when the Federal garrison surrendered to Confederate troops under General P. G. T. Beauregard after a prolonged bombardment—a site immediately associated with secession and, more generally, with the great epos of the Civil War. As early as 1948, the fort was designated as a national monument, making it a site of *American* memory, similar to the Andersonville prison camp and Stone Mountain. However, a brochure produced during the Civil War centennial celebrations (1961–1965) showed how the narrative and imagery offered to visitors of the fort was anything but neutral or purely American. Although it was the centennial of the Civil War, the brochure was titled *Fort Sumter: Centennial of the Confederacy*, while its text exclusively celebrated the courage of southern soldiers.[76] At that moment in history, celebrating the Confederacy and, consequently, the regional past also responded to political needs. As Jon Wiener points out, the centennial celebration of the Civil War in the mid-1960s also became a way for many southerners to express resentment about and to protest against what they interpreted as an attempt by the federal government to disrupt the traditional southern way of life.[77] Even during the 1970s, the Lost Cause was more than visible in the narrative offered by Fort Sumter.[78]

However, by the 1970s, the fort, like other places usually associated with the white southern narrative, began to be the object of African American countermemory tourism, which contributed to the downplaying of some of the more radically traditional aspects of southern historic sites and thus, indirectly, enhancing the variety trope. This is evident, for example, from a 1972 *Ebony* travel article in which readers are invited to visit Fort Sumter and the surrounding bay, which recounts: "The fort was later to become the scene of great heroism when a black boat pilot named Robert Smalls captured a steamboat from the Confederacy. . . . The Charleston harbor was also the scene of the famous charge on Ft. Wagner by blacks of the 54th Massachusetts Volunteers."[79]

Once again, Black society has reclaimed a historic tourist site by symbolically wresting it away from the oppressive white southern narrative that permeated the regional landscape. By associating these places with Black memory, in this case the heroism of Black Union soldiers, African Americans could visit Fort Sumter and the Charleston Harbor without feeling disconnected from them, as they would if they followed the nostalgic pro-Confederate mainstream narrative of those same places. Clearly, local promotional materials did not yet take this counternarrative view into account, adhering instead to the classic white-centric approach. Locally, outside the confines of the South Carolina Department of Parks, Recreation, and Tourism's state-sponsored ads, Charleston and Fort Sumter were still ideally placed along the same interpretative path that relied on an intrinsically nostalgic view of the Lost Cause, as was almost always the case at southern historical sites at the time. The Charleston Museum, which celebrated a record of seventy-seven thousand visitors in 1977, was no exception. It presented its Confederate relics and memorabilia to the public in a manner that was not immune to pro-southern partisanship, and it also promoted "a reverential attitude toward the Hunley," the famous Confederate Navy submarine that sank the USS *Housatonic* in 1864 in the city's harbor, of which the museum kept a life-size replica.[80] A 1979 article written by one of the museum's curators and published in the official Historic Charleston guide went so far as to refer to the Civil War as the "War for Southern Independence."[81]

The power of Black tourism to symbolically claim southern places of memory also affected the quintessential regional attractions: plantations. A 1973 travel article in *Black Enterprise* invited Black tourists to visit the region's "languid antebellum plantations."[82] While the plantation and its manor house mostly evoked forms of romantic nostalgia for white Americans, for Blacks they could only represent true sites of Black heritage, with the focal point lying not in the beautiful columned mansion, but in the slave quarters. An example of this inversion of meaning ascribed to a tourist site can be observed in another *Black Enterprise* travel article from 1977, which invited Blacks to visit the slave cabins of the plantations located between Charleston and Savannah, since that was where slaves lived and "prepared much of the food, raised most of the children and entertained the adults, thereby enabling Low Country men to become the finest and most Southern of fine Southern gentlemen, and their ladies the most gracious and most genteel of Southern Belles."[83] The myth of the moonlight-and-magnolias South was not denied, but Blacks were included in the picture, the core of the myth now transferred to the slave cabins, since that was where those who made the myth possible had lived. The revolutionary idea behind this tourist promotion piece was that without slaves there would be no Scarlett O'Hara. Jean Muteba Rahier and Michael Hawkins, studying the case of Louisiana in the 1990s, identified two metanarratives or grand narratives regarding plantations as tourist sites. They define them as the "*Gone with the Wind* meta-narrative" and the "*Roots* meta-narrative," i.e., a white-centric, supremacist view and a view that denies the alleged historicity of the former, seeking instead to bring the experience of slavery to the surface.[84] This new, dual nature of plantation tourism itself, however, originated decades before Rahier and Hawkins were writing—specifically during the 1970s. By the mid-1960s, in fact, two new powerful ideologies of Black American nationalism had been taking form, "the slavery narrative" and "the African nobility-redemption narrative," both embodying new ways of reading the past and experience of African American culture, accepting and even finding a source of pride in the hardships endured by one's ancestors.[85] Therefore, it is not surprising that in this period plantations apparently became a sought-after destination for a certain type of Black tourist, who saw slavery and the misery it brought no longer as a source of embarrassment, but rather as a cause for pride.

Sometimes this reversal of the implications associated with a tourist attraction became a suitable opportunity to propose more far-reaching and in-depth reflections on American society. In other words, the southern tourist system was sometimes used as a symbol of the internal contradictions of American history and the treatment inflicted on Black society. In a 1971 article for the magazine *Black Experience*, Vertamae Smart-Grosvenor reflected on the image of her birthplace, the southernmost part of South Carolina, a place known for its legends of ghosts and spectral apparitions, cleverly exploited by the tourism industry: the ghost of the pirate Blackbeard, for example, who had his base in South Carolina, or the famous lady in the blue dress who would appear on Hilton Head Island, or the gray men of Pawleys Island. Everyone took for granted that these were ghosts of white people, Grosvenor wrote, and thus they were imagined and depicted for tourists by the local tourism industry. However, Mae suggested that if some visitors wanted to look for ghosts in South Carolina, they would do better to try spotting Black ghosts, that is, the souls of the men and women who were dragged to those shores as slaves.[86] This was clearly a provocative statement rather than actual tourist advice, yet it is emblematic of the cultural confrontation over the interpretation of the past that by the 1970s had reached even the travel and leisure industries.

If Georgia's advertising materials displayed an ongoing tension between old and new, tradition and innovation, the same was not entirely true for South Carolina. Here, by the late 1970s, the transition seemed firmly established. In the mid-to-late 1970s the antebellum theme of the Old South was virtually absent from the Palmetto State's tourist-promotional material. At the beginning of the seventies South Carolina was still producing ads specifically dedicated to the moonlight-and-magnolias South, relying on the southern belle/Scarlett O'Hara cliché.[87] However, by the end of the decade, this type of message had disappeared from the DPRT's tourism advertisements.

The first general guide to the attractions of the state produced from 1980 was *Come See S.C.*[88] It remained in circulation only a few years, replaced in 1983 by a new publication simply titled *South Carolina*.[89] Much like the Georgia guidebook, *Come See S.C.* contained only brief descriptions of each of the ten subregions, devoting almost all of its space to enumerating the various state attractions. It other words, both the Georgia and South Carolina guides lacked the structure found in the Alabama and Mississippi booklets, with their thematic, descriptive, and panoramic chapters on the culture and history of the state as a whole. This difference can be attributed to two closely related causes. First, Georgia and South Carolina already had a positive image; their tourism bureaus did not need to create one, so to speak, through long descriptions. Second, and more importantly, Alabama and Mississippi had a serious lack of attractions; filling their guides with generic introductory overviews to local history and culture was a good way to take up space. It is not true, as one might think, that the state with the strongest tourist sector must also have the most articulate and complex guide. On the contrary, a comprehensive and descriptive guide is especially useful for a state that is not very well placed on the market. More generally, there is no close correlation between the amount of promotional material and the actual number of visitors to the state. Florida, for example, did not even have an official booklet in 1977, even though it was the number-one tourist destination in the entire South; South Carolina did not produce its own booklet until 1980, yet its tourism industry was already much stronger than Mississippi's. Georgia's booklet, too, was quite slim compared to those produced by its competing sister states.

Come See S.C. presents the division into tourism subregions even more vaguely, succinctly, and generically than the booklets from the other three states. These regions still appear in embryonic form, likely due in part to their large number (ten in total), which causes thematic overlaps on more than one occasion. Actually, it seems that the order in which the regions are presented in the guide corresponds to some criterion of relevance. The first three listed, in fact, are those best defined, with the most immediately recognizable image; they are also the ones most visited by tourists, namely Grand Strand, Historic Charleston, and Lowcountry and Resort Islands. Then, almost progressively, the regions become vaguer and more generic; the small amount of descriptive text devoted to each certainly does not contribute to the formation of an accurate image. Compared to the seven regions of Georgia, Carolina's ten have names that clearly do not facilitate thematic identification. With the exception of Grand Strand, Historic Charleston, and Capital City, they all seem to correspond almost exclusively to geographic characteristics. In some cases, the names are even misleading. The text on the Old Catawba Nation region, for instance, whose name seems to conjure up Indian lore, actually contained only sporadic references to Native American culture. The booklet's cover showcases the same hodgepodge of different themes, featuring a collage of seventeen photographs covering every possible type of attraction, from beaches to sports to water activities. What is most striking, however, is the absence of the historical theme; Charleston itself does not clearly appear on the cover. This is a first major clue to the general trend of this booklet and to South Carolina's overall promotional strategy, which show a substantial penchant for images related to leisure, sports, and outdoor activities. Of the 127 photographs in the booklet, only eleven are related in any way to historical attractions, including houses, buildings of various kinds, reenactment venues, art, and monuments. Notably, only two photographs are dedicated to the antebellum theme, fewer than those devoted to local flora and fauna and the Columbia Zoo animals. Strange as it may seem, even in the eight pages that make up the chapter on the Historic Charleston region, there is not a single photograph immediately identifiable with the historical theme. Furthermore, very little space is devoted to the Civil War, still inconsistently referred to as either the Civil War or the War between the States. However, it is interesting to note how one of these rare mentions of the war conveys a different message. Here the Civil War is defined as "four years which were to be the blackest in our nation's history," a markedly different image from that "awesome War Between the States" advertised in 1977 by Travel South USA.[90]

All in all, this booklet conveys the idea of a South Carolina extremely inclined toward general entertainment, outdoor activities, and leisure in general. This would not be particularly surprising were it not for Charleston's reputation as "America's most historic city." In *Come See S.C.* the very idea of South Carolina as a historical destination seems consigned to the background. From this we can infer that the project of establishing a viable promotional image to sell the state to tourists had clearly focused on recreational activities and modern amenities.

The paper advertisements produced by South Carolina between 1975/1976 and 1981 reflect the preponderance of the purely recreational theme shown in *Come See S.C.*; cultural and historical tourism was definitely consigned to the sidelines. Note for example the order in which the main ad listed the state's attractions in 1976: "All the things South Carolina has to offer. Like beaches, mountains, hunting, fishing, camping, golf, tennis, lakes, boating, gardens and historical cities."[91] The color advertisement produced that year was of the same kind: the large image, depicting shells on the beach, immediately emphasized the state's main characteristic, that of a seaside tourism destination. The text lists all of the state's beaches, golf courses, tennis courts, and fishing lakes, saving for last the "historic homes, world-famous gardens and cities like Charleston."[92] Even the so-called "Travel Kit Ad" (1977) left no doubt as to what were South Carolina's main attractions. Although the brief text made no mention of any specific attraction, the image (figure 6) clearly hinted at a tourism based on seaside activities and sports.

Golf courses and tennis seem to have been particularly exploited attractions for promotional purposes. Between 1975 and 1976, a special bicenten-

Figure 6. South Carolina Travel Kit, advertisement, 1977, South Carolina Department of Archives and History.

nial ad was created, advertising the Palmetto State as the place "where golf in America begins,"[93] accompanying it with an image of an eighteenth-century gentleman intent on playing. In 1977, the Travel South insert announced that "only one state in the South—Florida—is as rich in tennis resorts as South Carolina."[94] The same insistence on the recreational and sporting aspects of tourism can be seen in another large color advertisement of 1976–1977—this too a collage of various photos in which several people, all white families, are portrayed in an obvious "tourist" attitude on the beach, engaged in excursions, or strolling around town.[95]

Relegating the historical theme to the background was the result of precise strategic choices by the tourism sector, based on studies and surveys carried out in the mid-1970s. Beginning in 1978, South Carolina's advertising agency had identified five different types of tourists across the state, and for each a specific ad was created. There was of course the "beach vacationer," the "Colonial sightseer," the "highlands vacationer & camper," the "fisherman," and the "second-home vacationer." It is evident that of these five categories, four were focused on nature and recreational tourism. The one market segment apparently interested in historical/cultural tourism, the Colonial sightseer, was identified as consisting of couples without young children, middle aged or retired, upper class and highly educated—the type of tourist also interested in the colonial past rather than traditional southern antebellum history.[96] The emphasis on the old nineteenth-century plantation South, in short, found little room in the DPRT's strategic approach.

Only in rare cases did South Carolina produce advertisements in which the historical theme was prominent. One such case is the 1977 ad "Walk along the Battery through Azaleas, Sea Breezes and History." Although a general ad, it appears almost as a real promotional piece about historic Charleston. Set above a color photo showing the city at sunset, the text reads: "Come to the waterfront in Charleston and go back to Colonial times. Amidst the historic homes. The formal gardens. The flower stands and cobblestone streets. Come and see why many people have been calling Charleston America's most enchanting city. For more than 300 years."[97] Once again, the idea of history associated with Charleston was that of a colonial past. Not that the city lacked antebellum-related attractions, quite the contrary. Boone Hall, "the most photographed [plantation] in the South,"[98] was even chosen by a British film crew to represent the antebellum South in an early 1970s television documentary, probably because it was one of the locations where *Gone with the Wind* was filmed.[99] However, it is clear that a general attempt was made to present Charleston as a place of colonial and Revolutionary War history, despite the fact that the Lost Cause and the Confederate image were widely visible in the city's landscape and, like in Atlanta, many visitors came to Charleston precisely because they were attracted to that kind of image. A 1974 brochure almost seems to be redirecting Charleston visitors when it comments: "For a state which played such a large role in the American Revolution, it is remarkable that many people probably never think of South Carolina except in connection with Confederate history."[100]

There was an evident discrepancy between the material conceived and produced by the state's official tourist board, the DPRT, and the real tourist landscape offered to visitors in Charleston. The traditional antebellum charm and Confederate imagery appear to be completely absent from the official advertising of the state and the city. Charleston was associated exclusively with the colonial era. The most blatant example of this thematic preference is probably an ad produced from 1977 to 1978 in which Charleston was simply "a living museum of Colonial America."[101] In other cases, the city's image was more fictional than historical, as in a 1980 ad that emphasized Charleston's "cobblestoned streets that have seen the passing of pirates and presidents. The Port City echoes the America of 300 years ago."[102] Within the destination image, the colonial past was a true thematic image in its own right. It would have been strategically incorrect, from the perspective of an advertising professional, to present the same destination as a place of both colonial and antebellum past at the same time—a dangerously confusing overlap. This is well demonstrated by the case of Georgia, which like South Carolina could exploit colonial imagery. In the Peach State an entire subregion had, in fact, been dedicated to the colonial theme: the Colonial Coast, structured for the most part around the city of Savannah. It seems equally interesting to note that in no instance was Fort Sumter ever mentioned in the South Carolina ads, despite being such a central place in the Civil War and in American history in general.

The launch of the Come See S.C. campaign altered earlier ads, but their thematic focus did not change. Indeed, there is an impression of an even greater emphasis on the seaside/recreational theme. This is evident from three advertisements produced for the 1981–1982 campaign. All centered on oceanside images, they were also the first ads to make clear use of sexualized content, portraying (white) girls in bikinis in a vaguely provocative attitude, a clear example of the promotional strategy typical of beach tourist imagery in the age of mass tourism, which revolved around the five s's: sea, sun, sand, sex, and spirit.[103] Even the state's main booklet produced that year is the only one among the four states examined to show images of this type.

Charleston continued to be one of the most popular destinations in the entire state, as well as one of the few major urban destinations in the Deep South, along with Atlanta and New Orleans. In an interview, Robert Liming of the

DPRT reported a list of the most visited areas in the state, a ranking that seems to have remained unchanged during 1976–1980 period.[104] In first place was, of course, the Grand Strand, the long coastal area that includes Myrtle Beach, accounting for around 3.6 million visitors in 1980. Then came Charleston (2.5 million visitors in 1980). In third place was the capital, Columbia, with 1.1 million visitors), followed by Greenville and Spartanburg (705,851 and 527,000 respectively).[105] These last three locations however were mainly visited for business purposes or conventions, not for tourism. In 1980 Charleston recorded nearly twice the number of visitors as Savannah, Georgia, its main competitor as the most historical city of the South.[106] However, as was also the case with Atlanta, the popularity and appeal of Charleston went somewhat beyond the space devoted to the city in the DPRT materials. The image most commonly associated with it was that of a city where the past was still alive: "Charleston: Where America Really Began,"[107] triumphantly proclaimed a Canadian travel article in 1976, or Charleston, the "city that is itself a living museum,"[108] according to a 1979 brochure. Once again, the organic image of a destination did not match the induced image produced by a state office.

Furthermore, few places in the South have received as much academic attention as Charleston. Most of this attention has been devoted precisely to the complex relationship between memory and tourism. As in many other southern tourist sites, the memory of the past offered in Charleston, until quite recently, has been exclusively centered on a white-centric vision steeped in racist paternalism. This process appears all the more relevant since Charleston is a city that historically played a key role in the Atlantic slave trade, acting arguably as the most important American port of entry for African slaves until the early nineteenth century. The cityscape offered to visitors had, however, almost completely erased all traces of that past. Stephanie Yuhl has conducted one of the most in-depth studies of the issue. In her book *A Golden Haze of Memory*, she demonstrates how Charleston's image was planned and constructed by the local elite from the 1920s onward. The shameful signs of its slave past were selectively erased, while, at the same time, they brought to the forefront the image of a social and racial order typical of a city based on slavery.[109] Emphasis was primarily on architecture and works of art. As W. Fitzhugh Brundage indicates, the idea behind the entire operation was to sell the Old South as a golden age of civilization, as opposed to a more barbaric and unappealing modernity.[110]

The tourist image of the city reflected, and to a large extent still reflects, this very situation. Ethan Kytle and Blain Roberts show that there is still a real discrepancy between narratives offered to visitors.[111] The process of historic preservation, which began at the turn of the century, has also led to the gentrification and segregation of the downtown area, just as in many other tourist cities of the South.[112] In Charleston, this seems even more paradoxical, given that in the 1970s the African American population exceeded 60 percent of the city's total.

Tourism reflected the complex situation. During the 1970s and into the mid-1980s, the city guide used by tour operators still totally omitted African American history.[113] This meant that tourists who participated in tours would virtually never come into contact with the city's history of slavery. Although since the 1960s the civil rights movement had begun to transform Charleston, the narrative offered by the local tourism industry was much slower to change. Still in the 1970s, in fact, the plantations outside the city offered an account of the past almost identical to the one presented fifty years earlier, namely one of wonderful gardens ruled by benevolent masters. The issue of slavery was hushed or conveniently whitewashed. The underlying motivation, Kytle and Roberts demonstrate, was that Charleston tourism officials simply did not imagine that they would have to deal with Black tourists or white tourists interested in Black history. South Carolina and Charleston, in other words, had not yet engaged with the fast-growing African American tourism market.[114] In other cases, a subordinate image of Blacks was highlighted more explicitly. The official advertisement for Charleston produced by the DPRT in 1977/1978, features a white couple elegantly riding in a vintage carriage, driven by an African American coachman (figure 7).[115] This portrayal is notably reminiscent of the phenomenon highlighted by Bryant Simon in his examination of Atlantic City, New Jersey, during the first half of the twentieth century. During this period, being served, particularly by a Black man, had evolved into a significant symbol of social ascendancy for middle-class American tourists, particularly those of the white demographic.[116]

Unlike in Savannah and Atlanta, there is no clear record of Black heritage tours of Charleston during the 1970s. The only attraction that the DPRT acknowledged as relevant to Black cultural tourism in the city appears to have been the Old Slave Mart, a museum that a 1978 city brochure promoted as a place that could "give your family a new understanding of the Negro culture and of the years of slavery prior to the War Between the States."[117] It was also the only Charleston tourist site reported in a 1977 *Black Enterprise* travel article.[118]

This site had actually a complex and particular history. The museum had been in existence since 1938. Until 1959, it was run by Miriam B. Wilson, a woman originally from Ohio who nonetheless set the narrative of the Old Slave Mart by resorting to the idea of slavery as a positive, beneficial system for African Americans. In 1960, the museum passed to two sisters, Ju-

Figure 7. "South Carolina's Great Vacation No. 2: Charleston," advertisement, 1977–1978, South Carolina Department of Archives and History.

dith Wragg Chase and Louise Alston Graves. They hoped to make the museum a catalyst for Black tourism, especially after the important victories of the civil rights movement of the 1960s. Indeed, the site was absolutely one of a kind, being the only slavery museum in the entire United States. Yet it never became a center of Black tourism. Even Black Charlestonians, for the most part, ignored it. Kytle and Roberts indeed note how Asians and whites always outnumbered Black visitors. The museum eventually closed temporarily in 1987 due to economic problems, ironically just when Black heritage tourism was becoming important in South Carolina as well. Again, the problem was that the museum's interpretation of slavery was still very much the same as in previous decades, deliberately withholding the crudest aspects of the slave system. During the 1970s, the museum was even praised by members of the United Daughters of the Confederacy as an excellent response to all those who criticized the Old South plantation system.[119]

Black music was another important asset for the entertainment industry in South Carolina, but official state-sponsored promotion completely ignored it throughout the 1970s, even though some tourist areas of the state were deeply connected to the local music scene and to renowned Black musicians. In Atlantic Beach, for example, artists such as Ray Charles, James Brown, Little Richard, and B. B. King had often performed in front of Black and white crowds. In fact, the DPRT ignored music as a promotional asset in general, even more so than Alabama and Mississippi. One native genre, beach music, which had deep connections with local Black music, had been popular on the Grand Strand since the 1950s, yet the state tourist office did not mention it in its promotion, evidently considering beach music too local and regionally circumscribed to be of statewide significance on the national market. It should also be mentioned that during the 1970s, the genre had partially gone out of fashion and would only have a revival in the 1980s.[120] South Carolina began to be associated at a national level with live music mostly after country musician Calvin Gilmore started his Carolina Opry Theater in 1986, a country music show which is still an important part of the state's destination image. Since 1995 Gilmore has also been running the historic Charleston Music Hall, which reopened after sixty years.

Nevertheless, as in other parts of the South, by the mid-1970s a Black tourism system existed in South Carolina that ran mostly parallel to the official tourism image and promotional materials. If Black tourists did not visit the Old Slave Mart, they would still attend other destinations in the state. Atlantic Beach, for example, South Carolina's famous "Black Pearl," was one of the very few beach areas opened to Blacks during the Jim Crow era and thus a place still frequented by African Americans even in the seventies, the true

Black counterpart to the "white" Myrtle Beach.[121] The Palmetto State also featured another particularly distinctive attraction related to Black culture—although referring to it as an attraction seems somewhat inadequate—and it was scarcely highlighted by state promotional material. Oyotunji, the replica of a real African village, was located in Beaufort County, in the far south of the state. As a brochure states, this was "a Yoruba African village founded in 1970 by His Highness Oseijeman Adefunmi I. The community is composed of 125 Black Americans and islanders who live in the same way that their Yoruban ancestors lived."[122] His Highness Oseijeman Adefunmi I was anything but a true African prince. Born in Detroit with the name of Walter Eugene King, he had been an artist and a dancer before embarking on a series of journeys across the United States, to Haiti, and eventually to Africa where, in addition to Black nationalism, he had been initiated into the Yoruba priesthood. He then moved to South Carolina and founded Oyotunji, proclaiming himself king.

Considering this village as a simple tourist site is certainly not accurate. Even though a fee was charged to enter and visit, with "housing and primitive camping facilities" made available to conjure in tourists' mind the ancestral charm evoked by the village,[123] the *Encyclopedia of Religion in American Politics* actually lists Oyotunji as a Utopian society, one of those community experiments typical of the 1970s whose purpose was to unite "black nationalist ideals with the African Yoruba religion to promote African religion and culture."[124] Oyotunji, in short, had several natures. A 1978 article that appeared in *Ebony* probably gave the most accurate description of the site: "part social experiment, part tourist attraction, part African culture show-and-tell."[125] It is difficult to determine how many visitors this village was actually able to draw and, more interestingly, whether white tourists were also taking part in tours of Oyotunji. A 1977 article in a Texas newspaper told of about two hundred visitors per week, most of whom, in all likelihood, were African American.[126] The author of that article rightly placed emphasis on the influence that the television series *Roots* had on visits to the village, citing Adefunmi himself: "King Efuntola [another name for King Oseijeman Adefunmi] said the Roots phenomenon had eased the financial pressure on the village: 'Black people come from all over the country to see for themselves how African villagers live. We charge them $1.50 admission, plus 75 cents for watching our dances.'"[127] As opposed to the redneck charm of *Dukes of Hazzard* or the everlasting Old South myth conveyed by *Gone with the Wind*, the ultra-acclaimed series *Roots* was a catalyst for Black tourism, and not just to Oyotunji. Africa, above all, was the destination that benefited most from the television success of the story of Kunta Kinte and his family.[128]

Given its nature as a tourist attraction as well as small ethnic and cultural community, it is difficult to speculate on where the tourist kitsch began at Oyotunji, that is, to what extent the display of customs and folklore was sincere and how far it was constructed just to meet visitor expectations. Undoubtedly, many aspects of the experience at Oyotunji seem to have had purely commercial implications. If we are to believe the article in the Texas newspaper, visitors could pay a small surcharge to have their fortunes read or have sacrifices made in their name; elsewhere there was mention of black magic performed in the village for the visitors.[129] What is certain, however, is that the village's existence depended on the dollars spent by tourists. Therefore, it is not surprising to find very different opinions about this peculiar site. In 1977 the aforementioned article in *Ebony* gave a positive image of Oyotunji, as a site seriously involved in the preservation and promotion of Yoruba culture. The same was done in another Black magazine, *Jet*, in 1974.[130] Elsewhere, however, as in a 1977 article published in several newspapers, the portrayal of the village was strongly sarcastic, considering it essentially a tourist scam.[131] What is more important here is that the opening of Oyotunji was cofunded by the DPRT, the official state body in charge of tourism in South Carolina, which evidently saw it as an attraction potentially capable of drawing Black visitors to the state. Yet there was little or no mention of Oyotunji in the state promotional material. In the official South Carolina booklet, the village was dismissed in just two lines that say very hardly anything about the original project behind its foundation: "A Yoruba African village where over 100 black Americans and islanders live in primitive thatched huts and worship the African gods of the Yoruba religion."[132]

Despite the limited space devoted to the village of King Efuntola, which the DPRT had nonetheless helped fund, South Carolina's advertisements show a peculiar attitude in their focus on ethnic-cultural minorities. A good example dates back to 1977. This was a fifteen-page large-format brochure with text occupying 90 percent of each page and small images inserted here and there for ornamental purposes. It was titled *South Carolina: A Lot of It Looks a Little Like a Foreign Country*, and its central theme was the assumption that traveling through the Palmetto State one could find something of many other (and much more famous) tourist destinations.[133] The Caribbean, the South Sea Islands, Scotland, France, Jamaica, Barbados, Europe, England, and even Australia were named as benchmarks for the state's beauty. The long text is basically a list of the various local peculiarities and attractions. Thus one page is dedicated to beaches, one to golf, another to hunting parks, and so on. There was, of course, room for the "beautiful, aristocratic Old Charleston." In presenting it, however, all references to the Old South were omitted, with the city described as follows: "It does bear the mark of the West Indies. (A bit of Jamaica here, a little Barbados there, and a lot of charm everywhere.) It's been said of Charleston that it's the only city in America where you can eat as well as you can eat in Europe." This is not the only remarkable element. The text also celebrates the multiracial and multicultural society at the heart of the old city, illustrating the contribution of English, Irish, Welsh, French, Scottish, African, Jewish, Swiss, and German peoples. One might think that this particular brochure was designed for the international market, were it not for the fact that at that time South Carolina only advertised internationally in Canada. Not only was there no mention of the Confederacy (and only twice of the Civil War), but references to the state's history were almost exclusively to the colonial and Revolutionary periods, while antebellum homes were mentioned only a couple of times in fifteen pages of text. Once again, this publication was very much focused on leisure and seaside attractions.

The idea of establishing a relationship between the state and other international destinations seems to have been unique to South Carolina. Cole Graham and William Moore refer to a number of ads published during the 1970s by the Palmetto State titled *South France? No, South Carolina!*[134] Even an advertisement dedicated exclusively to Charleston did not shy away from mentioning the city's multicultural fabric, as the text reads: "A living museum of Colonial America, spiced with touches of the West Indies, nestles gracefully in the 20th century. An open-air market throbs with the beguiling music of the vendors' Gullah dialect. And fine European cuisine."[135]

Comparisons were also made with other areas of the United States. A 1977–1978 ad states that "along our Grand Strand you'll find a little bit of Coney Island and Miami Beach rolled into one."[136] In 1981, the Myrtle Beach Area Chamber of Commerce produced ads that claimed "you'll find everything at Myrtle Beach that you'd expect to find in Florida."[137] While referring to Hilton Head Island, one ad asked rhetorically, "Is there a bit of the romantic Caribbean in South Carolina? Believe It!"[138] It is clear that the promotional image pursued by South Carolina was precisely an attempt to capitalize on its being a transitional destination on the way to Florida, presenting to the public a destination similar to the great tourist giant of the South with fashionable resorts, beaches, and a Caribbean feel. A completely different kind of image from the rest of the Deep South.

It should be noted that the Palmetto State's promotional materials did not go so far as to truly acknowledge Black heritage in its general image. The same can be said for Georgia. Overall, the space that both states devoted to Black tourism was very limited. In the *Come See S.C.* booklet, seven photos depicted African Americans, while in *Georgia Days* there were three and in the later *This Way to Fun* six. Nevertheless, the visual component of both the Georgia and South Carolina guides remained very traditional in its representation of African American figures (i.e., underrepresenting them). Tourists shown enjoying their time at state attractions were almost exclusively white; Blacks, when portrayed as tourists, were always shown with other Blacks and almost exclusively intent on visiting Black heritage sites. In the "Big A" section of *This Way to Fun*, one of the rare photographs of Black people shows an African American family in front of Martin Luther King's grave. As in a similar case found in Alabama, the choice to portray African Americans mainly in the context of Black heritage tourism indicates both the recognition of the existence of such a phenomenon and a decision, on the part of the state tourism office, to separate it from mainstream tourism, almost setting it apart.

Of the seven photographs in the South Carolina booklet, at least five clearly portray people who are not tourists at all, but locals more or less aware that they are being photographed. Two of these showed Black women at work (one weaving a wicker basket and others tending tobacco plants). Something similar is also found in a Georgia brochure for the This Way to Fun campaign, dating from 1978/1979; here the main photograph depicts two elderly African American men weaving wicker baskets.[139]

Neither Alabama nor Mississippi presented similar cases in those years. The idea of using photographs of this kind is interesting and carries several complex implications. On the one hand, it seems to suggest the desire to show potential visitors some folkloristic scenes linked to the typically southern idea of a life far removed from the frenetic rhythms of contemporary existence; on the other, it seems to include African American figures in the overall design of the local culture theme or, to be more precise, the "local handicrafts" theme (following the thematic subdivision proposed by Robert Dilley), another colorful image still present today in the promotional material of Georgia and other southern states.[140] Lastly, showing Black people intent on traditional crafts in a tourist brochure also conveyed a clear message to white audiences, a message about the preservation of the old (but by that time partly faded) racial status quo in the South.

Another example of the inclusion of Blacks in the overall state narrative can be found in the Georgia Archives. This is a promotional photograph from around 1976, the focal point of which is a group of reenactors (figure 8). The setting, although not specified, is clearly recognizable as Fort Frederica on St. Simons Island, the fort established by James Oglethorpe between 1736 and 1748 to defend Georgia from Spanish forces based in Florida. In the foreground, next to a cannon, a white man armed with a rifle is looking out to sea; he is accompanied by two women, one white and one African American, apparently preparing to load flintlock pistols. The scene is clearly a reenactment of the battle that took place there in 1742 during the Anglo-Spanish War, in which the British defeated the Spanish forces, safeguarding the independence of the colony. The deeper meaning of this photograph is also clear. The man in the foreground is not wearing a red uniform, a sign that he is not a British soldier but rather a settler; likewise, the white woman next to him is also a settler, while the Black woman is clearly a slave. They are all, however, ready to defend the newly founded colony. In other words, the colonial spirit, which would soon become the American spirit, was inherent in both Black and white, men and women, slaves and freemen. Not surprisingly, this promotional photograph was produced for the national bicentennial and constitutes the only example of this type found in Deep South advertising during those years.

At this point, it is worth noting how the representation of minorities within the promotional material was not left to chance, but rather carefully thought out and discussed by tourism professionals. The focus on niche markets in

Figure 8. Promotional photo of Fort Frederica, 1978–1979. Georgia Archives.

1970s advertising was combined with the political need to underscore the changes taking place in the New South. Some evidence of this process can be seen in both Georgia and South Carolina. Minutes from a DPRT Commission meeting in 1979 show that while discussing the details of the 1979–1980 Come See S.C. promotional campaign, it was suggested that "more minorities should appear in the advertisements."[141] A letter attached to the original script for *Georgia: State of Surprise*, a promotional TV spot produced between 1975 and 1976, contained a "list of blacks who appear in the Georgia tourist film [*State of Surprise*]. The total time of the different scenes is somewhere between 30 and 60 seconds."[142] Ten scenes in the film, totaling less than a minute, showed Black people, four of these focusing on sports, an example of what Marilyn Kern-Foxworth demonstrates about African Americans in American advertising: between the 1970s and 1980s, ads showed Blacks primarily as athletes or entertainers.[143] But this letter, which so carefully specified the scenes and their duration, also addressed the need to achieve a minimum number of minutes dedicated to the African American population, otherwise disproportionately underrepresented in Georgia's tourism image. It is certainly no coincidence that during the film production phase, the Tourist Division requested the agency producing it to delete a scene showing a rock band performing with a flashy Confederate battle flag and replace it with something else.[144] The film was clearly intended for a broad and diverse audience.

Advertisements dedicated exclusively to Black heritage tourism do not seem to have existed during that period. However, in 1979, Georgia produced what appears to have been its first generic ad for a Black audience. This was published in the Black magazine *Ebony* and portrayed a group of African American tourists on a beach, as well as in a smaller sidebar playing golf.[145] The text does not directly mention Black heritage or particular historical-cultural sites, but was merely a general ad listing several services. Nevertheless, its publication is quite important precisely because the people portrayed were Black tourists. As previously discussed, in fact, sports and beach recreational activities had traditionally been Jim Crow strongholds. Thus, showing Black tourists engaged in these activities is the evidence that the Tourism Division was beginning to target, albeit still in a limited manner, the Black travel market.

In the booklets, brochures, and ads produced by the two states, only sporadic references were made to historical or cultural sites of importance to Black society. In Georgia, the promotional material could not avoid mentioning the Martin Luther King Jr. National Historical Site as one of its attractions, although King himself was only mentioned as a Nobel Prize winner and never in his role as the leader of the civil rights movement. King, along with activist and politician Andrew Young as well as the Atlanta Braves baseball star Hank Aaron, were the three famous Black Georgians featured in a 1978/1979 children's guide to the Peach State.[146] Even Atlanta, the great southern metropolis so important in state promotion, was never presented with direct references to its importance for Black culture. Occasionally some vague hints of the old myth of the "city too busy to hate" seemed to resurface in the publicity material. In the section devoted to the Big A in *This Way to Fun*, for example, neither King nor the civil rights struggles are mentioned, but the city is described as a "center of contrasting elements and widely divergent lifestyle," with the writer specifying, "The Big A projects an image of solidarity and depth."

In short, the multicultural approach of Georgia's state tourism industry was not so different from that of Alabama or Mississippi. It was not until the late 1970s that a greater inclusion of Black society in the overall design seemed to appear, albeit with a significant gap between the state's official promotion and the actual situation of local tourism, this last much more inclined toward the old traditional narratives and imagery. However, even though by the late 1970s the representation of African American people no longer appeared as taboo as it did in the previous decade, it remained very common to portray them not as tourists, but as intent on work or in vaguely folkloristic attitudes, as the case of another brochure produced in 1979 (figure 9). Actually it was Alabama, driven by pressing image issues, that surpassed its sister states in opening up its state-sponsored destination image to Black society. In South Carolina, the idea of multiculturalism was managed through multiple references to a state that was as diverse as many other places, although this did not result in an effective recognition of local Black culture in the state's narrative.

With regard to Native culture and history, Georgia and South Carolina's promotional materials shared a similar consideration with those of Alabama and Mississippi. It must be said that because they were more elaborate, describing the state as a single entity, booklets such as *Mississippi: It's Like Coming Home* and *Alabama the Beautiful* also had more space to highlight aspects inherent to Native American culture. Frequent references were also present in the Georgia and South Carolina booklets. In *Come See S.C.*, three out of ten tourist miniregions had one or more aspects of local Indian culture as attractions along with the use of names and words in tribal languages to appeal to the reader: "Ashepoo, Coosawhatchie, Combahee, Pocotaligo. . . . Names in this area reflect the Indian heritage of the Lowcountry. You might be lucky enough to find an arrowhead, a piece of clay pipe, or some other artifact. Lots of them are around. That's Ash-he-poo, Koos-a-hatch-e, Come-baa-he and Poke-a-tail-he-go." In Georgia, one of the seven tourist regions inaugurated by Spivia in 1978, Pioneer Territory, was mainly centered on the Native theme. A

Figure 9. Cover of a pamphlet from the This Way to Fun campaign, ca. 1979. Georgia Archives.

brochure dedicated to the state's festivals featured on its cover a photo (figure 10) showing the reenactment of an encounter between a British officer, most likely James Oglethorpe, founder of the colony of Georgia in 1733, and two tribal leaders of the Creek Nation.

This kind of image was part of a real trend to show the Natives in friendly attitudes toward the Europeans, with the obvious purpose of projecting the idea of a peaceful transition of power between the Natives and the newly arrived settlers. The same, for example, can still be seen in the reenactment of the landing of Pierre d'Iberville at Ocean Springs, Mississippi. Even in its official booklet, Georgia acknowledged the Natives' status as "Georgia's earliest settlers," thus partially inserting them in the overall narrative of state history. Even more interesting in this regard is another ad from 1976, "A Portrait of Our Historic Past," clearly inspired by the national bicentennial and dedicated to the history of Georgia.[147] Here the main color photo shows four men and a woman dressed as historical state figures, standing statuesquely with their eyes fixed on the viewer. The text names them one by one. From left to right are James Oglethorpe; Juliette Gordon Low, organizer of America's first girl scout troop; Hernando De Soto, the conquistador who "discovered" Georgia; Sequoyah, creator of the Cherokee alphabet; and George Walton, the Georgian governor who signed the Declaration of Independence. One might be struck by the absence of historical figures associated with the classic South or the Confederacy, but the context of the U.S. bicentennial would obviously have been ill-suited for such personages. Also missing was a historical repre-

Figure 10. *Georgia: Where Festivals Are Fun*, brochure, 1977–1978, Georgia Archives.

sentative of Georgia's Black culture, while the Native world was symbolized by Sequoyah.

Georgia and South Carolina, along with Virginia, Florida, and North Carolina, were also part of the Coastal Plains Regional Commission. This group produced collective ads in parallel with individual advertisements from each of its five member states. The area was promoted as "Coastal South," and despite the tendency to present it as a purely seaside and recreational destination, the promotional material also showed a concurrence of different images.[148] Thus, for example, in 1976 the commission produced a long promotional insert titled "The Coastal South's Got Everything You Want in a Beach Vacation," to be published in various newspapers with a very short text dedicated to each of the five states. Georgia advertised not only its beaches and maritime beauty, but historic Savannah, while South Carolina continued to promote itself as a beach destination, along with a few nods toward Charleston's historic colonial charm.[149] The 1980 edition of the *Coastal South Travel Guide* claims: "Broad white beaches and lush sea forest of pine, palm and magnolia contrast the excitement of the night clubs, restaurants, sports facilities, stock car races and even amusement parks found in and around South Carolina's major cities."[150] "Beaches of the Coastal South," the main ad of Coastal South group, was also entirely dedicated to beach and maritime tourism,[151] as were the images in the official brochure *Map of the Coastal South*.[152] Once again it was the triumph of the five *s*'s.

In terms of advertisement produced for the international market, few examples seem to be documented. By the late 1970s South Carolina was still only targeting the Canadian market, while Georgia was reaching out to new potential markets farther afield, such as Europe and Asia. An unusual case in this regard is an insert on Georgia that appeared in 1977 in the Japanese *Shukan Playboy* magazine (figure 11).

The main feature in the ad was a photograph of a "peanut version" of the then Georgia state flag, clearly chosen because it contained the evocative Confederate battle flag and the peanut, the latter a symbol closely associated with

Figure 11. Ad for the Japanese market. GAR, RCB 54412 Industry and Trade, Director's Subject files 1978, U.S. Dept. of Commerce 1978.

newly elected President Carter. The text demonstrates that the public image the authors were trying to convey was precisely the antebellum South: "The southern part is the setting for novels like Gone with the Wind and Tom Sawyer: the atmosphere is quite nostalgic and the streets still look the way they used to. In short, the classic atmosphere of the Deep South that you can discover by visiting Georgia."[153] The myth of Scarlett O'Hara had very strong appeal in Japan. Even in a country so culturally distant from the West, the Deep South was considered to be gifted with a "classic atmosphere" that was immediately recognizable to the reader. In other words, the Deep South was itself a commercial brand, as was the Wild West. Japan, just like Europe, had also been drawn into the rustic appeal of southern music. In 1977 Governor Busbee proudly stated that a Japanese radio station had begun a six-week program on Georgia music.[154]

The ads produced for foreign markets by South Carolina were few and did not stray from the general promotional themes of the state. There do not seem to have been any advertisements specifically aimed at the European market, while those published in Canada were simple remakes of the same products employed for the domestic market, centered on the three main themes of beaches, Charleston, and generic leisure. Even the photographs were the same as those used for material published in the United States.[155] The only television commercial produced by South Carolina in 1980 was aired in the United States and Canada, the first ever to be produced for the state's tourism promotion, which exploited as state attractions only Myrtle Beach, Charleston, and the Resort Islands.[156]

In conclusion, the case of South Carolina appears to be the most distinctive and the one that differs most from the rest of the Deep South. The only three real state attractions were all located along the coast: the Grand Strand with its beaches, Charleston, and the islands with their fashionable resorts. There were no other major attractions that could differentiate the state on a national level; consequently the local tourist image was built around these three elements, and beach tourism in particular, leaving little room for anything else. South Carolina also represents a unique case in terms of its relationship to the classic image of the South. While Mississippi, Georgia, and Alabama were still making the antebellum South theme one of their promotional assets in the early 1980s, in South Carolina this theme had certainly been of secondary importance since the late 1970s. Charleston provided the only real concentration of historical attractions that could be promoted nationally and internationally; yet in doing so the DPRT's main references were to the colonial and Revolutionary past. Very little was said about nineteenth-century plantation society, the Confederacy, or the Civil War. This is not to say that visitors to America's most historic city were not exposed to a type of tourist image tied to those themes, quite the contrary. Many of Charleston's tourists came precisely because they were attracted by an imagery that was much more southern than that reflected in promotional materials. Many colonial homes were often also antebellum mansions, originally built in the 1700s, but still in use in the following century. The choice to refer to them in the ads just as "Colonial houses" reveals a different kind of image, one less charged with subtext—in a sense, a way to convey a more *American* and less *southern* message. Compared to the rest of the Deep South, South Carolina had a substantial Revolutionary and colonial past on which to mold its tourism image; therefore it is not surprising that in an attempt to differentiate the state from its direct competitors the DPRT chose to focus on a theme that was largely unique in the Deep South context. In this regard, Savannah was somewhat of a contender, but by the mid-1970s Charleston seems to have taken the lead as the city with the most colonial charm in the South.

The other peculiarity unique to the Palmetto State was a promotional strategy based on comparisons with other destinations, both national and international. This was a fitting policy for a state that suffered from a blurry destination image. By associating itself with the already established image of other destinations, South Carolina partly obviated the problem. It was the only case in which a southern state appeared eager to move beyond the regional concept of the South. The reason why this happened in South Carolina is most likely the state's own image problem. The need to carve out a clear and recognizable space for itself to compete effectively with other southern states in the tourist market must have generated this need to distance its destination image from the rest of the classic tourist South. The almost total absence of references to the antebellum era and the limited attention given to the Confederacy and the Civil War are proof of this. Additionally, the promotional strategy followed by the DPRT in the 1970s also helped reassure the public that South Carolina was not part of the backward Deep South that had been shown on television until only so very recently.

Undoubtedly, beneath the surface of the official state-sponsored advertising, the local tourist landscape was not too different from that of Alabama or Mississippi, especially in privately operated attractions and facilities. Slavery remained taboo and African American society underrepresented, and in general the narrative of the past offered to visitors still passed through the filter of the Lost Cause. However, the difference with the other three cases is striking, showing how the classic image of the Deep South as an antebellum garden had lost ground here. It is not easy to say when this process actually began in South Carolina, as available promotional material for the pre-1977 period is sparse. Two brochures produced during the gubernatorial terms of James F. Byrnes (1951–1955) and George Bell Timmerman Jr. (1955–1959) still showed elements of the traditional southern image, which no longer featured in the mid-1970s.[157] The modernization of South Carolina's tourist image appears to have begun toward the second half of the 1960s, under the governorship of Robert McNair.[158]

Georgia, on the other hand, was more similar to Mississippi and Alabama in the overall structure of its promotion. Certainly, the Peach State benefited from the cosmopolitan metropolis that was Atlanta, a symbol of modernity and progress, yet nothing had been removed from the classic image of the Lost Cause. On the contrary, one cannot help but notice how Georgia seemed much more at ease than Alabama and Mississippi with insisting on the use of that theme, even at the expense of the idea of modernity. Of the seven thematic regions created by the Georgia Tourism Division in 1978, modernity was applied as a theme only to the Big A, that is, Atlanta. The rest of the state was presented as a place filled with all sorts of attractions, but with no special care taken to emphasize the general modernity of the state and each of its regions. By contrast, Alabama and especially Mississippi inserted references wherever possible to a new course toward modernity. The reason, clearly, was that Georgia did not have the same problems of perceived backwardness and therefore did not feel the same need to underscore the idea of progress and innovation. Likewise, it is not surprising that it was Alabama and not Georgia that initiated a true recognition of Black society in the tourism context of the state, since Georgia, especially because of Atlanta, had for a decade already adopted a self-image as a more modern, business-bound state *too busy to hate.*

Epilogue

By 1981, with the end of the Carter administration, much of the southern craze that had raged in the United States during the previous decade had subsided. This occurred partly in parallel with the decline in the president's popularity, but there were clearly other, deeper causes as well. The crisis in the values and mission of the United States had reached its peak under Carter, but the subsequent confidence boost during the Reagan presidency came as a rapid cure to that malaise. The South ceased to represent the cultural antidote to many of the nation's problems, while that sense of curiosity and novelty for southern imagery that had engaged American pop culture during the decade also largely vanished. On a more general level, the South was no longer in the national spotlight as it had been five years earlier, for at that point American culture in general had assimilated much of the southern image and the region now appeared more similar to the rest of the country than it had a decade before.

Nevertheless, new questions about the role of the South within the United States and about the persistence of its cultural uniqueness emerged from this newly acquired status. What had the South actually become? It is no coincidence that the monumental work that was the *Encyclopedia of Southern Culture* first appeared in 1989, reflecting a need to take stock of the situation and attempt to answer this question. The encyclopedia, edited by the Center for Southern Studies, was based on the observation, expressed by William Farris, that "Southern culture is much broader and more complex today, but in many ways it remains unchanged."[1] To try to understand what the South was all about in the early 1990s, one needed the seventeen hundred pages of the *Encyclopedia of Southern Culture* and those prestigious academic names who had edited its contributions. Only fifteen years later, the revised and updated version of that massive opus would be expanded to include twenty-four volumes totaling nearly ten thousand pages.

A transition had occurred, although this had by no means taken the form of a sudden and radical revolution. Indeed, even the classic images associated with the region and the Deep South in particular did not disappear and would never truly disappear from the overall picture. This is because even though the *induced destination image* stopped emphatically promoting that kind of imagery, it was now something very much ingrained in the South's *organic destination image*. In the 1980s, tourist offices, travel agencies, and travel writers were still exploiting the idea of a rural, romantic, and timeless South; however, along with this symbolic paraphernalia was added a new emphasis on modernity, casual entertainment, multiculturalism, and even some tentative opening toward African American society and Black heritage tourism. Even food and music tourism, now so important to the overall image of the South, seemed to be going through an embryonic phase in the mid- to late 1970s. Individual destinations had exploited these themes before; what was new here was the idea of making them key parts of the destination image of an entire state or the whole South. The same is true of the local crafts theme, another crucial element in the promotional image of the Deep South today. Studies on New Orleans confirm that the 1970s represented a time of transition for the destination image of the Crescent City, which embraced, over the course of the decade, a greater number of themes.[2] In short, the tourist image projected by the South by the 1980s was more complex than it had been in previous years. It was still the land of plantations and antebellum homes, the Old South still available to American culture and popular imagination, ready to make a powerful comeback when needed, but it could no longer be *only* that. Tara McPherson notes a huge revival of American interest in the classic southern myths toward the end of the 1980s as a reaction to the turbulence of late capitalism, as well as an ambiguous manifestation of racial nostalgia.[3] As Michael O'Brien puts it, the South can also function as "an idea, used to organize and comprehend disparate facts of social reality."[4] For the American people, the region was, and still is, a "South of the Mind," as Zachary Lechner evocatively defined it, a South to be looked at in the present with the eyes of the imagination turning to the past.[5] The same happened in the revolutionary decade that was the seventies, when certain aspects of southern tradition allowed many to find a cultural refuge from the uncertainties of the present.

The process of reshaping and expanding the destination image of the South went hand in hand with broader, less easily definable cultural processes that affected the region, but also the nation as a whole. The increasing hunt for new themes to attract tourists as well as encourage economic profit was accompanied by an equally frantic search for new ways to assert the southern identity on a broader scale, a search that gained significant momentum during the 1980s and 1990s.[6] At the same time, the disruption of past structures within society and American culture in general would result in the culture wars of the turn of the millennium. This is not as much to say that southern tourist offices somehow led those cultural struggles as to place emphasis on the American dimension of the phenomenon. What the tourism industry did was help make the South more American, precisely in its effort to address the search for a new complex identity suitable for all.

The relationship between the tourism industry and southern culture was one of mutual influence. On the one hand, tourist promoters needed to find viable images to sell not only their states but the entire region to the public; on the other hand, in doing so, they further reinforced those very images that they promoted. Just as the early twentieth-century South had become an antebellum paradise largely due to the interest of the local tourism industry, today's South has become the indefinable land of variety thanks also to the influence of the tourism promotional sector.

The questions facing southern tourist professionals in the 1970s were complex and multifaceted. Where did the South and "southernness" begin and end now that faith in the myth of the rural, white South was giving way to this New South? What ideas could be conjured up to sell Dixie effectively to tourists? But there was also another challenge: the new pillars of the southern destination image had to be as inclusive as possible, shared by various social groups and addressing different national and international market niches.[7] Thus, the tourism sector enhanced universally accepted myths, such as culinary and musical traditions or the myth of a biracial South, rapidly adopting them with newfound energy as emblems of local identity. Moreover, by the 1980s, southern society was more stratified than it had been twenty years earlier, transformed by migratory flows that had inevitably made it more flexible and willing to explore new ways of understanding and expressing regional identity. In other words, it is crucial not to overlook the transnational and global nature of these processes.

Part of the current tourist image of the Deep South, namely the variety theme, seems to have been developed between the seventies and early eighties in response to these questions and novelties, taking the form of a gradual accumulation process. The moonlight-and-magnolias South remained, but other equally representative elements were placed alongside it, including the idea of cosmopolitanism, food, ethnicity, native folklore, sports, youth entertainment, and even Black history. It was a South that swallowed up themes and concepts, without doing the actual work of selection. At the same time, motives related to southern reputation clearly drove tourism promoters to stop overemphasizing certain controversial aspects of the classic tradition.

In some cases, the old images seem to have evolved into new forms. The traditional rural and antimodern charm of the South has not disappeared from the regional destination image, but evolved over these last thirty years, reaching a friendly, chic, and trendy dimension that hinges on small-town

American imagery, another place of the mind where the allure of comfort and modern entertainment meets an ideal rustic setting located off the beaten path.[8] Again, the origins of the process can be traced back to the 1970s and have clear cultural subtexts. Both yesterday and today, small-town America serves as a form of reassurance regarding the values and the integrity of the American identity rather than as an escape from social anxiety. Yet, this is certainly not a southern myth, but rather an American one.

It seems increasingly clear that the transformation of the image of the South must be included in a larger perspective of American history, and therefore cannot be read as an exclusively hyperregional phenomenon. The emergence of the variety theme was not a revolution, an abrupt turning point, or a sudden awakening of consciousness, but rather a long-lasting process whose roots can be identified in the post–World War II mass tourism boom. This process gained momentum in the 1970s due to social issues and other motives related to the world of advertising. It is indisputable, however, that the end of that decade was a crucial moment. The embarrassment of Mississippi's tourism director over the excesses of a Civil War–related promotion, Cavanaugh's attempt to remove "Civil War" from Alabama's official booklet, Jimmy Carter and Jefferson Davis's appearance side by side on a billboard in Georgia— in all of this, both change and resistance to change were clearly visible. It was not until the late 1970s that new elements in the tourist promotional discourse began to appear systematically rather than occasionally in every state of the Deep South.

As an agent deeply involved in the construction of the South's image, each state's tourism promotion industry fully reflected the 1970s' stance between tradition and the urge for change. It is also critical to understand that the southern tourism promoters of the seventies did not want to radically transform the destination image of the South, nor could they have done so even if they had wanted. Such a radical choice would have been disastrous from the perspective of the destination's image, with potentially damaging effects on the tourism industry. The goal, therefore, was to adapt what already existed to the new status quo and respond to the new dictates of tourism marketing, while exploiting a range of themes that could satisfy all Americans (and foreigners), whether they were southerners or not. The development of a successful image is also a dialogical relationship between those who propose it and those who receive it; the receiver must be inclined to accept a certain set of messages, as in the case of the myth of the Old South, which was never simply a nostalgic fad of the South alone, but a real part of American culture tout court. In the tourist material of today, the casual emphasis on evoking southern heroes or antebellum magnificence has ceased; however these themes have never completely disappeared from the overall picture. It can be argued that the major difference today is that this type of message and tourist experience is offered primarily to those who *explicitly seek it*, through websites or specific promotional articles, and no longer as one of the main themes presented in the overall general promotion. Visiting the websites of the Alabama and Mississippi tourism offices, one easily understands the extent of the transition. Here the potential visitor is confronted with sections corresponding to the main themes of the two states' current destination image: for Alabama, "Arts & Culture," "Beaches," "Civil Rights Legacy," "Food & Drink," "History," "Music," "Outdoors," "Science & Discovery," "Sports," "Golf"; for Mississippi, "Arts & Music," "Attractions and Events," "Food & Drink," "History & Culture," "Sports & Outdoors." It is only by navigating through these subpages that one will be able to find information about antebellum homes or historic sites related to the Confederacy, now presented with texts far removed from the sentimental nostalgia still in use during the seventies. Here is how Georgia's official tourist guide now presents that Classic South region that still in 1980 depended exclusively on the antebellum South and the Lost Cause: "Sure, classic may be in the name, but this region is anything but traditional. In recent years, it has seen an explosion of new restaurants and breweries catering to the next generation."[9] Has the Old South, then, actually disappeared from Georgia's destination image? Obviously not, but in order to find it, one must now navigate to the Tourism Division's website, go through two different submenus, and only there, under a large photo of an African American family in front of Dr. King's grave, learn more about the "grit and grace of Georgia's antebellum trail of historic towns."[10]

However, neither the persistence of negative clichés about southern states, which continued into the seventies, nor the internal revolutions taking place in the world of advertising singlehandedly explain the fragmentation of the southern destination image around the time of the Carter administration. Another key factor was a new level of competitiveness among states in the region, based on a general increase in domestic U.S. tourist traffic. Any state that wanted to capitalize on tourism had to address the needs of niche travelers while trying to create a recognizable brand, differentiating it from other similar destinations in a way that would stick in the mind of the public. One could go so far as to say that there is no single variety trope, or rather, that such a unified trope cannot exist. By its very nature, this jumble of different themes will always leave some in the foreground with respect to others, perhaps changing them over the years, depending on the various promotional campaigns launched by the promoters. In the late 1970s and early 1980s, Georgia's destination image can perhaps be defined as the variety trope focused on cosmopolitan Atlanta and the classic South; South Carolina's variety trope, on the other hand, was centered on beach activities. But these are imprecise definitions precisely because the state tourism offices themselves were not looking for these kinds of clear-cut juxtapositions. In the case of Alabama and Mississippi, things were even more confusing as it is harder to even vaguely identify some kind of message that stands out from the rest. Without wishing to venture too far into this kind of impression-based consideration, we can perhaps describe the destination image of these two states as a variety trope with the message "we are no longer what we were ten years ago" placed in the foreground.

These variations in their respective destination images also reflected the differences that existed between states. One must not be led into imagining a single, uniform South, as Bennett H. Wall warned in the mid-1970s.[11] Each state had to deal with its own specific issues and the peculiarities of its tourism industry. Alabama and Mississippi were still slowed down by image problems and the scarcity of attractions that could be promoted on a national level, while South Carolina was clearly trying to carve out its own space, presenting itself as a version of Florida suitable for cultural tourism. All of this clearly affected the scope and shape of their respective variety themes. In the late 1970s, South Carolina in particular seemed to be the state least anchored to classic, traditional promotion. Almost totally devoid of any reference to the antebellum South, the Palmetto State's promotional image was virtually set apart from the tourist Deep South, more represented by Georgia, Alabama, and Mississippi. Georgia, despite the presence of Atlanta, the center of Black heritage and southern cosmopolitanism par excellence, actually gave the impression of a tourist destination with an image more like Alabama than South Carolina, still caught between an attachment to the traditional canon and an interest in new, burgeoning trends. At the same time Georgia was also the state with the largest and most successfully established variety theme, thanks to its accomplished and self-sufficient thematic subregional images.

Certainly, there has been no shortage of complaints about this chaotic new portrait of the South, which now appears perhaps more welcoming and enticing than it once was but is at the same time more indistinct and culturally confusing. However, as Ted Ownby concludes, to reject this complex image would be hazardous, since the alternative would be nothing more than a return to the old celebratory discourse of the antebellum South.[12] This is a situation that has much in common with the mid-1970s, when American culture was fiercely debating the future of the South as a distinct regional entity.

There is another important consideration with regard to the link between the current promotion of the South and that seen in the late 1970s. Not only are most of the themes within the overall image the same, although more have accumulated over time, but also the strategic ways they are presented are similar and in direct continuity with the past. It is especially worth noting the way in which Black heritage has been included in the overall design. The advertisement produced by Alabama in 1979 to 1980 declaring that "no other state in the union is as rich in Black history as Alabama the Beautiful" appears quite modern in its approach. If one looks at the current promotional material from Alabama, Georgia, or Mississippi, one can observe the same tendency of each to present itself as the premier destination for Black heritage and civil rights tourism. Consider, for example, these two short texts from the 2018 guides to Mississippi and Alabama: "Mississippi is a state known to inspire and create leaders. Our nation's Civil Rights Movement was no exception," and "Follow a newly developed U.S. Civil Rights Trail to get a full understanding of America's Civil Rights Movement and Alabama's role in it."[13] In other words, the tendency is to highlight the fundamental role that the various states played in the history of civil rights. The promotion thus suggests that one cannot truly understand Black American history without visiting Mississippi, Alabama, Georgia, and so on. Again, competition among neighboring states and the need to keep the door open to specialized markets during the second half of the 1970s gave rise to this policy. Above all, rivalry for tourist dollars is the key element here, as demonstrated by the fact that, following the example of Alabama, other southern states began to produce official tour guides for African Americans during the 1980s. However, it is also easy to perceive a broader design that goes beyond the tourism industry, responding to the cultural climate of the period. Between the 1970s and 1980s, what Charles Wilson calls "the myth of the biracial South" spread across the United States. Racial problems were no longer confined to the South, and indeed the region that had once belonged to Jim Crow now seemed well intentioned, giving lessons of peaceful coexistence to all of America by presenting itself as a place of racial harmony.[14] Therefore, it is no coincidence that during this period tourism promoters also began to exploit this idea, reinforcing it through this very exploitation.

The individual state travel offices and Travel South USA obviously took on the main roles in the process of updating the tourist image of the South. In so doing, they also played the part of political agents, considering that travel office directors were personally appointed by state governors. Thus they represented the new face of southern politics. The seventies were also the period in which state tourist offices became more modern and competitive, in constant direct contact with one another—thanks also to Travel South USA—and therefore always up to date both on the general promotional image of the South as a tourist region as well as on the strategies and themes adopted by the other southern states. Within this competitive framework, tourism offices operated a successful collaboration through an exchange of information and reports, thus making the entire tourist South more closely connected than it once was. Consider, for example, the idea of dividing the various states into small tourist subregions, a strategy clearly at the heart of the establishment of the variety theme. It was a strategy that South Carolina had undertaken following the example and data provided by Georgia. Speaking of the links between past and present, it should be noted that the tourist subregions are also a legacy of the 1970s that still continue to this day. Consequently, this process of destination image development can also be seen as a path undertaken communally by the South, which in fact, judging by the Travel South promotional material produced in the late 1970s, had already begun collectively to promote itself as a more complex and varied destination than the original antebellum garden.

More challenging is the assessment of the extent to which tourism advertisement of that period succeeded in changing the American perception of the Deep South. There is no need to point out, of course, that the perception of the South during the 1970s, 1980s, and 1990s depended only in part on promotional efforts, influenced also, more importantly, by various other forms of information beyond the control of any tourism bureau. This is the complexity of the destination image, divided between its organic and induced parts. It is also true that the image-building power of tourism advertising was much more profound in the 1970s and 1980s than it is today and therefore should not be underestimated. In a time when one could not use the internet to plan a vacation, the promotional material produced by Alabama, Mississippi, Georgia, and South Carolina was a tool with which the potential visitor frequently came into contact. From the late 1990s onward, the first step for anyone considering a vacation to Alabama has become to type something like "travel to alabama" into a web browser and access an endless array of information, comments, and opinions produced by third parties, private enterprises, or other visitors. In the 1970s and 1980s, on the other hand, it was normal to request the official state booklet by mail, since this was the only sure source of information about the various attractions and their accessibility. In this way, potential visitors came into direct contact with the destination image planned by the state tourism offices.

That said, has anything actually changed in the perception of the South thanks to tourism promotion? As will be evident by now, my guess is that it has. Again, it could be argued that by imprinting itself on the American mindset and the self-perception of the South, the variety theme of tourism effectively contributed to shaping today's image of the South as a cultural region with hard-to-define boundaries, both geographical and cultural. Of course, some are alarmed by the end of clear regional individuality, and the fact is that the uniqueness of the South seems to be slipping away, as it is so difficult not to compare the region of today to "an earlier South that was somehow more authentic, real, more unified and distinct."[15] Yet even that earlier South was largely the result of precise choices by southern and national elites and promoters.

One might say that between the 1970s and the present the South has done more than shed its distinctive image, successfully transforming itself from the "Nation's region," to borrow Leigh Anne Duck's definition,[16] into a broader, more self-sufficient destination. At least until the 1960s, the South was promoted primarily as a *particular region* of the United States—the region most closely connected to traditions, the past, family ties, and the land. Now it appears as a *country*, touristically self-sufficient because equipped with every possible attraction and theme, on the same level as the rest of the country. A quick look at the Travel South USA webpage is enough to confirm this. It is a region perceived as a self-sufficient entity, moreover, because its discrepancy with the broader United States (a discrepancy that was full of meaning and that lent strength to the idea of a region similar yet different from the rest of America) has mostly disappeared. This step has been keenly felt by several scholars in the field of southern studies, though not necessarily in relation to tourism. A critical reinterpretation of the field of inquiry in southern studies has challenged the North-South dichotomy (the South exists only if it is in relation to something other than the South) precisely because a rigid interpretation of the South is now proving to be too strained, crushed by decades of preconceptions and no longer useful for understanding an increasingly complex reality.[17] As Urszula Niewiadomska-Flis suggests, if it is no longer conceived as part of the North-South dyad, then the South "is no longer positioned as the exotic/peculiar Other at the margins of the American imagery."[18]

The 1970s tourism promoters, the state tourist offices, and Travel South USA deserve credit for having envisioned a self-sufficient South that no longer necessarily had a subordinate role to the North—a South that did not have to be the "Nation's region." In realizing this, they slowly deconstructed the regional fantasies of the classic South, reshaping them into a new set of narratives that originated from different experiences, memories, and pasts. In Barbara Ladd's words, they were truly "dismantling the monolith."[19] To look at it from a different perspective, the South has benefited culturally from the fragmentation of its image; while losing certain distinctive but burdensome elements, it acquired many new ones. Some it shares with the rest of the country, while others were born and developed in the region, yet without actually becoming local myths. The South has not lost all of its distinguishing features, as pessimists feared, but has allowed itself to create, highlight, and discuss new ones. The challenge of understanding the current role and scope of the idea of the South in America is far from over; indeed it has just begun, for this new complexity, with all the new cultural centers and peripheries in what was once the Nation's Region, is yet to be understood and explained. This, I would argue, is the fascinating task that awaits southern studies.

NOTES

Introduction

1. Starnes, introduction to *Southern Journeys*, 3.
2. Cox, *Destination Dixie*; Starnes, *Southern Journeys*.
3. Cox, *Dreaming of Dixie*.
4. Stanonis, *Dixie Emporium*.
5. McIntyre, *Souvenirs of the Old South*; Hillyer, *Designing Dixie*.
6. Slade, Givens-Carroll, and Narro, *Mediated Images of the South;* McPherson, *Reconstructing Dixie*; Stager and Carver, *Looking beyond the Highway*.
7. For example in Brundage, *Southern Past*, 310.
8. Santangeli Valenzani, "La sfida sul ruolo del turismo negli Stati Uniti."
9. Gregory, *Southern Diaspora*; Poston and Weller, *Population of the South*.
10. Stanonis, *Creating the Big Easy*.
11. M. J. Souther, *New Orleans on Parade;* Souther, "Making 'America's Most Interesting City.'"

Chapter 1. The Tourist South, Jimmy Carter, and the Southernization of America

1. Urry, *Tourist Gaze*; Pearce, *Social Psychology of Tourist Behaviour*; Sirkaya and Woodside, "Building and Testing Theories." Dilley's quote is from Dilley, "Tourist Brochures and Tourists Images," 59.
2. Chronis, "Between Place and Story," 1798. See also Cohen, Prayag, and Moital, "Consumer Behaviour in Tourism," 872.
3. Crompton, "Assessment of the Image," 18. For other definitions, see Gallarza, Saura, and Garcia, "Destination Image," 58.
4. Chronis, "Between Place and Story," 1799.
5. Camprubi, Guia, and Comas, "Analyzing Image Fragmentation," 138.
6. Jenkins, "Understanding and Measuring," 2.
7. Gunn, *Vacationscape*, 111.
8. Molina and Esteban, "Tourism Brochures," 1041.
9. On the importance of visual elements in tourism advertising see Leiss, Kline, and Jhally, *Social Communication in Advertising*; Barnes and Duncan, *Writing Worlds*.
10. Francesconi, "Images and Writing," 344.
11. Dann, *Language of Tourism*.
12. Aron, *Working at Play*, 41.
13. Cox, *Destination Dixie*, 7.
14. Nora, *Les lieux de mémoire*.
15. Archibald, "Personal History of Memory," 80.
16. Brundage, *Southern Past*, 221.
17. Crumley, "Exploring Venues of Social Memory," 42.
18. Hopkins, "Signs of the Post-rural," 78.

19. Dietzel, "Consuming Southern Landscape."
20. See the introductions of the two seminal volumes edited by Richard Starnes and Karen Cox: Starnes, *Southern Journeys;* Cox, *Destination Dixie.* See also McIntyre, *Souvenirs of the Old South;* Hillyer, *Designing Dixie.*
21. Rebecca McIntyre noted how the South's regional identity has been largely shaped by the image that northern tourists have of it, although at the same time local images and culture have been historically manipulated, to a large extent, for the very purpose of attracting visitors. See McIntyre, *Souvenirs of the Old South.*
22. Cobb, *Away Down South*, 316.
23. See, for example, Vinitzky-Seroussi, "Commemorating a Difficult Past," 32.
24. Budrytė, "Experiences of Collective Trauma," 55.
25. Cash, *Mind of the South*, 61.
26. Ownby, "Nobody Knows the Troubles," 241.
27. Nolan, "Anatomy of the Myth," 14
28. Vann Woodward, *Origins of the New South*, 155–157.
29. Smith, *Myth, Media and Southern Mind*, 22.
30. Cox, *Destination Dixie*, 2.
31. Regarding current official brochures in Alabama, Mississippi, Georgia, and Louisiana, see Santangeli Valenzani, "Advertising the Deep South."
32. On the evolution of southern tourism, see Lowery, "Monument to Many Souths," 224; Starnes, *Southern Journeys*, 2.
33. Brundage, "No Deed but Memory," 10
34. Selwyn, *Tourism Image*, 1–21.
35. A clear separation between "South" and "Dixie" was first adopted by John Shelton Reed in his study on the prevalence of the two terms in American business names. The author observed how "Dixie" was a word that connoted the South mainly in its historical-cultural character. See Reed, *Heart of Dixie.*
36. Cox, "Branding of Dixie."
37. Simon, *Boardwalk of Dreams*, 21.
38. Blight, *Race and Reunion*, 265.
39. Foster, *Ghosts of the Confederacy.*
40. Eskew, "From Civil War to Civil Rights," *International Journal of Hospitality.*
41. Janiskee, "Historic Houses and Special Events," 399.
42. See, for example, Hall, "Civil War Reenactors," 9.
43. Kammen, *Mystic Chords of Memory*, 626.
44. Fowler, "Heritage," 60.
45. Bowes, "Tourism and Heritage," 36.
46. Weeks, *Gettysburg*, chap. 6. See also Ashworth, "Heritage and Tourism," 95.
47. Bajc, "Introduction to Collective Memory," 2.
48. Hoelscher, "Where the Old South," 239.
49. Hoelscher, 239.
50. Davis, *Race against Time*, 175
51. Benjamin et al., "Heritage Site Visitation and Attitudes."
52. Starnes, *Southern Journeys*, 6–7.
53. Draves, "It's Easier to Pick," 90. A nearly identical phrase is attributed elsewhere to an unspecified citizen of Tennessee. See Wolf, "These Southerners Just Love Yankees," 47.
54. Starnes, *Southern Journeys*, 14.

55. Rugh, *Are We There Yet?*
56. Doering, "Geographical Aspects," 309.
57. Weeks, *Gettysburg*, chap. 6.
58. Nelson, "Art of Queuing Up," 2. Marguerite Shaffer also notes the same nationalist function in the tourism of the 1880–1940 period. See Shaffer, *See America First*.
59. Palmer, "Ethnography of Englishness"; Pretes, "Tourism and Nationalism"; Frew and White, *Tourism and National Identity*.
60. See, for example, Fousex, *To Lead the Free World*.
61. Quoted in Pretes, "Tourism and Nationalism," 129.
62. Slotkin, *Gunfighter Nation*, 655.
63. Alabama Bureau of Publicity and Information, "Alabama to Participate in Presidential Patriotic Parade," newsletter, 1981, sg014556, Alabama Department of Archives and History (hereafter adah) (Tourism and Travel Administration, Bureau Policy 1972–1982, Travel, Publicity and Press Release 1981.
64. C. Bates, "'Oh, I'm a Good ol' Rebel,'" 197.
65. Bonner, *Colors and Blood*, 177.
66. Schulman, *Seventies*, 5.
67. Quoted in Coski, *Confederate Battle Flag*, 130.
68. Clark, *Emerging South*, 142.
69. Wolcott, *Race, Riots, and Roller Coasters*, 119.
70. Stanonis, *Faith in Bikinis*, 96–97.
71. Lollar and Van Doren, "U.S. Tourist Destinations," 632.
72. Rugh, *Are We There Yet?*, 11.
73. "Driving Vacations 'Out,'" 11-a.
74. Smith, *Hosts and Guests*, 232.
75. Fox, *Mirror Makers*, 329.
76. Fasce, *Le anime del commercio*, 167–172.
77. Page and Connell, *Tourism*, 149.
78. Brundage, *Southern Past*, 310.
79. Ownby, "Nobody Knows the Troubles," 248.
80. Santangeli Valenzani, "Advertising the Deep South."
81. Eckes, "South and Economic Globalization."
82. Quoted in Borstelmann, *1970s*, 136.
83. On the transformations that occurred in the South during the 1970s, see Scranton, *Second Wave*; Cobb, *Selling of the South*; Schulman, *Seventies*; Borstelmann, *The 1970s*, 133–137.
84. Smith, *Myth, Media and Southern Mind*; Reed, *Minding the South*.
85. Smith, *Myth, Media and Southern Mind*, 133.
86. Ashmore, *Epitaph for Dixie*, 25.
87. Cobb, *Away Down South*, 238.
88. Cumming, "Been Down Home So Long," 84.
89. Roland, "Ever-Vanishing South," 6.
90. Cobb, "Epitaph for the North," 6.
91. Murphy, "South as the New America."
92. The percentage is calculated according to data reported for each state in American Revolution Bicentennial Administration, *The Bicentennial of the United States of America*.

93. Jimmy Carter, "Restoration of Citizenship Rights to Jefferson F. Davis Statement on Signing S. J. Res. 16 into Law," American Presidency Project, accessed July 1, 2024, https://www.presidency.ucsb.edu/node/244072.

94. Prunty, "Two American Souths," 18. The quote, taken from D. H. Donald, "When the United States Rejoined the South," commencement address, Millsaps College, Jackson, Mississippi, June 1976, is cited in Prunty, "Two American Souths."

95. Cowie, *Stayin' Alive*, 174.

96. Egerton, *Americanization of Dixie*; Vann Woodward, "South Tomorrow," 68.

97. Grimlin, *American Regionalism*, 28.

98. On this subject, see Wilson, "Myth of the Biracial South."

99. Cobb, *Away Down South*, 318.

100. Huber, "Short History of Redneck."

101. Raines, "Todd and Stabler Offseason Game," b-5; Jackson, Rise and Decline.

102. Bowden, "Plains," 4-e.

103. Wilson, "Carter Era."

104. Zaretsky, *No Direction Home*.

105. Francaviglia and Franklin, *Main Street Revisited*.

106. On this subject, see Rees, "Plains and Simple."

107. Cohen, "Trailing Jimmy Carter in Search," C1

108. Johnson, "Small Town," 4D

109. Smith, *Hosts and Guests*, 4–5.

110. *Come See S.C.,* brochure, 1981, South Carolina Department of Archives and History (hereafter scdah) (s200044, 232k03, General Travel Brochures 1970–1989).

111. On this subject, see, for example, Schulman, *Seventies*, 115–117; and Crespino, *In Search of Another Country*, 172

112. Dunn, "Quest for the South's Future."

113. Eckes, "South and Economic Globalization," 39.

114. Percy, "Going Back to Georgia," in *Signposts in a Strange Land*, 26–38.

115. Schulman, *From Cotton Belt to Sunbelt*, 220.

116. Eckes, "South and Economic Globalization," 44.

117. Terrill, "No More Dixie?," 241

118. *Program Report of the United States Travel Service; Summary and Analysis of International Travel to the U.S.*

119. Hudman and Jackson, *Geography of Travel and Tourism*, 65.

120. Gibbons and Fish, "Dynamics," 18.

121. *U.S. News & World Report*, June 27, 1977, 38, Jimmy Carter Library (from now JCL) (Domestic Policy Staff, Stern's Subject Files, Special Projects, box 92, Tourism).

122. On this subject, see de Grazia, *Irresistible Empire*.

123. Dudziak, *Cold War Civil Rights*, 11; Layton, *International Politics*, 59–60.

124. Dudziak, *Cold War Civil Rights*, 240.

125. Dudziak, 240.

126. Tellex Report, "Come to Alabama," press release for BBC Oxford, 1981, ADAH (Tourism and Travel administrative files 1940–2010, sg014981, Alabama Publicity UK1980–82.

127. Hayes, "Congressional Travel and Tourism Caucus," 124.

128. Hayed, 124.

129. *Five Year Program for the Southern Travel Directors Council, Inc.,* report, July 17, 1974, Georgia Archive (from now on GAR) (RCB 19492 Industry and Trade, Tourist Division, Director's Subject Files 1980, Travel South 1980). These member

states included Alabama, Arkansas, Florida, Georgia, Kentucky, Louisiana, Mississippi, North Carolina, South Carolina, Tennessee, and Virginia—the classic definition of "the South" as the area that comprised the eleven states of the former Confederacy, plus Kentucky and minus Texas.

130.   *Regional Analysis of International Travel,* 59.
131.   *Regional Analysis of International Travel,* 59.
132.   "Travel in the South," *Alabama Hospitality* 3, no. 3 (August 1980), GAR (RCB 19492, Industry and Trade, Tourist Division, Director's Subject Files 1980, Travel South 1980).
133.   Stanonis, *Faith in Bikinis,* p.53
134.   Mohl, "Miami," 72.
135.   Division of International Marketing, South Carolina Department of Parks, Recreation and Tourism, *Outside Interests: Selling South Carolina Tourism to the World, International Marketing Program 1980–1990,* report, SCDAH(S200016, Administrative Correspondence Files 1976–1992, box 20).
136.   The figure refers to international arrivals, excluding Canada, with Atlanta as the U.S. port of entry. The figures were reported by the *Atlanta Constitution.* See Morgan, "Atlanta Makes Headway," 9-c.
137.   *A Regional Analysis of International Travel to the United States,* U.S. Department of Commerce, 59.
138.   U.S. Department of Commerce, United States Travel Service, *International Tourism: Travel Issues and Answers,* second quarter 1978, JLC (Domestic Policy Staff, Stern's Subject Files, box 93, National Tourism Policy Study).
139.   Christensen, "'Wild West,'" 310.
140.   U.S. Travel Service, *Publications and Materials of the United States Travel Service: 1977.*
141.   U.S. Travel Service, *Publications and Materials of the United States Travel Service: 1977.*
142.   U.S. Travel Service, *Publications and Materials of the United States Travel Service: 1968.*
143.   U.S. Travel Service, "Examples of USTS Involvement with States/Cities," JLC (Domestic Policy Staff, Stern's Subject Files, box 95, Tourism, U.S. Travel Service 7/8/80–12/2/80).
144.   *South Magazine,* January/February 1976 GAR (RCB 5296 Industry and Trade, Tourist Division, Director's Subject Files 1977, Savannah 1975–1976).
145.   "Florida Jumpy," G-4.
146.   "Busbee Speech at Governor's Conference on Tourism," transcript, 1977, GAR (RCB 31076 Industry and Trade, Public Relations, Promotional Speeches, Scripts and Correspondence 1970, 1972, 1976, 1978, 1977 Gov. Busbee Speeches/ Correspondence).
147.   On the clash between the USTS and the Carter administration, see Santangeli Valenzani, "La sfida sul ruolo del turismo negli Stati Uniti."
148.   In 1979, Travel South director Michael Sarka appeared before a Senate subcommittee to emphasize the need to keep the USTS alive. See *Hearing before the Subcommittee,* 43.
149.   "The South Rises Again—as Draw for Tourists," *Orlando Sentinel,* July 31, 1977, 13-D; "South Rises Again in Tourism Picture," Travel Trade, September 15, 1980, GAR (RCB 19492, Industry and Trade, Tourist Division, Director's Subject Files 1980, Travel South 1980).

150. "The South Reports Record Year in Travel," *Southern Traveler*, October 1980, GAR (RCB 19492, Industry and Trade, Tourist Division, Director's Subject Files 1980, Travel South 1980).

151. "Travel in the South," *Alabama Hospitality* 3, no. 3 (August 1980), GAR (RCB 54412 Industry and Trade, Tourist Division, Director's Subject Files 1978, U.S. Dept. of Commerce 1978).

152. *South Magazine*, January/February 1976, 20.

153. These include New England, the Eastern Gateway, George Washington Country, Travel South USA, the Great Lakes Country, the Mountain West, the Far West, and Hawaii.

154. U.S. Travel Data Center, *1979 Travel South Economic Analysis: Preliminary Report*, May 27, 1980, GAR (RCB 19492, Industry and Trade, Tourist Division, Director's Subject Files 1980, Travel South 1980).

155. The definition of "leisure travel" here is based on the category used by the *Census of Transportation*, which lists the following as reasons for travel: "outdoor recreation, entertainment, sightseeing, and personal and family affairs." It should also be noted that the *Census of Transportation* considered Texas and Oklahoma as the South, unlike Travel South USA. See U.S. Census Bureau, 1967 Census of Transportation,

156. Birdsall, "Changing Images," 141–142.

157. "Governor Cliff Finch Report," sec. 2, p. 2 (emphasis added).

158. Bay, *Traveling Black*.

159. "Democracy Defined at Moscow," 105.

160. "Questions and Answers," *Pittsburgh Courier*, October 14, 1961, 10.

161. Williams, *This Is My Country Too*, 29–30.

162. Sundown towns are localities (sometimes entire counties) where Blacks were forbidden after sunset, under penalty of arrest or worse. They were not exclusive to the South; between 1890 and 1968 thousands of towns "for whites only" were founded all over America. See Loewen, *Sundown Towns*.

163. Adams, "Highways of Hope," 1.

164. Graves, "Black Travel and Leisure Time," 4.

165. Broadus, "Black Tourist Boom," 13-D.

166. Burns, Introduction to Tourism and Anthropology, 76.

167. Gordon, "Take Amtrak to Black History," 55.

168. B. Hayes, "Black Tourist Looking," F-15.

169. Williford, "Traveling America's South," IX-2.

170. Clarke, "Mapping Transnationality," 133–134.

171. Gordon, "Take Amtrak to Black History," 57.

172. Cobb, *Away Down South,* p. 262.

173. Weathers, "Travelling through the Lowlands," 45.

174. Brundage, *Southern Past*, p. 312.

175. Eskew, "From Civil War," *International Journal of Hospitality*, 205.

176. Santangeli Valenzani, "Advertising the Deep South."

177. *Destination USA*, 67.

178. Kern-Foxworth, "Colorizing Advertising"; Kern-Foxworth, *Aunt Jemima, Uncle Ben;* O'Barr, *Culture and the Ad;* Ohmann, Selling Culture.

179. See Foley and Lennon, "Heart of Darkness," 196–197; Tunbridge and Ashwort, *Dissonant Heritage*.

180. Dwyer and Alderman, *Civil Rights Memorials*, 39.

181. Shackel, *Memory in Black and White*, 15.

1. "Memo Travel South," memorandum, 1977–1978, GAR (Travel South meeting, July 1977, RCB 24902 Industry and Trade, Director's Subject Files 1977).
2. Arkansas Department of Parks and Tourism, "Arkansas Tourism Division," 1-B, and "USTS-Assisted Travel Mission," FY 1980, in United States Department of Commerce, *USTS Report*, June 1980, ADAH (SG014979 Pageants, Personal Files, USRS Travel Service 1979–1981); letter from George William to Betty Blake, Delta Queen Steamboat Company, May 24, 1977, MDAH (box 11532, row 22, bay 5, shelf 2, S1663, Delta Queen).
3. *Five Year Program for the Southern Travel Directors Council, Inc. Adopted by the Board of Directors*, July 17, 1974, GAR (RCB 19492 Industry and Trade, Tourist Division, Director's Subject Files, Travel South 1980).
4. "The South—Location and Legend," advertisement, *House & Garden*, February 1975, 34.
5. Travel South, "State Advertisement Participation in Travel South USA Print Media Promotions," 1977, GAR (RCB 24902 Industry and Trade, Director's Subject Files 1977, Travel South Marketing Committee).
6. "Travel South," advertisement script, 1977, GAR (1977 Speeches/Scripts,RCB 31076, Industry and Trade, Public Relations, Promotional Speeches, Scripts and Correspondence 1970, 1972, 1976, 1978).
7. "You'll Find Adventure in the Changing Middle South," advertisement, *Daily Oklahoman*, February 6, 1966, 7.
8. "Alabama, the State Where the Stars Fell," advertisement, *Akron Beacon Journal*, December 14, 1941, 41.
9. Buchanan, "Magnolias and Manufacturing," 96. Buchanan's essay contains an important analysis of the promotional tourist-industrial material produced in Mississippi between 1945 and 1955.
10. *Travel South USA: Come to the Warm*, booklet, 1979, GAR (RCB 16066, Industry and Trade, Director's Subject Files 1979, Georgia Press Institute, Athens).
11. *Travel South USA: Come to the Warm* (emphasis added).
12. Cohen Ferris, *Edible South*, 323–325.
13. "Rebel Soldiers Charge North," C-1.
14. Tellex Report, "Alabama the Beautiful," press release for BBC Radio Scotland, 1982, ADAH (Tourism and Travel Administrative Files 1940–2010, SG014981, Alabama Publicity United Kingdom 1980–82).
15. Egerton, *Southern Food*.
16. McDaniel, *Irresistible History of Southern Food*.
17. Memorandum by Travel South, 1980, GAR (RCB 19492, Industry and Trade, Tourist Division, Director's subject files 1980, Travel South 1980).
18. *Honeymoon South, Travel South*, brochure, 1981, ADAH (Tourism and Travel Administrative files, 1940–2010, SG014977, Alabama the Beautiful campaign 1980–1981) (emphasis added).
19. "South Carolina Tourism Advertising—Proposal, Leslie Advertising," 1979–1980, SCDAH (S200039, dprt, Marketing Office, Advertising Proposal 1975–1998).
20. Travel South, *The Nation's Greatest Vacation Area,* brochure, mid-1970s, ADAH (SG014284, Tourism and Travel, Communication Division, Program Administrative Files 1961–1979).

21. Travel South USA, *Southern Travel Economic Analysis & Annual Report*, 1976, GAR (RCB 54412 Industry and Trade, Tourist Division, Director's Subject Files 1978).

22. U.S. Travel Data Center, *1979 Travel South Economic Analysis: Preliminary Report*, May 27, 1980, 2–3, GAR.

23. TTG Europa, "Southern Team-Work," newspaper clipping, October 24, 1980, GAR (RCB 19492, Industry and Trade, Tourist Division, Director's Subject Files 1980, Travel South 1980).

24. Chart printed in *The South Magazine*, January/February 1976, 20. The table takes into account the budgets available to the tourism offices of the various states and the earnings of the local tourism industry in each. Data should, however, be taken with a grain of salt.

25. The figure for tourist numbers in southern California was reported by the director of the San Diego Zoo and Wild Animal Park in Volkart, "Surrey Zoo Success," 4. For tourists in Florida, see Beamguard, "Florida's Greenest Year," 6.

26. *Report and Recommendations of the Tourism Study Commission to the Legislature of Mississippi*, February 1978, p. 40, Mississippi Department of Archives and History (hereafter MDAH) (757.1:TS1978).

27. Report and Recommendations of the Tourism Study Commission, 1978, p. 89.

28. Alabama Bureau of Publicity and Information, "Doug Benton Renamed to Head Alabama's Travel Department," memorandum, ADAH (SG14286 Tourism and Travel, Communications Divisions, Program Administrative Files 1962–1986, Press Release 1970–1977).

29. "West," 14.

30. Martin, "Ed Hall's Job," 5.

31. Doering, "Reexamination of the Relative Importance," 16.

32. Peirce, *Deep South States of America,* 307.

33. Dameron and Murphy, "International City Too Busy," 47.

34. Allen, *Atlanta Rising*, 188.

35. Meyers, *Empire State of the South*, 321.

36. Abbott, *New Urban America*, 6.

37. Bartley, *Creation of Modern Georgia,* 236. See also Main and Gryski, "George Busbee and the Politics," 273, 278.

38. Mickey, *Paths Out of Dixie,* 345

39. On Busbee and tourism, see Cook, *Governors of Georgia*, 298.

40. In January 1977, Governor Busbee reported seventy-four major productions up to that time, which had earned the state about eighty-nine million dollars. See "Department Speech, 1/31/1977," transcript, January 31, 1977, GAR (Gov. Busbee Speeches/Correspondence,RCB 31076, Industry and Trade, Promotional Speeches, Scripts and Correspondence 1970, 1972, 1976, 1978).

41. *GHTA News*, 1979, GAR (GHTA 1979,RCB 16065, Industry and Trade, Director's Subject Files 1979).

42. Krane and Shaffer, *Mississippi Government and Politics*, 84.

43. "My Position on Tourism," 48.

44. On Finch's plan for tourism, see "Finch Points Out State's Need," 8; "Finch Creates New Tourism Organization," 2B; "Economy," 12.

45. Biographical and professional notes on George Williams can be found in: "Starkville Man Hired to Head," 49; "Tourism Official Says Potential," 9.

46. "Sunbelt South Emerges," 8.

47. Bolton, *William F. Winter*, 198.
48. Sumners, *Governors of Mississippi*, 145; Nash and Taggart, *Mississippi Politics*, 88.
49. Krane and Shaffer, *Mississippi Government and Politics*, 85, 215.
50. Bolton, *William F. Winter*, 214–125.
51. Peirce, *Deep South States of America*, 381.
52. Grahm and Moore, *South Carolina Politics and Government*, 152.
53. J. B. Edwards, *State (Condition) of the State: 1977*, January 18, 1977, https://dc.statelibrary.sc.gov/handle/10827/658.
54. Peirce, *Deep South States of America*, 422.
55. Peirce, 418.
56. "Fred P. Brinkman: Biographical Sketch," n.d., SCDAH (S200016, box 18, 310A2, Administrative Correspondence Files 1976–1992, Reorganization Commission, DNR Program 1977).
57. Mitchell, "Executive Cites 'New Realism,'" 12-A.
58. King, *Sombreros and Motorcycles*, 24–25.
59. King, *Sombreros and Motorcycles*, 32; Edgar, *South Carolina: A History*, 579.
60. "South Carolina Chamber of Commerce Annual Meeting: Fred Brinkman Remarks," January 25, 1979, SCDAH (Dept. of Parks, Recreation and Tourism S200015, Speeches, 1974–1987).
61. Rogers et al., *Alabama*, 596.
62. "Inaugural Address of Governor George Wallace," transcript, 1963, ADAH (Administrative Files, SG030847).
63. Frederick, *Stand Up for Alabama*, 378.
64. Hollins, *See Alabama First*, 134.
65. Bass and Devries, *Transformation of Southern Politics*, 57–59.
66. Frederick, *Stand Up for Alabama*, p. 348.
67. Harvey, "Wallaceism," 171. In his monograph on Wallace, Dan T. Carter notes how "with the exception of a few hard-line right-wingers like Patrick Buchanan, the former Alabama governor has been a prophet without honor, remembered (if at all) for his late-life renunciation of racism." However, Carter concluded with a less negative assessment of the governor, emphasizing the influence Wallace's policies would have in laying the groundwork for the new conservative political trend from the 1980s onward. See Carter, *Politics of Rage*.
68. Rogers et al., *Alabama*, 596. With regard to the economic growth boasted by the Wallace administration, the arbitrary or overtly optimistic use of the data presented has often been called into question. See Flint, *Alabama in the Twentieth Century*, 111; Bass and Devries, *Transformation of Southern Politics*, 71.
69. Webb and Armbrester, *Alabama Governors*, 279.
70. Flint, *Alabama in the Twentieth Century*, 118.
71. Flint, 150.
72. Letter from Caroline S. Cavanaugh to Dan Young, April 15, 1981, ADAH (Bureau of Tourism and Travel, Tourism and Travel Administrative Files, 1940–2010, Pageants, Personal Files, SG014979, USTS #2 1979–1981); *Travel-ALA*, July 1979, ADAH (SG020098 Tourism and Travel, Communications Divisions, Information and Promotional Publications 1972–1991, Travel-ALA, 1972–1983).
73. Gibbons and Fish, "Dynamics," 21.
74. Herring, "Smokeless Tourist Industry," 11-B.
75. The *Alabama Journal* called Benton "Wallace's warm-up man at rallies" (a defini-

tion that the same Benton applied to himself). Duncan, "Benton Denies His Politicking," 45.

76. Duncan, 45.

77. *Travel-ALA*, June 1979, ADAH (SG016201, Historical Commission Administrative Correspondence 1968–1980, Alabama Promotion Publications).

78. "Firm Gets Tourism Contract," 17.

79. *Montgomery Advertiser*, March 3, 1978, 30.

80. For biographical and professional data on Caroline Cavanaugh, see archival material in ADAH (SG036739, Director's Correspondence, Cavanaugh Personal Folder 1979–1982); "Chamber Vice President," 25; "Cavanaugh Loses Spending Authority," 2.

81. *Survey of State Travel Offices: 1977–1978*, 311.

82. The national average for advertising abroad was $40,000 in 1977–1978, rising to $70,000 in 1980–1981. The calculation is based on data found in the surveys of state travel offices in 1977–1978 and 1980–1981.

83. This was probably another misunderstanding. There is no record in the Mississippi State Archives of these advertisements being published in Germany, the United Kingdom, or anywhere else. Presumably, Mississippi was declaring as its own state ads some Travel South promotional materials that included a small space for each of the southern states, including Mississippi. Alternatively, it is possible that Mississippi was declaring as advertising expenses generic promotion expenses for the familiarization project with German travel agents. Mississippi tourism personnel were planning some familiarization tours of the state for German visitors, as a way to capitalize on the meeting of the Deutsches Reisebüro, Germany's major travel agency organization, held in New Orleans in December 1977. See "State Focuses Tourism Effort," 15

84. *Survey of State Travel Offices: 1980–1981*. Again, there seems to have been some confusion on data. Alabama, for example, did not report any foreign promotion expenditures for 1981, yet it is evident from its tourism office materials and records that such activity existed.

85. "Amenities," March 1978, GAR (RCB 54412 Industry and Trade, Tourist Division, Director's Subject Files 1978, GHTA 1978).

86. Alabama Bureau of Publicity and Information, *Recreation and Tourism, General Situation Statement*, report, 1979, ADAH (SG014976 Tourism and Travel Administrative Files, Transportation, Travel, Tourism, 1979–1981).

87. "Tourism Efforts Are Paying Off," 4.

88. U.S. Travel Service, *Domestic Tourism Program: FY 1977–FY 1979*, MDAH (Dept. of Tourism Subject Correspondence, B2, r170, b5-s2, box 11534).

89. *1979 Travel South Economic Analysis: Preliminary Report*, GAR.

90. *Objectives for 1978: Department of Industry and Trade*, 1977, GAR (RCB 24901, Industry and Trade, Director's Subject Files 1977, FY'78 Planning Presentation Joint House and Senate Tourist Committee).

91. *Summary of Discussion: Advisory Council on Tourism*, 1978, GAR (RCB 54412 Industry and Trade, Tourist Division Director's Subject Files 1978, Coastal APDC 1978).

92. In addition to the nationwide magazines, the ads were in newspapers from Ohio, Pennsylvania, North Carolina, Michigan, Indiana, Florida, Tennessee, Alabama, the District of Columbia, Virginia, and West Virginia. See Letter from Ed Spivia

to Miss Hanna Ledford, June 26, 1978, GAR (Tourist Correspondence 1978, RCB 20025, Industry and Trade, Director's Subject Files 1978).

93. That year Georgia spent $388,000 in magazine ads alone. See *Survey of State Travel Offices: 1979–1980*. Milt Folds also talked about full-page advertising in Pittsburgh, Washington, D.C., Philadelphia, Cincinnati, and Cleveland newspapers. See James Hightower, "All Stops Pulled for Tourists," Newspaper Clipping, Atlanta Constitution. March 5, 1978, GAR (Tourist Correspondence 1978).

94. Georgia Tourism Division, "Remarks on FY 1980 Amended Budget Report," December 19, 1979, GAR (1980 Budget, RCB 19491, Industry and Trade, Director's Subject Files 1980).

95. "South Carolina Tourism Advertising—Proposal, Leslie Advertising," memorandum, 1979–1980, SCDAH (S200039, DPRT, Marketing Office, Advertising Proposal 1975–1998).

96. South Carolina Department of Parks, Recreation, and Transportation, "Advertising Schedule for 1976–1977," SCDAH (S108165, Administrative Reference and Correspondence Files, PRT Files and Miscellaneous, 1965–1979, box 34, PRT 12–3–76).

97. "South Carolina Tourism Advertising—Proposal, Leslie Advertising," SCDAH.

98. "South Carolina," *Business and Economic Dimensions* 16, no. 2 (1980), ADAH (SG014977, Steiner-Bressler Advertising General 1980–1981).

99. Travel South USA meeting minutes, July 27, 1979, GAR (RCB 16066 Industry and Trade, Tourist Division, Director's Subject Files 1979, Travel South Minutes).

100. Bureau of Publicity and Information, *1978 Budget Proposal*, ADAH (SG14285, Tourism and Travel, Communications-administrative files, 1963–1989).

101. Mississippi Agricultural and Industrial Board financial data for fiscal year 1977–1978, MDAH (box 11532, row 22, bay 5, shelf 2, s-1663); Tourism Development Department, *1978 Activity Report,* January 1979, MDAH (Governor's Office of Planning and Coordination Files, 76–80, box 28627 B1/R002/B 01/503 Box 28627 shelf 6, s.2635).

102. "Questionnaire, Tourism Promotion," 1977–1978, MDAH (Department of Tourism Correspondence, B2/R170/B5/B2, S1163).

103. Mississippi Agricultural and Industrial Board, Tourism Development Department, *1978 Activity Report,* January 1979, MDAH (RG 76 Board of Economic Development SG1:A&I Board).

104. Data for 1977 and 1978 can be found in *Travel in Alabama 1977* and *Travel in Alabama 1978*, both located in ADAH (Tourism and Travel Communications Division, Program Administrative Files 1962–1986, SG14286). Data for 1979, 1980, and 1981 are in *Travel Survey Highlight*s, located in ADAH (Tourism and Travel, Communications Division, Program Administrative Files [Mr. Hardy] 1963–1985, SG14288; Auburn Study Slide Presentation ALA-T-0341, Tourism and Travel Administration, SG014977, Steiner-Bressler Advertising General 1980–1981, and also Tourism and Travel, Communications, Administrative Files, 1963–1989, SG14285).

105. Among the statistical abstracts of South Carolina, data on the state of origin of "non-resident travelers" appears only in 1981 for the previous year. See South Carolina Budget and Control Board, *Statistical Abstract of South Carolina*, 1981, https://dc.statelibrary.sc.gov/handle/10827/19472.

106. The ranking then continued with New Jersey, Texas, Alabama, and Pennsylvania. Other states worthy of mention were Virginia, Tennessee, Maryland, Minnesota, Canada, North Carolina, and Indiana. See Letter from Ed Spivia to E. Y. Chapin,

Rock City Gardens, August 21, 1978, GAR (Correspondence 1978, RCB 20025, Industry and Trade, Director's Subject Files 1978).

107. "Governor's Conference on Tourism, Round Table Discussions, Advertising—Session 2," transcript, July 12, 1979, ADAH (Bureau of Tourism and Travel, Communications Division, Program Administrative Files, SG020099, Governor's Tourism Conference 1979, 81, 82).

108. Harrison, "State Tourism Support Urged," 2-B.

109. "Governor's Conference on Tourism, Round Table Discussions, Advertising—Session 2," ADAH

110. Mississippi Tourism Study Commission, *Report and Recommendations of the Tourism Study Commission to the Legislature of Mississippi*, 1975, MDAH (757.1:TS1975).

111. On this subject, see Hobson, *Tell about the South*; Maxwell, *Indicted South*.

112. Tellex Report, "Alabama," press release for bbc Manchester, 1981, ADAH (Tourism and Travel administrative files 1940–2010, SG014981, Alabama Publicity UK 1980–82).

113. Tellex Report, "Come to Alabama," press release for bbc Oxford, 1981, ADAH (Tourism and Travel Administrative Files 1940–2010, SG014981, Alabama Publicity UK 1980–82).

114. Tellex Report, "Alabama the Beautiful," ADAH.

115. Letter from George Busbee to Ed Spivia, GAR (RCB 16064, Industry and Trade, Tourist Division, Director's Subject Files 1979).

116. French newspaper clipping, December 1979, GAR (RCB 19492, Industry and Trade, Tourist Division, Director's Subject files 1980, Travel South 1980).

117. Pallister, "How to Live a Life," 4–5

118. Pallister, 4–5.

119. "Travel Alabama the Beautiful," advertisement, *Canadian Readers Digest*, January 1981, ADAH (Tourism and Travel Administrative files, 1940–2010, Adv. Publication, cuts 1940–2000, SG026784, Tourism advertising and publications 1980–1990); "Alabama's Antebellum Mansions Still Part of Today's Scene," script, 1981, ADAH.

120. *Report and Recommendations of the Tourism Study Commission to the Legislature of Mississippi*, 1975, MDAH.

121. Smith, *Myth, Media and Southern Mind*, 114.

122. "Try-Harder State Shoots," 6-A.

123. "Miss-understood Mississippi," advertisement, *Black Enterprise*, June 1976, 192.

124. Memorandum from George Williams to Bill Hackett, June 4, 1980, MDAH (Department of Tourism, 1979–1980, RG 76 Board of Economic Development, SG1: A&I Board).

125. "Promote Tourism," 4.

126. "South Carolina Tourism Advertising—Proposal, Leslie Advertising," 1979–1980, SCDAH.

127. Judd, "Promoting Tourism," 178.

128. Coastal Plains Regional Commission, *Travel Industry Development Advisory Committee Annual Report*, June 30, 1980, GAR (RCB 19491, Industry and Trade, Tourist Division, Director's subject files 1980, Coastal Plains Regional Commission, 1980).

129. U.S. Travel Service, *Examples of USTS Involvement with States/Cities*, 1980, JCL (U.S. Travel and Tourism Administration, S.1097, Domestic Policy Staff, Jeffrey Farrow's Subject Files, Box 95, Tourism).

130. Ed Spivia, speech transcript, 1976, GAR (Ed Spivia Speeches, Correspondence 1976,

RCB 31076, Industry and Trade, Promotional Speeches, scripts and correspondence 1970, 1972, 1976, 1978).

131. "Mid-Year Tourism on Upswing," memorandum, July 25, 1977, GAR (Tourist Correspondence 1977, RCB 24900 Industry and Trade, Tourist Division Director's Subject Files 1977).

132. "Joint Meeting: Coastal Georgia/Colonial Coast," meeting minutes, December 15, 1977, GAR (Coastal APDC 1978, RCB 54412 Industry and Trade, Tourist Division Director's Subject Files 1978).

133. Transcripts of George Busbee's speech at the Governor's Conference on Tourism, December 2, 1977, GAR (Gov. Busbee Speeches/Correspondence, RCB 13510, RCB 31076, Industry and Trade, Promotional Speeches, scripts and correspondence 1970, 1972, 1976, 1978).

134. Governor George Busbee, "Negatives and Positives of the Georgia Travel Industry," luncheon address, transcript, December 2, 1977, GAR (Gov. Busbee Speeches/Correspondence, RCB 31076, Industry and Trade, Promotional Speeches, scripts and correspondence 1970, 1972, 1976, 1978).

135. *Suggested Implementation and Promotional Strategies for Plains Country Tourism Master Plan*, GAR (Lower Chattahoochee APDC 1977, RCB 24901, Industry and Trade, Director's subject files 1977).

136. *Suggested Implementation and Promotional Strategies*, 1977, GAR.

137. Tharpe, "1981 Becoming 'Gold Rush,'" 2.

138. Advisory Council on Tourism, summary of meeting minutes, January 19, 1978, GAR (Coastal APDC 1978, RCB 54412, Industry and Trade, Director's Subject Files 1978).

139. Department of Industry and Trade, "Remarks on FY 1981 Budget Proposal Presented to Joint Appropriations Committeees of the House and Senate," GAR (1980 Budget, RCB 19491, Industry and Trade, Director's Subject Files 1980).

140. Memorandum from Caroline S. Cavanaugh, ADAH (Tourism and Travel administrative files, Bureau Policy, 1972–1982, SG014556, Travel, Publicity and Press Releases 1980).

141. *Mississippi Economic Growth Programs: Hearing before the Subcommittee on Economic Growth of the Joint Committee*, 94th Cong. (1976).

142. Fred Brinkman, "Marine-Based Recreation and Tourism," presentation at the Coastal Plains Conference on Marine Resources, December 1974, SCDAH (S200015, Speeches 1974–1987).

143. *Plains Country*, brochure, 1978/1979, GAR (DOC2–752 Industry and Trade, Public Relations, Publications 1978–1979).

144. Shipp, "Think of Autumn Colors," 4.

145. Smith, "Georgia Hopes to Capitalize," 7-B.

146. Letter from Ed Spivia to Bob King, August 1977, GAR (Governor's Policy Statement Input 1977, RCB 24900 Industry and Trade, Director's Subject Files 1977).

147. Letter from Ed Spivia to John Watkins, January 6, 1977, GAR (Governor's Policy Statement Input 1977, RCB 24900 Industry and Trade, Director's Subject Files 1977).

148. *Take the Presidential Route*, brochure, 1978, GAR (Presidential Route, RCB 54412 Industry and Trade, Director's Subject Files 1978).

149. *Travel the Presidential Route*, brochure, 1979, GAR (Georgia Gov. Conference on Tourism 1979, RCB 16006 Industry and Trade, Director's Subject Files 1979) (emphasis added).

150. "Plains Draws Visitors," 4-C.

151. "Plains Businessmen Hope Tourists Will Return with Carter," *Atlanta Constitution,* December 23, 1980, 12-b.
152. *Georgia: This Way to Fun,* booklet, 1979, GAR (DOC2–752, Industry and Trade, Public Relations, Publications 1978–1979).
153. Blanco, "Becoming Billy Carter," 7.
154. "What Made News Last Year, Makes a Great Vacation This Year," advertisement, 1977, GAR (RCB 27169, Industry and Trade, Public Relations, State Advertising Files, 1974–1978).
155. *Travel Tips in Georgia's Plains Country,* brochure, GAR (RCB 19492, Industry and Trade, Tourist Division, Director's Subject files, DATO Gasoline Shortage Impact Survey).
156. *Suggested Implementation and Promotional Strategies for Plains Country Tourism Master Plan,* 1977, GAR.
157. Foote, *Shadowed Ground,* 313
158. Flansburg, "Campaign '76," 14-A
159. Letter from John H. Flister, U.S. National Park Service, to Roy Burson, Department of Community Development, January 1977, GAR (Andersonville Trail Study 1976, RCB 5296 Industry and Trade, Director's Subject Files 1977).
160. Lamb, "Andersonville's Future in Past," 2-A
161. Friedman, "Seeking Truth, Healing Scars," E-1.
162. Wells, "Andersonville Stirs Sad Memories," 50-T.
163. See, for example, White and Frew, "Exploring Dark Tourism," 2.
164. Letter from Flister to Burson, GAR.
165. Salter, "Andersonville Has Grim Kind," 8-G.
166. Lowry, "Old South's 1st White House," 10-A.
167. Lowry, 10-A.
168. Lowry, 10-A.
169. On this topic, see Santangeli Valenzani, "La sfida sul ruolo del turismo negli Stati Uniti."
170. Kerr, *Tourism Public Policy,* 78.

Chapter 3. Alabama and Mississippi

1. For an introductory overview of slogans in tourism advertising, see Pan, "Tourism Slogans."
2. U.S. Travel Data Center, *Survey of State Travel Offices* 1977–1978, report, GAR (Industry and Trade, Tourist Division, Director's Subject files 1978, RCB 54412).
3. See, for example, "Alabama Has It All," advertisement, *Tuskegee Progressive Times,* May 6, 1971, 8, or the supplement "Alabama Has It All," *Montgomery Advertiser,* May 19, 1974, 17.
4. "Alabama, Star Variety! Star Values!," advertisement, Dayton Daily News, May 10, 1964, 49.
5. *Travel-ALA,* July 1975, ADAH (Tourism and Travel, Communications Division, Information and Promotional Publications, 1972–1991, SG020098, Travel-ALA, 1972–1983).
6. Hummon, "Tourist Worlds," 187.
7. "Alabama the Beautiful," ADAH (Tourism and Travel Administration, Pageant, Personal Files, SG014979, UK1980–1981).

8. "Governor's Conference on Tourism, Round Table Discussions, Advertising—Session 2," ADAH.

9. "Governor's Conference on Tourism, Round Table Discussions, Advertising—Session 2," ADAH.

10. "Roundtable on Special Events," transcript, ADAH (Bureau of Tourism and Travel, Administration Files 1940–2010, SG014974, Governor's Conference on Tourism 1979).

11. Funk, "Selling Alabama a New Way," 4-B.

12. The rocking chair on the front porch is what Charles P. Roland referred to as a "Southern institution." See Roland, *History of the South*, 154.

13. *All the Things You're Missing . . . Are Yours in Mississippi,* booklet, 1982, MDAH (Mississippi Agricultural and Industrial Board, Department of Tourism Development Miscellaneous Publications, Box I, 411TD, 7:MP). David Hummon uses this very slogan as an example to explain the concept of tourist promotion based on the abundance of attractions. See Hummon, "Tourist Worlds," 185.

14. *Travel in Alabama 1977* and *Travel in Alabama 1978,* booklets, ADAH (Tourism and Travel Communications Division, Program Administrative Files 1962–1986, SG14286). "Travel parties" is another term used to calculate roughly the number of tourists. It refers to groups of two or more individuals traveling within state boundaries.

15. *Travel in Alabama 1977; Travel in Alabama 1978; Travel Survey Highlights,* ADAH.

16. Bryant, "James Gang," C1

17. Steiner/Bressler Advertising, "Alabama's Top Ten Travel/Tourist Attractions," memorandum, 1979, ADAH (SG14288 Tourism and Travel, Communication Division, Program Administrative Files 1963–1985).

18. Depriest, "Tourism Said Big Business," 17.

19. "Noccalula Favorite of Tourists," 1-A and 5-A.

20. For this data, see "Visitor Use Statistics," National Park Service, accessed July 1, 2024, https://irma.nps.gov/Stats.

21. See J. J. Johnson, "Planned Growth Tuskegee Goal," 4 AA. According to reports in the *Advertiser*, the goal was not met, and Tuskegee recorded just below 100,000 visitors in 1984. For further details, see C. Chandler, "VictoryLand Proves Helpful to Shorter," 2C.

22. "Questionnaire, Tourism Promotion, 1977/1978," MDAH.

23. "Questionnaire, Tourism Promotion, 1977/1978," MDAH.

24. Letter from George Williams to Mrs. Irwin K. Brown, July 25, 1977, MDAH (Department of Tourism Correspondence, B2/r170/B5/B2,S1163). Dixieland USA would have been a park "themed around the South, old and new. It will have rides, games, shows and exhibits," as stated by Dr. John W. Murphy, the president of the Mississippi company working to set up the project. See "Dixieland USA," 7.

25. *Report and Recommendations of the Tourism Study Commission,* 1975, MDAH.

26. *Report and Recommendations of the Tourism Study Commission,* 1975, MDAH.

27. Marilyn Mills and Judy Guice, Local and Area Planning, Mississippi Research and Development Center, "Local Historical Society in Mississippi," July 1977, MDAH (917.62 M656s).

28. *Mississippi's Travel Industry Quarterly Report,* 4, no. 1 (1978); *Mississippi's Travel Industry Quarterly Report,* 4, no. 4 (1978); *Mississippi's Travel Industry Quarterly*

Report, 5, no. 4 (1979). These reports can be found in the archives of Beauvoir, the Jefferson Davis Home and Presidential Library.

29. Advertisement, *Chicago Tribune,* February 13, 1955; advertisement, *House Beautiful,* March 1978, 67.

30. "Spring Time Is Pilgrimage Time in Mississippi," advertisement, HOUSE BEAUTIFUL, March 1978, 67.

31. " Alabama the Beautiful," radio advertisement transcript, ADAH (Tourism and Travel Administrative files, 1940–2010, SG014977, Alabama the Beautiful campaign 1980–1981).

32. The State Archives in Jackson, Mississippi, hold a copy from 1978. See *Mississippi Pilgrimage Guide,* 1978, MDAH (Miscellaneous Publications, Box I, 411TD, 7:MP).

33. *Tourism in Historic Columbus,* 1977, MDAH (Department of Tourism Correspondence, B2/r170/B5/S2, S 1663).

34. *Alabama Has It All,* brochure, n.d. [1977?], ADAH (Tourism and Travel, Communications Division, Program Administrative Files, 1961–1979, SG014284, Photo, Brochures, Pamphlet).

35. *Travel-ALA,* October 1975, ADAH (Tourism and Travel, Communications Division, Information and Promotional Publications, 1972–1991, SG020098, Travel-ALA, 1972–1983).

36. *Alabama Has It All,* ADAH. The exact year of publication is unknown, but without a doubt after 1975 and before 1979.

37. *Ebony,* May 1981, 144. Apparently the photo was part of a kit that was sent to the press by the Alabama tourist office.

38. On this topic, see Giltner, *Hunting and Fishing.*

39. Bryant, "James Gang."

40. Leiss, Kline, and Jhally, *Social Communication in Advertising;* Scarles, "Mediating Landscapes."

41. Barnes and Duncan, *Writing Worlds.*

42. Scarles, "Mediating Landscapes," 47.

43. *Alabama Has It All,* ADAH.

44. Obviously this strategy is not exclusive to the Deep South or the South in general, but is clearly one of the new paradigms in states' tourism promotional strategy at the time. For an overview on travel subregions, see Polovitz Nickerson, *Foundations of Tourism,* 277.

45. "Alabama Has It All," advertisement, *Selma Times-Journal,* June 24, 1973, 21. The W. C. Handy Museum was a fairly new attraction, which might explain why it held such an important place in this ad. The museum had opened three years earlier, in 1970.

46. *Alabama Has It All,* ADAH.

47. *Alabama the Beautiful,* booklet, 1981, ADAH (Tourism and Travel, Communications Division, Program Administrative Files, 1961–1979, SG014284, Photo, Brochures, Pamphlet).

48. Jenkins, "Apparitions of the Past," 213.

49. "Deletions and Corrections for the *Alabama the Beautiful* Booklet," ADAH (Tourism and Travel Administrative files, 1940–2010, SG014977, Alabama the Beautiful campaign 1980–1981).

50. See the campaign materials in ADAH (SG037009, Tourism and Travel Adminis-

trative Files, Director's correspondence, Alabama the Beautiful ad campaign 1980–1982).

51. Quoted in Wilson, "Myth of the Biracial South," 10.

52. Santangeli Valenzani, "Advertising the Deep South," 149.

53. "Alabama the Beautiful," advertisement, 1979–1980, ADAH (SG037009, Tourism and Travel Administrative Files, Director's Correspondence, Ads, circa 1979).

54. "Alabama the Beautiful," advertisement, Ebony, May 1981, 142. This ad was mentioned also by Eskew, "From Civil War," in Dann and Seaton, *Slavery, Contested Heritage, and Thanatourism*, 205.

55. "Alabama the Beautiful," radio advertisement transcript, ADAH.

56. "Alabama Has It All," advertisement, *Selma Times-Journal*, June 24, 1973, 21.

57. Alabama Bureau of Publicity and Information, *Summary of Activities Report*, October 1979–March 1980, ADAH.

58. Memorandum from Caroline S. Cavanaugh, February 22, 1980, ADAH (Tourism and Travel, Communications Division, Record of Administrative Head of Agencies 1979–82, SG014971, Audio Visual 80–81).

59. "Berkovitz Tries to Capture," 13.

60. *Travel-ALA*, February 1979, ADAH (Tourism and Travel, Communications Division, Information and promotional publications, 1972–1991, SG020098, Travel-ALA, 1972–1983).

61. *Travel-ALA*, February 1979, ADAH.

62. *Audio-Visual/Research Division Report*, July 1979, ADAH (Tourism and Travel Administrative Files 1940–2010, SG014979, Monthly Reports July, August, Sept. 1979).

63. *A Preliminary Treatment, a Promotional Film on Historic Alabama Attractions*, ADAH (Tourism and Travel, Communications Division, Record of Administrative Head of Agencies, 1979–1982, SG014972, Audio Visual 80–81).

64. *16mm Travel Film on Alabama the Beautiful*, film script, 1981, ADAH (Tourism and Travel, Administrative files, 1940–2010, Director's Correspondence, SG036739, Movie Script 1981).

65. This was an annual event with African dance, art, cooking, and music. There is no data on the actual attendance. Peter Applebome, who attended the Selma Extravaganza of 1995, described it as an event with an almost exclusively African American crowd. It is reasonable to assume that the situation in the 1970s and 1980s was no different. See Applebome, Dixie Rising, 78–80.

66. *Historical Highway Markers in Alabama*, ca. 1977, ADAH (SG014284, Tourism and Travel, Communication Division, Program Administrative Files 1961–1979).

67. *Mississippi: It's Like Coming Home*, brochure, 1978, MDAH (Mississippi Agricultural and Industrial Board, Department of Tourism Development miscellaneous publications, Box I, 411TD, 7:MP).

68. *All the Things You're Missing . . . Are Yours in Mississippi*, 1982, booklet, MDAH (Mississippi Agricultural and Industrial Board, Department of Tourism Development miscellaneous publications, Box I, 411TD, 7:MP).

69. Saggus, "A&I Board," 20.

70. Foster, *Ghosts of the Confederacy*, 57.

71. *All the Things You're Missing . . . Are Yours in Mississippi*, MDAH.

72. Apparently this occurred at a blues concert in Jackson attended by some of Mississippi's greatest black musicians during the national bicentennial celebrations.

Waller's proclamation does not seem to have attracted particular attention—so little, in fact, that accounts of the event can only be found in local newspapers. See Sanford, "Blues 'King' Paid His Dues," 6.

73. King, *I'm Feeling the Blues,* 56.
74. King, 57.
75. King, 57.
76. King, 58.
77. See for example Tiede, "The King," 19; Arnold, "In Memphis and Tupelo," 7-L. See also Bertrand, "Tradition-Conscious Cotton City."
78. Bertrand, "Tradition-Conscious Cotton City," 98.
79. See the relevant material in MDAH (box 19769, row 27, bay 22, shelf 5, series 303, Rg:76, Promotional Materials [1980–2007], and also box 29178, B1/R0021/B09/S03, shelf 5, series 2651, Dept. of Economic Development, Annual Report [411–1: An1980]).
80. "The Hills Region," MDAH (box 19769, row 27, bay 22, shelf 5, series 303, Rg:76, Promotional Materials [1980–2007])
81. *Rich in Memories: Mississippi,* booklet, 1985, MDAH (Promotional Materials (1980–2007), box 19769, row 27, bay 22, shelf 5, series 303, Rg: 76 Tourism, 1980s, 1990s—Travel Guides 1985–1991).
82. Travel South advertisement, 1980, GAR (RCB 19492, Industry and Trade, Tourist Division, Director's Subject Files, 1980, Travel South).
83. Rawls, "Hank," 4D.
84. Letter from Fob James to Bill Fowler, Southbound Glory, April 28, 1981, ADAH (SG014977, Alabama the Beautiful Campaign 1980–1981).
85. Letter from Caroline Cavanaugh to Bob A. Davis, April 2, 1980, ADAH (SG014556, Tourism and Travel Administration, Travel Publicity and Press Releases 1980).
86. Letter from Cy Steiner to Honorable Joe McCorquodale, Speaker of the House of Alabama, March 4, 1981, ADAH (SG014977, Transportation, Travel and Tourism, Steiner-Bressler News Releases 1981).
87. Bill Crowe, "Song That Meshed with Night Says It Right about Alabama," newspaper clipping from *Birmingham View,* ADAH (SG014977, Transportation, Travel and Tourism, Steiner-Bressler Advertising General 1980–1981).
88. See, for example, Gibson and Connell, "Music, Tourism," and Souther, "Making the 'Birthplace of Jazz.'"
89. A more in-depth analysis of this guidebook would be beyond the scope of the present work, but it is still interesting to focus briefly on the booklet cover. The difference with other promotional images or state guide front covers is immediately evident. There are no monuments, flowers, or pleasant places, nor any other images typically used in tourism promotion, but instead a picture of three middle-aged Black women, laughing while sewing. Without wishing to delve too deeply into such observations, the gap between white and Black female representation is very clear, despite the fact that this booklet was intended primarily for African Americans. *Alabama's Black Heritage: A Tour of Historic Sites,* brochure, 1983, ADAH (Tourism and Travel, Communications Division, Program Administrative Files, 1961–1979, SG014284, Photo, Brochures, Pamphlet).
90. Gates, "Information Sought," C1.
91. Grahm, "Black Mississippi Tour Guide," N1.
92. Bates, *The Other Movement,* 143, 168. See also Ellis, "There's a Dance Every Weekend."

93. Bates, *The Other Movement,* 124, 163. In 1977 there are reports of an inaugural Native music festival in Phoenix City, Alabama. See Wesley, "Music Highlights Festival," 8-A.

94. Smalhout and Hoseman, "A Fond Salute to Dresses," C-1.

95. "Tour Romantic Alabama," advertisement, *Courier-Journal,* December 8, 1940, 35.

96. *Huntsville,* brochure, 1979–1982, ADAH (SG014971, Tourism and Travel, Communications Division, Record of Administrative Head of Agencies 1979–1982).

97. "Alabama: Stone Age to Space Age," 1st version, 1979, ADAH (Tourism and Travel, Communications Division, Program Administrative Files, 1961–1979, SG014284, Photo, Brochures, Pamphlet).

98. Travel South, "Tennis in the South," advertisement, 1977, GAR (DOC2-760, Industry and Trade, Public Relations, News from the Georgia Dept. of Industry and Trade).

99. Buchanan, "Magnolias and Manufacturing," 102.

100. *Mississippi: It's Like Coming Home,* 1978, MDAH.

101. The *Mississippi Magic* magazine studied by Buchanan, while greatly emphasizing the theme of the state's industrial progress as early as 1945, was not an advertisement, nor it was intended to promote tourism. It was simply a bimonthly bulletin distributed by the A&I Board intended primarily for companies interested in investing in the state. See Buchanan, "Magnolias and Manufacturing."

102. "Discover Your Own Mississippi Hideaway," advertisement, *Delta Democrat-Times,* July 31, 1969, 27.

103. "Deletions and Corrections for *Alabama the Beautiful* Booklet," ADAH.

104. *Alabama the Beautiful: What's Going On, Where to Go,* brochure, 1979, ADAH (SG014284, Tourism and Travel, Communication Division, Program Administrative files, 1961–1979).

105. *Report and Recommendations of the Tourism Study Commission,* 1977, MDAH. This number, however, is probably extremely inaccurate and in reality must have been much lower. *Mississippi's Travel Industry Quarterly Report* states that only 186,376 tourists visited Vicksburg National Military Park in 1975. See *Mississippi Travel Industry Quarterly Report,* 1977, MDAH (box 15084, row 14, bay 6, shelf 5, R6 76, s6 2, n.15). This discrepancy in figures might also be explained by a different method of visitor recording. The larger number likely took into account all park entries, thus including, for example, joggers and passersby. The lower number, on the other hand, may have considered only paying visitors.

106. Fassler, "Why the Whole Town."

107. Letter from George Williams to Carol Ann, 1978, MDAH (box 11533, row 20, bay 26, shelf 1, s1663, Rg 76, Sg1, Memorandum).

108. Letter from George Williams to Senator Caroway, April 1978, MDAH (box 11533, row 20, bay 26, shelf 1, s1663, Rg 76, Sg1, Memorandum).

109. Polner, "Vicksburg at Peace," 317.

110. *South Magazine,* January/February 1976.

111. "Middle South Utilities," 1979–1980, MDAH (box 11533, row 20, bay 26, shelf 1, Rg:76, Sg1).

112. "Middle South," advertisement, *Chicago Tribune,* April 13, 1980; "Middle South," advertisement, Chicago Tribune, May 8, 1977.

113. "Come South for the Winter," advertisement, *Ottawa Citizen,* February 17, 1979, 60.

114. *Tourism in Historic Columbus,* MDAH (emphasis added).

115. *Rosemont Plantation,* brochure, MDAH (Tourism Division Subject Correspondence

1973–1980, General Correspondence 1978 July–December Department of Tourism Development, box 11531, row 23, bay 13, shelf 4, Rg 76 Sg1, N.5).

116. "First White House of Confederacy," 5D.
117. *Cruise the Rivers of America,* brochure, 1977, MDAH (Tourism Division Subject Correspondence, 1973–1980, box 11532, row 22, bay 5, shelf 2, S 1663, Delta Queen 1977).
118. *MS Queen and Delta Queen Steamboating,* brochure, 1979, MDAH (Tourism Division subject correspondence, 1973–1980, box 11532, row 22, bay 5, shelf 2, S 1663, Delta Queen Steamboat Co).
119. *Cruise the Rivers of America,* MDAH.
120. Draper, "Expo 1850," E-1.
121. Letter to the editor, Greenwood Commonwealth, September 11, 1974, 4.
122. Letter to the editor.
123. Elliot, "Black Leaders' Opinions Vary," 2.
124. Elliot, 2.
125. Wickenberg, "Natchez Pilgrimage," H-1.
126. *Alabama the Beautiful* 52 Weeks a Year, booklet, 1979–1980, ADAH (Tourism and Travel, Communications Division, Program Administrative Files, 1961–1979, SG014284, Photo, Brochures, Pamphlet).
127. Souther, "Making 'America's Most Interesting City,'" 136–137.
128. These ads are in ADAH (SG037009, Tourism and Travel Administrative Files, Director's Correspondence, Alabama the Beautiful ad Campaign 1980–1982).
129. Ownby, "Nobody Knows the Troubles," 248
130. *Internacional* 3, no. 9 (1980), ADAH (Bureau of Tourism and Travel, Tourism and Travel administrative files, 1940–2010, SG014981, Publications International, 1981).
131. "Examples of USTS Involvement with States/Cities," JCL (Domestic Policy Staff, Stern's Subject Files, Box 95, Tourism, U.S. Travel Service 7/8/80–12/2/80).
132. The text in *Internacional* is obviously in Spanish; the quote is from the English version of the same article.
133. "Belgian" folder, ADAH (Bureau of Tourism and Travel, Tourism and Travel Administrative Files, 1940–2010, SG014981, Publications International, 1981).
134. *Why Alabama?,* booklet, ADAH (Bureau of Tourism and Travel, Tourism and Travel Administrative Files, 1940–2010, SG014981, Publications International 1980–82).
135. *Alabama, a Culinary Delight,* booklet, ADAH (Bureau of Tourism and Travel, Tourism and Travel administrative files, 1940–2010, SG014981, Publications International 1980–82).
136. *Alabama, a Culinary Delight* ("Culinary Experience" section).

Chapter 4. Georgia and South Carolina

1. Lee, Cai, O'Leary, "WWW.Branding.States.US."
2. This catchphrase had been used before; there is at least one trace of it in 1974. For further details, see Ford, "PRT Officials Discuss Tourism," 9-A.
3. "Introductory Information," memorandum, 1981–1982, SCDAH (s200015, Speeches, 1974–1987).
4. Slide presentation, September 1976, GAR (1976 Speeches/Scripts, RCB 31076, Industry and Trade, Public Relations, Promotional Speeches, Scripts and Correspondence).
5. Address of Governor George Busbee at the Pre-Legislative Forum, transcript, November 9, 1977, GAR (RCB 31076, Industry and Trade, Public Relations, Promotional Speeches, Script and Correspondence, 1977 Governor Busbee Speeches/Correspondence).

6. "Joint Meeting: Coastal Georgia/Colonial Coast," GAR. For the names of the subregions, see the above-cited slide presentation from September 1976, GAR.

7. *Georgia: This Way to Fun*, GAR.

8. The new regional thematic subdivision associated Savannah with the colonial and Revolutionary past, not the antebellum period.

9. Sites listed on the national monument register for the state of Georgia at that time were Fort Frederica, Fort Pulaski, and Ocmulgee, an archaeological site related to the Creek Nation.

10. *Georgia Travel Report* 5, no. 6 (June 1978), GAR (Tourist Correspondence 1978, RCB 20025, Industry and Trade, Director's Subject Files 1978).

11. Shipp, "Think of Autumn Colors," 4.

12. Letter from Spurgeon Richardson to Ed Spivia, February 7, 1977, GAR (Six Flags Over Georgia 1977, RCB 24900 Industry and Trade, Director's Subject Files 1977).

13. "Summary of Policy Statement on South Carolina's Beaches," 1976, SCDAH (S108165, Administrative Reference and Correspondence Files PRT Files Miscellaneous, 1965–1979, PRT Commission 6/30/76).

14. News release, 1978, South Caroliniana Library, University of South Carolina (Tourism in South Carolina Vertical Files Collection, 1920–2000, News Releases).

15. Sumter Chamber of Commerce Breakfast Club, opening remarks, April 9, 1980 SCDAH (S200015, Speeches 1974–1987).

16. *This Is Georgia: Georgia Days*, booklet, 1975, GAR (DOC2–752, Industry and Trade, Public Relations, Publications 1978–1979). The first mention of a brochure with this name is in the *Atlanta Constitution* in 1973. See Harell, "'Georgia Days' Is Much Book," 20-C.

17. *Georgia: This Way to Fun*, GAR.

18. *Mississippi, Your Guide to Travel*, 1975, MDAH (Department of Tourism Development, Miscellaneous Publications, box I, 411NTD, 7:MP).

19. *Classic South*, brochure, 1979, GAR (RCB 19492, Industry and Trade, Tourist Division, Director's Subject Files, 1980).

20. "Madison, Treasure Chest," 42.

21. *Georgia: So Much, So Near*, booklet, 1974, GAR (DOC2–752, Industry and Trade, Public Relations, Publications 1978–1979).

22. *Georgia: State of Adventure, Historic Homes*, GAR (DOC2–752, Industry and Trade, Public Relations, Publications 1978–1979).

23. Silver, "'Deliverance' Factor."

24. Morse, "Politics Provoking 'Georgia on Minds,'" E-13

25. Georgia Film Office advertisement, 1978, GAR (Coastal APDC 1978).

26. *Atlanta Guidebook*, booklet, 1979, GAR (Correspondence 1979, RCB 16064, Industry and Trade, Director's Subject Files 1979).

27. *Gone with the Wind Memorabilia Collection*, brochure, attached to a letter from Patrick Duncan to Lawrence E. Bergman, January 21, 1980, GAR (RCB 19490, Industry and Trade, Director's Subject Files 1979–1980, Memos Big 1979–1989).

28. Stillman, "46 Black Women Tour," 4.

29. Dickey, "Tough Little Patch," 1.

30. "Atlanta in Vintage Airline Travel Posters," Sunshine Skies, accessed July 1, 2024, https://www.sunshineskies.com/atlanta-in-vintage-airline-travel-posters.html.

31. Heimann, *All American Ads*, 693.

32. Quoted in Dickey, "Tough Little Patch," 54.

33. "Scarlett's Atlanta," 36.

34. Dameron and Murphy, "International City Too Busy," 48.
35. "The Georgia Variety Show Opens This Summer," advertisement, *Morning Call*, April 22, 1978, 15-D.
36. K. Clark, "Saving 'The Dump,'" 75.
37. Memorandum from Ed Spivia to the Georgia Travel Industry, Canadian Dollar Program, 1980, GAR (Interoffice Correspondence, RCB 19491, Industry and Trade, Director's Subject Files 1980).
38. Memorandum from Spivia to the Georgia Travel Industry, GAR.
39. Avraham and Daugherty, "Step into the Real Texas," 1395.
40. Sibley, *Peachtree Street USA*, 93.
41. Newman, *Southern Hospitality*, 65. See also Butler, Carter, and Brunn, "African-American Travel Agents," 1029.
42. "Atlanta: The Hyperbole Is Justified," 56.
43. "America the Greatest Travel Bargain," 227.
44. Bessonette, "Bus Tours Show Off Atlanta," 14-E. A promotional piece that demonstrates how, alongside the mainstream tourism induced by movies and television (as in the case of *Gone with the Wind*), another kind of destination image ran parallel, centered on TV programs and cultural products related to Black culture.
45. *Tour Atlanta with TourGals, Inc.*, brochure, 1977, GAR (Tour Gals of Atlanta 1977, RCB 24901, Industry and Trade, Director's Subject Files 1977).
46. Farrissee, "Heritage Tourism," 103.
47. White, "Greetings . . . from Stone Mountain," 2-T.
48. For a story of Stone Mountain, see Hale, "Granite Stopped Time."
49. *Georgia: This Way to Fun*, GAR.
50. R. and M. Magruder, "Stone Mountain State Park," *Travel/Holiday*, May 1980, GAR (Big A Publicity, RCB 19490 Industry and Trade, Director's Subject Files 1979–1980).
51. Speech by Mrs. Busbee, transcript, December 1, 1977, GAR (RCB 31076, Industry and Trade, Public Relations, Promotional speeches, 1977 Speeches/Scripts) (emphasis added).
52. Autry, "Elastic Monumentality?"
53. Quoted in Nordheimer, "Agnew Mellow in Talk."
54. Autry, "Elastic Monumentality?"
55. Goldsmith, "State's Wonders," E-1.
56. Kalina, "Park Not to Be Taken," 17.
57. Magnotta and Magnotta, "Visit Georgia's Stone Mountain Park," H-7.
58. "See the USA," 27.
59. Vincent Lowery highlighted the implicit denialism of slavery at the Stone Mountain plantation. See Lowery, "Monument to Many Souths," 231.
60. *Georgia's Stone Mountain Park*, brochure, 1980, GAR (Atlanta Convention and Visitors Bureau 1980, RCB 19491, Industry and Trade, Director's Subject Files 1980) (emphasis added).
61. As Lowery explains, "Projecting King's face onto the Confederate monument momentarily permitted tourists to imagine a racially progressive South, without sacrificing the heritage Talmadge celebrated at the unveiling ceremony." Lowery, "Monument to Many Souths," 236.
62. Timothy and Nyuapane, *Cultural Heritage and Tourism*, 62.
63. Quoted in Lowery, "Monument to Many Souths," 236.
64. Salter, "History, Recreation Blend," 3-G.

65. *Mississippi's Travel Industry: Quarterly Report*, 4, no. 1 (1978); *Mississippi's Travel Industry: Quarterly Report*, 4, no. 4 (1978); *Mississippi's Travel Industry: Quarterly Report*, 5, no. 4 (1979). The reports can be found in the archives of Beauvoir, the Jefferson Davis Home and Presidential Library.

66. *Historic Homes—Liberty Hall*, brochure, 1978–1979, GAR (DOC2–752, Industry and Trade, Public Relations, Publications 1978–1979) (emphasis added).

67. *Alexander H. Stephens Memorial Park*, brochure, 1950s, GAR (DOC 3357, Parks and Historic Sites, Public Relations and Information, Publications) (emphasis added).

68. Georgia Travel Report 5, no. 6 (June 1978), GAR (Tourist Correspondence 1978, RCB 20025, Industry and Trade, Director's Subject Files 1978).

69. For a history of the painting, see Janney, "New and Unique Show," and Judt, "Cyclorama."

70. "A Resolution, Cyclorama," 1978, GAR (Cyclorama, RCB 29681, Natural Resources, Planning and Research, Director's Subject Files 1973–1978).

71. Reeves, "Mayor Rebuffs Attacks," C-1.

72. Blight, *Race and Reunion*, 388.

73. Reeves, "Mayor Rebuffs Attacks."

74. In the 1950s the United Daughters of the Confederacy accompanied schoolchildren through Cyclorama by carefully instructing them about "the glorious history of the valiant but losing effort to save the city from the Yankee invaders." See Lowe, "From 'Flag in the Dust,'" 118.

75. "Cyclorama," *Atlanta Constitution*, 3-A.

76. *Charleston, South Carolina: Home of Fort Sumter,* brochure, 1961–1965, SCDAH (P900358, Miscellaneous Tourism Brochures).

77. Wiener, "Civil War, Cold War," 242.

78. Brown, *Civil War Canon*, 197.

79. "Annual Vacation Guide," 182.

80. Brown, *Civil War Canon*, 197.

81. Article by J. Kenneth Jones, Curator of Decorative Arts, Charleston Museum, in *Gateway to Historic Charleston,* brochure, March 1979, GAR (RCB 16066 Industry and Trade, Tourist Division, Director's Subject Files 1979, S.C. Governor's Conference on Travel, 1–41979).

82. "See the USA," 25–30.

83. Weathers, "Travelling through the Lowlands," 47.

84. Rahier and Hawkins, "*Gone with the Wind,*" 205–206.

85. Clarke, "Mapping Transnationality," 133–134.

86. Grosvenor, "What Does South Carolina Low Country Mean?," 7.

87. "Holiday," advertisement, March 1970, 111. The text assured readers that "the Old South was a very romantic place. So it's no wonder South Carolina has so many beautiful gardens today."

88. *Come See S.C.*, SCDAH.

89. *Annual Report of the South Carolina DPRT*, 1983–1984, SCDAH (S200025, Annual Reports of the DPRT 1970–2000).

90. "Travel South," advertisement, 1977, GAR (1977 Speeches/Scripts, RCB 31076, Industry and Trade, Public Relations, Promotional Speeches, Scripts and Correspondence 1970, 1972, 1976, 1978).

91. "South Carolina Offers You the Vacation with All the Extras," advertisement, 1975–1976, SCDAH (S200039, DPRT, Marketing Office, Advertising Proposal 1975–1998, 1975–1976 Ads).

92. "These Are the Things That Litter Our Beaches," advertisement, 1975–1976, SC-DAH (S200039, dprt, Marketing Office, Advertising Proposal 1975–1979, 1975–1976 Ads).

93. "South Carolina: Where Golf in America Begins," advertisement, 1975–1976, SCDAH (S200039, DPRT, Marketing Office, Advertising Proposal 1975–1979, 1975–1976 Ads).

94. "Tennis in the South," GAR.

95. "Our First South Carolina Vacation (But Not Our Last!)," advertisement, 1976/1977, SCDAH (S200039, dprt, Marketing Office, Advertising Proposal, 1976–1977).

96. Leslie Advertising, "Come See S.C.: South Carolina's Tourism Advertising 1979–1980," SCDAH (S200039, dprt, Marketing Office, Advertising Proposal 1975–1998, Advertising Proposal 1979–1980, Leslie Advertising).

97. "Walk along the Battery through Azaleas, Sea Breezes and History," advertisement, 1976–1977, SCDAH (S200039, DPRT, Marketing Office, Advertising Proposal 1975–1979, 1977–1978 ads).

98. Tolf, "Charleston's Great Gardens," NSCJ-1.

99. "Old Homes Take Limelight," E-16.

100. South Carolina American Revolution Bicentennial Commission, *Major Sites of the Revolution in South Carolina*, brochure, 1974, South Carolina State Documents Depository, South Carolina State Library, https://dc.statelibrary.sc.gov/server/api/core/bitstreams/8ab2fbba-c6b8-4370-a31f-355355c7f1ae/content.

101. "South Carolina's Great Vacation No. 2, Charleston," advertisement, SCDAH (S200039, DPRT, Marketing Office, Advertising Proposal 1975–1979, 1977–78 Ads).

102. "South Carolina Beaches," advertisement, *Greenville News*, June 9, 1980, 15-E.

103. "Our Winter Vacation Gives You Two More Days in the Sun Instead of Two More Days in Your Car," "You're Getting Warmer," and "Summer Comes Early and Stays Later in South Carolina," advertisements, 1981–1982, SCDAH (S200039, dprt, marketing office, advertising proposal 1975–1998, 1981–1982).

104. *South Carolina Statistical Abstract 1977* (Columbia: South Carolina Division of Research and Statistical Services, 1977); *South Carolina Statistical Abstract 1981* (Columbia: South Carolina Division of Research and Statistical Services, 1981).

105. Tharpe, "1981 Becoming 'Gold Rush,'" 2.

106. Minis, "Savannah, Charleston Wage Gracious War," 13-E.

107. Neal, "Charleston," 23.

108. *Charleston S.C. Trip Planner*, brochure, GAR (RCB 16066 Industry and Trade, Tourist Division, Director's Subject Files 1979, S.C. Governor's Conference on Travel, 1–41979).

109. Yuhl, *Golden Haze of Memory*. Before the Civil War, Charleston had more slaves than any other city in the United States; an 1830 census showed that the majority of the city's white population owned slaves. See Litvin and Brewer, "Charleston, South Carolina Tourism," 73.

110. Brundage, *Southern Past*, 203.

111. Kytle and Roberts, "Is It Okay to Talk?," 144–145.

112. Bures, "Historic Preservation, Gentrification, and Tourism," 196.

113. Kytle and Roberts, "Is It Okay to Talk?," 144–145.

114. Kytle and Roberts, *Denmark Vesey's Garden Slavery*, pt. 4.

115. "South Carolina's Great Vacation No. 2, Charleston," advertisement, SCDAH (s200039, DPRT, Marketing Office, Advertising Proposal 1975–1979, 1977–78 ads).

116. Simon, *Boardwalk of Dreams*, 21.

117. *South Carolina Points of Interest*, brochure, ca. 1978, SCDAH (s200044, DPRT Marketing Office, Brochures 1940–1980, Points of Interest).

118. Weathers, "Travelling through the Lowlands," 50.

119. Kytle and Roberts, *Denmark Vesey's Garden Slavery*, pt. 4.

120. King, *Sombreros and Motorcycles*, 121–123

121. Stokes, *Myrtle Beach*, 199–200.

122. *South Carolina Points of Interest*, brochure, ca. 1978, SCDAH (s200044, DPRT Marketing Office, Brochures 1940–1980, Points of Interest).

123. *South Carolina Points of Interest,* SCDAH.

124. Schultz, West, and Maclean, "Utopianism," 251.

125. Popp, "Africa-American Style Village," 86.

126. Mok, "African King Has Six Wives," 9.

127. Mok, 9.

128. Clarke, "Mapping Transnationality," 140.

129. "Africa Lives in Dixie," 2-E.

130. "African Village in South Carolina," 50.

131. Tiede, "'Oyotunji'—Voodoo for Ripoff," 5. It should be noted that the three major Black magazines *Ebony, Jet*, and *Black Enterprise* covered very little about Oyotunji: between 1970 and 1981 only one article in Ebony, one in *Jet*, and none in *Black Enterprise*. This seems particularly curious given the emphasis and special attention with which these magazines treated Black heritage and the rediscovery of Black Africanist sentiment. One explanation, the most plausible, is that these Black newspapers actually had an ambiguous opinion about the village and its commercial trafficking of traditional culture. Not surprisingly, it was *Black Enterprise*, the magazine closest to the sentiments of educated, upper-middle-class Blacks, that never mentioned it.

132. *Come See S.C.*, booklet, 1980, SCDAH.

133. "South Carolina: A Lot of It Looks a Little Like a Foreign Country," 1977, SCDAH (s200044, Dept. of PRT Marketing Office, Brochures 1940–1998).

134. Grahm and Moore, *South Carolina Politics and Governments*, 161.

135. "South Carolina's Great Vacation No.2, Charleston," advertisement, SCDAH.

136. "South Carolina Beaches," advertisement, 1977–1978, SCDAH (S200039, Dept. of PRT, Marketing Office, Advertising Proposal 1975–1998).

137. "Kick Up Your Heels at the Beach without Giving Up an Arm and a Leg," advertisement, *Courier-Journal*, January 11, 1981, H-13.

138. "Is There a Bit of the Romantic Caribbean in South Carolina? Believe It!," advertisement, 1977–1978, South Caroliniana Library, University of South Carolina (Tourism in South Carolina Vertical Files Collection, 1920–2000, Promotion 1970s).

139. *Georgia: This Way to Fun*, GAR.

140. Dilley, "Tourist Brochures and Tourist Images."

141. South Carolina Parks, Recreation and Tourism Commission, meeting minutes, September 28, 1979, SCDAH (s200025, Annual Reports of the DPRT 1970–2000).

142. Letter from Ed Spivia to Jaqueline L. Clarke, January 9, 1978, GAR (Travel Films, RCB 54412, Industry and Trade, Director's Subject Files 1978); Gerald Rafshoon Adver-

tising Inc. to Roy Burson, December 10, 1975, GAR (DOC2–752 Industry and Trade, Public Relations, Publications, 1973–1978, Travel Movie 1976).

143. Kern-Foxworth, *Aunt Jemima, Uncle Ben,* xx.

144. Georgia Tourism Division to Gerald Rafshoon, September 9, 1975, GAR (DOC2–752, Industry and Trade, Public Relations, Publications, 1973–1978, Travel Movie 1976).

145. Advertisement, *Ebony,* January 1979, 34.

146. *Dasher Goes to School in Georgia,* brochure, 1978/1979, GAR (DOC2–752, Industry and Trade, Public Relations, Publications 1978–1979).

147. "A Portrait of Our Historic Past: This Is Georgia," advertisement, 1975–1976, GAR (DOC2–752, Industry and Trade, Public Relations, Publications 1978–1979).

148. "Beach Ads Draw Tourists to Coastal South," announced a 1979 CPRC Annual Report. The promotion was targeted at the neighboring states and Canada. See Coastal Plains Regional Commission, *Annual Report 1979,* GAR (RCB 16065, Industry and Trade, Director's Subject Files 1979).

149. "The Coastal South's Got Everything You Want in a Beach Vacation," advertisement insert, *Dayton Daily News,* March 28, 1976, 32.

150. *South Carolina: The Coastal South U.S.A,* booklet, 1980, GAR (RCB 19491, Industry and Trade, Director's Subject Files 1980).

151. Coastal Plains Regional Commission, *Annual Report 1979,* GAR.

152. *Map of the Coastal South,* brochure, ca. 1980, GAR (RCB 19491, Industry and Trade, Director's Subject Files 1980, Coastal Plains Regional Commission 1980).

153. Advertisement for the Japanese market, 1978, GAR (RCB 54412 Industry and Trade, Director's Subject files 1978, U.S. Dept. of Commerce 1978). I would like to thank Professor Oliviero Frattolillo for translation from the Japanese.

154. "Busbee Speech at Governor's Conference on Tourism," GAR.

155. Leslie Advertising, "Come See S.C.: South Carolina's Tourism Advertising 1979–1980," SCDAH.

156. "Come See S.C.," television commercial, 1980, SCDAH (S200039, Advertising Proposal 1979–1980, Leslie Advertising).

157. The first brochure, titled *Nothin' Could Be Finah Than to See South Carolina* (1951–1955), is in SCDAH (State Development Board, Tourism Promotional Brochure, S 149013, Columbia, South Carolina). The second, with the same name, produced between 1955 and 1959, is from a private collection. Although the coastal, recreational, and nautical features are already present, these brochures also make use of images such as costumed southern belles and antebellum homes. The second brochure also features a photo of a large Confederate flag waving during a sports match.

158. King, *Sombreros and Motorcycles,* 25.

Epilogue

1. Quoted in Klein, "Southern Encyclopedia," c-11.

2. See, for example, Souther, *New Orleans on Parade;* Atkinson, "'Shakin' Your Butt.'"

3. McPherson, *Reconstructing Dixie,* 16–18.

4. O'Brien, *Idea of the American South,* xi.

5. Lechner, *South of the Mind.*

6. Cobb, "We Ain't White Trash," 135.

7. Graham, "Since 1965," 156.

8. These observations are based on the analysis conducted on general brochures from

Alabama, Mississippi, Georgia, and Louisiana published in 2018. For further details, see Santangeli Valenzani, "Advertising the Deep South."

9. *Georgia Travel Guide 2020* (Atlanta: Georgia Department of Economic Development, 2020), 5.
10. Explore Georgia, https://www.exploregeorgia.org/.
11. Wall, "Epitaph for Slavery," 233.
12. Ownby, "Nobody Knows the Troubles," 249.
13. Ownby, 249.
14. Wilson, "Myth of the Biracial South," 14.
15. Ayers, "What We Talk About," 46.
16. Duck, *Nation's Region*.
17. See, for example, Coffey and Skipper, *Navigating Souths*; Romine and Greeson, *Keywords for Southern Studies*.
18. Niewiadomska-Flis, "(Re)imagined Souths," 19.
19. Ladd, "Dismantling the Monolith."

Abbot, C. *The New Urban America: Growth and Politics in Sunbelt Cities.* Chapel Hill: University of North Carolina Press, 1987.

Adams, S. "Highways of Hope Opening for Negroes in the South." *St. Petersburg Times,* November 8, 1964.

"Africa Lives in Dixie." *Tallahassee Democrat,* September 11, 1977.

"An African Village in South Carolina." *Jet,* January 3, 1974.

Allen, F. *Atlanta Rising: The Invention of an International City 1946–1996.* Marietta, Ga.: Longstreet Press, 1996.

"America the Greatest Travel Bargain." *Black Enterprise,* June 1980.

American Revolution Bicentennial Administration. *The Bicentennial of the United States of America: A Final Report to the People.* Vol 3. Washington, D.C.: American Revolution Bicentennial Administration, 1977.

"Annual Natchez Pilgrimage Helps Make City Well Known." *Clarion Ledger,* May 8, 1970.

"Annual Vacation Guide, Do Yourself Proud: Discover Black History." *Ebony,* June 1972.

Applebome, P. *Dixie Rising: How the South is Shaping American Values, Politics, and Culture.* San Diego, Calif.: Harcourt Brace, 1997.

Archibald, R. R. "A Personal History of Memory." *In Social Memory and History: Anthropological Perspectives,* edited by J. Climo and M. G. Cattell, 65–80. Walnut Creek, Calif.: Altamira Press, 2002.

Arkansas Department of Parks and Tourism. "Arkansas Tourism Division Seeking German Travelers." *Baxter Bulletin,* December 8, 1977

Arnold, C. "In Memphis and Tupelo, Memories and Souvenirs." *Miami Herald,* August 13, 1978.

Aron, C. S. *Working at Play: A History of Vacations in the United States.* New York: Oxford University Press, 1999.

Ashmore, H. S. *An Epitaph for Dixie.* New York: Norton, 1958.

Ashworth, G. J. "Heritage and Tourism: An Argument, Two Problems and Three Solutions." In *Spatial Implications of Tourism,* edited by C. A. M. Fleischer-van Rooijen, 95–104. Groningen, Netherlands: Geo Pers, 1992.

Atkinson, C. Z. "'Shakin' Your Butt for the Tourist': Music's Role in the Identification and Selling of New Orleans." In *Dixie Debates: Perspectives on Southern Cultures,* edited by R. H. King and H. Taylor, 150–164. New York: New York University Press, 1996.

"Atlanta: The Hyperbole Is Justified." *Black Enterprise,* February 1974.

Autry, R. "Elastic Monumentality? The Stone Mountain Confederate Memorial and Counter Public Historical Space." *Social Identities* 25, no. 2 (2017): 169–185.

Avraham, E., and D. Daugherty. "Step into the Real Texas: Associating and Claiming State Narrative in Advertising and Tourism Brochures." *Tourism Management* 33 (2012): 1385–1397.

Ayers, E. J. "What We Talk About When We Talk About the South." In *All Over the Map: Rethinking American Regions,* edited by E. L. Ayers, P. N. Limerick, S. Nissenbaum, and P. S. Onuf, 62–82. Baltimore, Md.: John Hopkins University Press, 1996.

Bajc, V. "Introduction to Collective Memory and Tourism: Globalizing Transmission through Localized Experience." *Journeys* 7, no. 2 (2006): 1–14.

Barnes, T. J., and J. Duncan, eds. *Writing Worlds: Discourse, Texts and Metaphors in the Representation of Landscape.* London: Routledge, 1992.

Bartley, N. V. *The Creation of Modern Georgia.* Athens: University of Georgia Press, 1990.

Bass, J., and W. Devries. *The Transformation of Southern Politics: Social Change and Political Consequence since 1945.* New York: Basic Books, 1976.

Bates, C. "'Oh, I'm a Good ol' Rebel': Reenactment, Racism and the Lost Cause." In *The Civil War in Popular Culture: Memory and Meaning,* edited by L. A. Kreiser and R. Allred, 191–222. Lexington: University of Kentucky Press, 2014.

Bates, D. E. *The Other Movement: Indian Rights and Civil Rights in the Deep South.* Tuscaloosa: University of Alabama Press, 2012.

Bay, M. *Traveling Black: A Story of Race and Resistance.* Cambridge, Mass.: Harvard University Press, 2021.

Beamguard, J. "Florida's Greenest Year." *Tampa Tribune,* July 28, 1978.

Benjamin, S., C. Kline, D. Alderman, and W. Hoggard. "Heritage Site Visitation and Attitudes toward African American Heritage Preservation: An Investigation of North Carolina Residents." *Journal of Travel Research* 55, no. 7 (2015): 919–933.

"Berkovitz Tries to Capture State's Essence in Documentary." *Montgomery Advertiser,* October 3, 1978.

Berry, B. J. L., and D. C. Dahmann. "Population Redistribution in the United States in the 1970s." *Population and Development Review* 3, no. 4 (1977): 443–471.

Bertrand, M. T. "A Tradition-Conscious Cotton City: (East) Tupelo, Mississippi, Birthplace of Elvis Presley." *In Destination Dixie: Tourism and Southern History,* edited by K. L. Cox, 87–109. Gainesville: University Press of Florida, 2012.

Bessonette, C. "Bus Tours Show Off Atlanta from Four Angles." *Atlanta Constitution,* November 16, 1980.

Birdsall, S. S. "Changing Images of the Tourist South Since 1950." *Southeastern Geographer* 26, no. 2 (1986): 135–143.

Black, E., and M. Black. *Politics and Society in the South.* Cambridge, Mass.: Harvard University Press, 1989.

Blanco, J. "Becoming Billy Carter: Clothes Make the Man (and His Many Characters)." *Southern Cultures* 16, no. 2 (2010): 6–30.

Blight, D. W. *Race and Reunion: The Civil War in American Memory.* Cambridge, Mass.: Harvard University Press, 2001.

Bolton, C. C. *William F. Winter and the New Mississippi: A Biography.* Jackson: University Press of Mississippi, 2013.

Bonner, R. E. *Colors and Blood: Flag Passions of the Confederate South.* Princeton, N.J.: Princeton University Press, 2002.

Borstelmann, T. *The 1970s: A New Global History from Civil Rights to Economic Inequality.* Princeton, N.J.: Princeton University Press, 2012.

Borstelmann, T. *The Cold War and the Color Line.* Cambridge, Mass.: Harvard University Press, 2009.

Bowden, J. E. "Plains: A Look Back at the South's Future." *Pensacola News Journal,* December 26, 1976.

Bowen, L., and J. Schmid. "Minority Presence and Portrayal in Mainstream Magazine Advertising: An Update." *Journalism & Mass Communication Quarterly* 74, no. 1 (1997): 134–146.

Bowes, R. G. "Tourism and Heritage: A New Approach to the Product." *Recreation Research Review* 14, no. 4: 35–40.

Brengholm Ren, C., and B. Stilling

Blichfeldt. "One Clear Image? Challenging Simplicity in Place Branding." *Scandinavian Journal of Hospitality and Tourism* 11, no. 4: 416–434.

Broadus, J. "Black Tourist Boom: A Sleeping Giant Rouses." *Detroit Free Press,* May 20, 1973.

Brown, T. J. *Civil War Canon: Sites of Confederate Memory in South Carolina.* Chapel Hill: University of North Carolina Press, 2015.

Brundage, W. F. "No Deed but Memory." In *Where These Memories Grow: History, Memory, and Southern Identity*, edited by W. F. Brundage, 1–28. Chapel Hill: University of North Carolina Press, 2000.

Brundage, W. F. *The Southern Past: A Clash of Race and Memory.* Cambridge, Mass.: Harvard University Press, 2005.

Bryant, T. "The James Gang: She's a Believer: Alabama Has It All." *Birmingham Post-Herald*, March 15, 1979.

Buchanan, B. "Magnolias and Manufacturing: Southern Imagery in Mississippi's Promotional Publication 1945–1955." In *Mediated Images of the South: The Portrayal of Dixie in Popular Culture*, edited by A. Slade, D. Givens-Carroll, and A. J. Narro, 89–105. Lanham, Md.: Lexington Books, 2012.

Buck, R. C. "The Ubiquitous Tourist Brochure: Explorations in Its Intended and Unintended Use." *Annals of Tourism Research* 4, no. 4 (1977): 195–207.

Budrytė, D. "Experiences of Collective Trauma and Political Activism: A Study of Women Agents of Memory in Post-Soviet Lithuania." In *Memory and Pluralism in the Baltic States*, edited by E.-C. Pettai, 55–74. London: Routledge, 2014.

Bures, R. M. "Historic Preservation, Gentrification, and Tourism: The Transformation of Charleston, South Carolina." *Critical Perspectives on Urban Redevelopment* 6 (2001): 195–209.

Burns, P. *An Introduction to Tourism and Anthropology.* London: Routledge, 1999.

Butler, D., P. L. Carter, and S. D. Brunn. "African-American Travel Agents: Travails and Survival." *Annals of Tourism Research* 29, no. 4 (2002): 1022–1035.

Camprubi, R., J. Guia, and J. Comas. "Analyzing Image Fragmentation in Promotional Brochures." *Journal of Hospitality & Tourism Research* 38, no. 2 (2012): 135–161.

Carter, D. T. *The Politics of Rage: George Wallace, the Origins of the New Conservatism, and the Transformation of American Politics.* Baton Rouge: Louisiana State University Press, 1994.

Carter, P. L. "Coloured Places and Pigmented Holidays: Racialized Leisure Travel." *Tourism Geographies* 10, no. 3 (2008): 265–284.

Cash, W. J. *The Mind of the South.* New York: Vintage Books, 1950.

Cavalli, A. "Lineamenti di una sociologia della memoria." In *Il senso del passato. Per una sociologia della memoria*, edited by P. Jedlowski and M. Rampazi, 31–42. Milan: Franco Angeli, 1991.

"Cavanaugh Loses Spending Authority." *Alabama Journal*, July 30, 1982.

"Chamber Vice President Makes Things Happen in Andalusia." *Montgomery Advertiser,* December 7, 1978.

Chandler, C. "VictoryLand Proves Helpful to Shorter." *Montgomery Advertiser,* January 14, 1985.

Christensen, P. "The 'Wild West': The Life and Death of a Myth." *Southwest Review* 93, no. 3 (2008): 310–325.

Chronis, A. "Between Place and Story: Gettysburg as Tourism Imaginary." *Annals of Tourism Research* 39, no. 4 (2012): 1797–1816.

Clark, K. "Saving 'The Dump': Race and the Restoration of the Margaret Mitchell House in Atlanta." In *Destination*

Dixie: Tourism and Southern History, edited by K. L. Cox, 69–86. Gainesville: University Press of Florida, 2012.

Clark, T. D. *The Emerging South.* New York: Oxford University Press, 1961.

Clarke, K. M. "Mapping Transnationality: Roots Tourism and the Institutionalization of Ethnic Heritage." In *Globalization and Race: Transformations in the Cultural Production of Blackness,* edited by K. M. Clarke and D. A. Thomas, 133–153. Durham, N.C.: Duke University Press, 2006.

Cobb, J. "We Ain't White Trash No More: Southern Whites and the Reconstruction of Southern Identity." In *The Southern State of Mind,* edited by J. Nordby Gretlund, 135–146. Columbia: University of South Carolina, 1999.

Cobb, J. C. "An Epitaph for the North: Reflections on the Politics of Regional and National Identity at the Millennium." *Journal of Southern History* 66, no. 1 (2000): 3–24.

Cobb, J. C. *Away Down South: A History of Southern Identity.* Oxford: Oxford University Press, 2005.

Cobb, J. C. *The Selling of the South: The Southern Crusade for Industrial Development 1936–1980.* Baton Rouge: Louisiana State University Press, 1982.

Coffey, M. G., and J. Skipper, J., eds. *Navigating Souths: Transdisciplinary Explorations of a U.S. Region.* Athens: University of Georgia Press, 2017.

Cohen Ferris, M. *The Edible South: The Power of Food and the Making of an American Region.* Chapel Hill: University of North Carolina Press, 2014.

Cohen, R. "Trailing Jimmy Carter in Search of Answers." *Washington Post,* October 26, 1976.

Cohen, S. A., G. Prayag, and M. Moital. "Consumer Behaviour in Tourism: Concepts, Influences and Opportunities." *Current Issues in Tourism* 17, no. 10 (2014): 872–909.

Cook, J. F. *The Governors of Georgia.* Macon, Ga.: Mercer University Press, 2010.

Coski, J. *The Confederate Battle Flag: America's Most Embattled Emblem.* Cambridge, Mass.: Belknap Press, 2005.

Cowie, J. *Stayin' Alive: The 1970s and the Last Days of the Working Class.* New York: The New Press, 2010.

Cox, K. L. "Branding of Dixie, The Selling of the American South, 1890–1930." In *Dixie Emporium: Tourism, Foodways, and Consumer Culture in the American South,* edited by A. Stanonis, 50–68. Athens: University of Georgia Press, 2008.

Cox, K. L., ed. *Destination Dixie: Tourism and Southern History.* Gainesville: University Press of Florida, 2012.

Cox, K. L. *Dreaming of Dixie: How the South Was Created in American Popular Culture.* Chapel Hill: University of North Carolina Press, 2011.

Crespino, J. *In Search of Another Country: Mississippi and the Conservative Conuterrevolution.* Princeton, N.J.: Princeton University Press, 2007.

Crompton, J. L. "An Assessment of the Image of Mexico as a Vacation Destination and the Influence of Geographical Location upon that Image." *Journal of Travel Research* 17, no. 4 (1979): 18–23.

Crumley, C. L. "Exploring Venues of Social Memory." In *Social Memory and History: Anthropological Perspectives,* edited by J. Climo and M. G. Cattell, 39–52. Walnut Creek, Calif.: Altamira Press, 2002.

Cumming, B. J. "Been Down Home So Long It Looks Like Up to Me." *Esquire,* August 1971.

"Cyclorama." *Atlanta Constitution,* April 6, 1985.

Dameron, R. J., and A. D. Murphy. "An International City Too Busy to

Hate? Social and Cultural Change in Atlanta 1970–1995." *Urban Anthropology and Studies of Cultural Systems and World Economic Development* 26, no. 1 (1997): 43–69.

Dann, G. *The Language of Tourism: A Sociolinguistic Perspective.* Oxford: CAB International, 1996.

Davis, J. E. *Race against Time: Culture and Separation in Natchez Since 1930.* Baton Rouge: Louisiana State University Press, 2004.

De Grazia, V. *Irresistible Empire: America's Advance through Twentieth-Century Europe.* Cambridge, Mass.: Belknap Press, 2005.

"Democracy Defined at Moscow." *The Crisis,* April 1947.

Depriest, W. "Tourism Said Big Business." *Montgomery Advertiser,* September 21, 1978.

Destination USA: Report of the National Tourism Resources Review Commission. 6 vols. Washington, D.C.: U.S. Government Printing Office, 1973.

Dickey, J. W. "A Tough Little Patch of History: Atlanta's Marketplace for *Gone with the Wind* Memory." PhD dissertation, Georgia State University, 2007.

Dietzel, S. B. "Consuming Southern Landscape: Visual Representations of the American South." *Southern Quarterly* 36, no. 4 (1998): 287–303.

Dilley, R. S. "Tourist Brochures and Tourists Images." Canadian Geographer/Le Géographe Canadien 30, no. 1 (1986): 59–65.

"Dixieland USA: Plans to Open by Summer." *Magee Courier,* October 7, 1976.

Doering, T. R. "A Reexamination of the Relative Importance of Tourism in State Economies." *Journal of Travel Research* 15, no. 1 (1976): 13–17.

Doering, T. R. "Geographical Aspects of State Travel Marketing in the USA." *Annals of Tourism Research* 6, no. 3 (1979): 307–317.

Draper, N. "Expo 1850 Recaptures Florewood Plantation Life." *Clarion-Ledger,* August 20, 1978.

Draves, I. "It's Easier to Pick a Tourist Than It Is a Bale of Cotton: The Rise of Recreation on the Great Lakes of the South." *Southern Cultures* 20, no. 3 (2014): 87–104.

"Driving Vacations 'Out.'" *Statesville Record and Landmark,* February 27, 1974.

Duck, L. A. T*he Nation's Region: Southern Modernism, Segregation, and U.S. Nationalism.* Athens: University of Georgia Press, 2009.

Dudziak, M. L. "Desegregation as a Cold War Imperative." *Stanford Law Review* 41, no. 1 (1988): 61–120.

Dudziak, M. L. *Cold War Civil Rights: Race and the Image of American Democracy.* Princeton, N.J.: Princeton University Press, 2011.

Duncan, C. "Benton Denies His Politicking." *Alabama Journal,* April 4, 1974.

Dunn, J. P. "The Quest for the South's Future: An Overview." In *The Future South: A Historical Perspective for the Twenty-First Century,* ed. J. P. Dunn and H. L. Preston, 1–9. Champaign: University of Illinois Press, 1991.

Dwyer, O. J., and D. H. Alderman. *Civil Rights Memorials and the Geography of Memory.* Athens: University of Georgia Press, 2008.

Echtner, C. M., and J. R. Brent Ritchie. "The Measurement of Destinagion Image: An Empirical Assessment." *Journal of Travel Research* 31, no. 4 (1993): 3–13.

Eckes, A. E. "The South and Economic Globalization, 1950 to the Future." In *Globalization and the American South,* ed. J. C. Cobb and W. Stueck, 36–65. Athens: University of Georgia Press, 2005.

"Economy." *Clarion-Ledger,* November 3, 1975.

Edgar, W. B. *South Carolina in the Modern Age.* Columbia: University of South Carolina Press, 2012.

Edgar, W. B. *South Carolina: A History.* Columbia: University of South Carolina Press, 1998.

Egerton, J. *Southern Food: At Home, on the Road, in History.* New York: Alfred A. Knopf, 1987.

Egerton, J. *The Americanization of Dixie: the Southernization of America.* New York: Harper's Magazine Press, 1974.

Elliot, J. "Black Leaders' Opinions Vary on Slave Quarters." *Clarion-Ledger,* August 6, 1974.

Ellis, C. "There's a Dance Every Weekend: Powwow Culture in Southeast North Carolina." In *Southern Heritage on Display: Public Ritual and Ethnic Diversity within Southern Regionalism,* edited by C. Ray, 79–105. Tuscaloosa: University of Alabama Press, 2003.

Eskew, G. T. "From Civil War to Civil Rights: Selling Alabama as Heritage Tourism." In *Slavery, Contested Heritage, and Thanatourism,* edited by M. S. Dann and A. V. Seaton, 201–214. New York: Routledge, 2013.

Eskew, G. T. "From Civil War to Civil Rights: Selling Alabama as Heritage Tourism." *International Journal of Hospitality and Tourism Administration* 2, nos. 3–4 (2001): 201–214.

Fan, Y. "Branding the Nation: Towards a Better Understanding." *Place Branding and Public Diplomacy* 6, no. 2 (2010): 97–103.

Farrissee, A. "Heritage Tourism: Telling the Rest of the Story." *Georgia Historical Quarterly* 83, no. 1 (1999): 101–107.

Fasce, F. *Le anime del commercio. Pubblicità e consumi nel secolo americano.* Rome: Carocci, 2012.

Fassler, S. "Why the Whole Town of Vicksburg Still Lives for the Civil War." *Globe & Mall,* August 19, 1978.

"Finch Creates New Tourism Organization." *Clarksdale Press Register,* August 26, 1976.

"Finch Point Out State's Need for Presidential Primary in '76." *Hattiesburg American,* June 23, 1975.

"Firm Gets Tourism Contract." *Alabama Journal,* June 6, 1979.

"First White House of Confederacy Opens." *Times and Democrat,* December 12, 1976.

Flansburg, J. "Campaign '76—a Footnote to the Civil War." *Des Moines Register,* October 24, 1976.

Flint, W. *Alabama in the Twentieth Century.* Tuscaloosa: University of Alabama Press, 2006.

"Florida Jumpy Over South's Tourism Bid." *Cincinnati Enquirer,* September 12, 1976.

Foley, M., and J. Lennon. "Heart of Darkness." *International Journal of Heritage Studies* 2, no. 4 (1996): 195–197.

Foote, K. E. *Shadowed Ground: America's Landscapes of Violence and Tragedy.* Austin: University of Texas Press, 2003.

Ford, W. "PRT Officials Discuss Tourism." *Florence Morning News,* April 26, 1974.

Foster, G. M. *Ghosts of the Confederacy: Defeat, the Lost Cause, and the Emergence of the New South, 1865 to 1913.* Oxford: Oxford University Press, 1987.

Fousex, J. *To Lead the Free World: American Nationalism and the Cultural Roots of the Cold War.* Chapel Hill: University of North Carolina Press, 2000.

Fowler, P. "Heritage: A Post-Modernist Perspective." In *The Natural and Built Environment,* edited by D. Uzzell. Vol. 1 of *Heritage Interpretation.* London: Belhaven Press, 1989.

Fox, S. R. *The Mirror Makers: A History of American Advertising and Its Creators.* Champaign: University of Illinois Press, 1984.

Francaviglia, R. V., and W. Franklin. *Main Street Revisited: Time, Space, and Image*

Building in Small Town America. Iowa City: University of Iowa Press, 1996.

Francesconi, S. "Images and Writing in Tourist Brochures." *Journal of Tourism and Cultural Change* 9, no. 4 (2001): 341–356.

Frederick, J. *Stand Up for Alabama: Governor George Wallace.* Tuscaloosa: University of Alabama Press, 2007.

Frew, E., and L. White, eds. *Tourism and National Identity: An International Perspective.* Abingdon, Va.: Taylor and Francis, 2011.

Friedman, S. "Seeking Truth, Healing Scars at Andersonville." *Detroit Free Press,* February 6, 1977.

Funk, T. "Selling Alabama a New Way." *Anniston Star,* July 30, 1983.

Gallarza, M. G., I. G. Saura, and H. C. Garcia. "Destination Image: Towards a Conceptual Framework." *Annals of Tourism Research* 29, no. 1 (2002): 56–78.

Gates, J. "Information Sought for Black Tour Guide." *Jackson Daily News,* May 7, 1984.

Gibbons, J. D., and M. Fish. "Dynamics of the U.S International Tourism Market, 1970–1984." *Journal of Travel Research* 24, no. 4 (1986): 17–24

Gibson, C., and J. Connell. "Music, Tourism and the Transformation of Memphis." *Tourism Geographies* 9, no. 2 (2007): 160–190.

Giltner, S. E. *Hunting and Fishing in the New South: Black Labor and White Leisure after the Civil War.* Baltimore: John Hopkins University Press, 2008.

Gimlin, H., ed. *American Regionalism: Our Economic, Cultural and Political Makeup.* Washington, D.C.: Congressional Quarterly, 1980.

Goldfield, D. *Black, White, and Southern: Race Relations and Southern Culture, 1940 to the Present.* Baton Rouge: Louisiana University Press, 1991.

Goldsmith, D. "State's Wonders Make a Fine Post Card." *Atlanta Constitution,* June 2, 1981.

Goldstein, N. "Treasure Hunt: States Go after Filmmakers' Money." *Akron Beacon Journal,* October 23, 1977.

Goodric, J. N. "A New Approach to Image Analysis through Multidimensional Scaling." *Journal of Travel Research* 16, no. 3 (1978): 3–7.

Gordon, T. S. "Take Amtrak to Black History: Marketing Heritage Tourism to African Americans in the 1970s." *Journal of Tourism History* 7, nos. 1–2: 54–74.

"Governor Cliff Finch Report to the People." *Magee Courier,* April 21, 1977.

Graham, H. D. "Since 1965: The South and Civil Rights." In *The South as an American Problem,* edited by L. J. Griffin and D. H. Doyle, 145–163. Athens: University of Georgia Press, 1995.

Graham, C. "Black Mississippi Tour Guide Is Planned." *Clarion Ledger,* May 17, 1984.

Graham, C. B., and W. V. Moore. *South Carolina Politics and Government.* Lincoln: University of Nebraska Press, 1994.

Graves, E. G. "Black Travel and Leisure Time—an Untapped Market." *Black Enterprise,* May 1972.

Gregory, J. N. *The Southern Diaspora: How the Great Migrations of Black and White Southerners Transformed America.* Chapel Hill: University of North Carolina Press, 2005.

Grosvenor, V. "What Does South Carolina Low Country Mean to Me? Home." *Tampa Bay Times,* April 20, 1971.

Gunn, C. A. *Vacationscape: Designing Tourist Regions.* Austin: Bureau of Business Research, University of Texas at Austin, 1972.

Hale, G. E. "Granite Stopped Time: The Stone Mountain Memorial and the Representation of White Southern Identity." *Georgia Historical Quarterly* 82, no. 1 (1998): 22–44.

Hall, C. M. *Tourism and Politics: Policy, Power, and Place.* New York: Wiley, 1994.

Hall, D. "Civil War Reenactors and the Postmodern Sense of History." *Journal of American Culture* 17, no. 3 (1994): 7–11.

Harell, B. "'Georgia Days' Is Much Book." *Atlanta Constitution,* January 24, 1973.

Harlow, J. "Last of Old Natchez Red Light Houses Comes Down." *Clarion Ledger,* May 4, 1975.

Harrison, R. "State Tourism Support Urged." *Mobile Press-Register,* September 5, 1979.

Hartshorn, T. A. "The Changed South, 1947–1997." *Southeastern Geographer* 37, no. 2 (1997): 122–139.

Harvey, G. E. "'Wallaceism Is an Insidious and Treacherous Type of Disease': The 1970 Alabama Gubernatorial Election and the 'Wallace Freeze' on Alabama Politics." In *History and Hope in the Heart of Dixie: Scholarship, Activism, and Wayne Flynt in the Modern South,* edited by G. E. Harvey, R. D. Starnes, and G. Feldman, 158–170. Tuscaloosa: University of Alabama Press, 2006.

Harvey, G. E. *A Question of Justice: New South Governors and Education, 1968–1976.* Tuscaloosa: University of Alabama Press, 2006.

Hayes, B. "Black Tourist Looking for More Travel Market Security." *Los Angeles Times,* July 11, 1971.

Hayes, B. J. "The Congressional Travel and Tourism Caucus and U.S. National Tourism Policy." *International Journal of Tourism Management* 2, no. 2 (1981): 121–135.

Hearing on S. 233 before the S. Subcommittee on Merchant Marine and Tourism of the Committee on Commerce, Science and Transportation, 96th Cong. (1979).

Heimann, J., ed. *All American Ads of the 70s.* Cologne: Taschen, 2004.

Herring, A. "Smokeless Tourist Industry Brings $2.3 Billion into State." *Montgomery Advertiser,* May 17, 1981.

Hillyer, R. *Designing Dixie: Tourism, Memory, and Urban Space in the New South.* Charlottesville: University of Virginia Press, 2014.

Hobson, F. *Tell about the South: The Southern Rage to Explain.* Baton Rouge: Louisiana University Press, 1983.

Hoelscher, S. "Where the Old South Still Lives: Displaying Heritage in Natchez, Mississippi." In *Southern Heritage on Display: Public Ritual and Ethnic Diversity within Southern Regionalism,* edited by C. Ray, 218–250. Tuscaloosa: University of Alabama Press, 2003.

Hollins, T. *See Alabama First: The Story of Alabama Tourism.* Mount Pleasant, S.C.: Arcadia Publishing, 2013.

Hopkins, J. "Signs of the Post-rural: Marketing Myths of a Symbolic Countryside." *Geografiska Annaler* 80, no. 2 (1998): 65–81.

Huber, P. "A Short History of *Redneck*: The Fashioning of a Southern White Masculine Identity." *Southern Cultures* 1, no. 2 (1995): 145–166.

Hudman, L. E., and R. H. Jackson. *The Geography of Travel and Tourism.* Cincinnati, Ohio: Thomson Delmar Learning, 2003.

Hummon, D. M. "Tourist Worlds: Tourist Advertising, Ritual, and American Culture." *Sociological Quarterly* 29, no. 2 (1988): 179–202.

Hunt, J. D. "Image as a Factor in Tourism Development." *Journal of Travel Research* 13, no. 3 (1975): 1–17.

Jackson, H. H. *The Rise and Decline of the Redneck Riviera: An Insider's History of the Florida-Alabama Coast.* Athens: University of Georgia Press, 2013.

Janiskee, R. L. "Historic Houses and Special Events." *Annual of Tourism Research* 23, no. 2 (1996): 384–414.

Janney C. E. "A New and Unique Show: The Rise and Fall of Civil War Cycloramas." In *Buying and*

Selling Civil War Memory in Gilded Age America, edited by J. Marten and C. E. Janney, 223–237. Athens: University of Georgia Press, 2021.

Jenkins, J. L. "Apparitions of the Past and Obscure Visions for the Future: Stereotypes of Black Women and Advertising during a Paradigm Shift." In *Black Women and Popular Culture: The Conversation Continues*, edited by A. Y. Goldman, V. S. Ford, A. A. Harris, and N. R. Howard, 199–224. Lanham, Md.: Lexington Books, 2014.

Jenkins, O. H. "Understanding and Measuring Tourist Destination Images." *International Journal of Tourism Research* 1, no. 1 (1999): 1–15.

Johnson, D. "'Small Town in Texas' No Big Deal." *Orlando Sentinel Star*, June 18, 1976.

Johnson, J. J. "Planned Growth Tuskegee Goal." *Montgomery Advertiser*, March 27, 1977.

Judd, D. R. "Promoting Tourism in the U.S. Cities." *Tourism Management* 16, no. 3 (1995): 175–187.

Judt, D. "Cyclorama: An Atlanta Monument." *Southern Cultures* 23, no. 2 (2017), https://www .southerncultures.org/article/ cyclorama-atlanta-monument/.

Kalina, M. "Park Not to Be Taken for Granite." *Pittsburgh Post-Gazette*, November 27, 1979.

Kammen, M. *Mystic Chords of Memory: The Transformation of Tradition in American Culture*. New York: Alfred A. Knopf, 1991.

Keenan, K. L. "Skin Tones and Physical Features of Blacks in Magazine Advertisements." *Journalism and Mass Communication Quarterly* 73, no. 4 (1996): 905–912.

Kern-Foxworth, M. *Aunt Jemima, Uncle Ben, and Rastus: Blacks in Advertising, Yesterday, Today and tomorrow*. Westport, Conn.: Greenwood Press, 1994.

Kern-Foxworth, M. "Colorizing Advertising: Challenges for the 1990s and Beyond." *Black Issues in Higher Education* 4, no. 64 (1992).

Kerr, W. R. *Tourism Public Policy, and the Strategic Management of Failure*. Oxford: Elsevier, 2003.

King, P. N. *Sombreros and Motorcycles in a Newer South: The Politics of Aesthetics in South Carolina's Tourism Industry*. Jackson: University Press of Mississippi, 2012.

King, S. A., *I'm Feeling the Blues Right Now: Blues Tourism in the Mississippi Delta*. Jackson: University Press of Mississippi, 2011.

Klein, G. "Southern Encyclopedia, New Set of Books Defines What Makes Region Unique Part of Nation." *Town Talk*, August 2, 1987.

Krane, D., and S. D. Shaffer. *Mississippi Government and Politics: Modernizers versus Traditionalists*. Lincoln: University of Nebraska Press, 1992.

Kytle, E. J., and B. Roberts. "Is It Okay to Talk about Slaves? Segregating the Past in Historic Charleston." In *Destination Dixie: Tourism and Southern History*, ed. K. L. Cox, 137–159. Gainesville: University Press of Florida, 2012.

Kytle, E. J., and B. Roberts. *Denmark Vesey's Garden Slavery and Memory in the Cradle of the Confederacy*. New York: New Press, 2018.

Ladd, B. "Dismantling the Monolith: Southern Places—Past, Present, and Future." *Critical Survey* 12, no. 1 (2000): 28–42.

Lamb, R. "Andersonville's Future in Past." *Atlanta Constitution*, June 7, 1976.

Layton, A. S. *International Politics and Civil Rights Policies in the United States: 1941–1960*. Cambridge: Cambridge University Press, 2000.

Lechner, Z. J. *The South of the Mind: American Imaginings of White Southernness, 1960–1980*. Athens: University of Georgia Press, 2018.

Lee, D. L. "The South and the American Mainstream: the Election of Jimmy Carter." *Georgia Historical Quarterly* 61, no. 1 (1977): 7–12.

Lee, G. L., L. A. Cai, J. O'Leary. "WWW. Branding.States.US: An Analysis of Brand-Building Elements on the U.S. State Tourism Websites." *Tourism Management* 27, no. 5 (2006): 815–828.

Leiss, W., S. Kline, and S. Jhally. *Social Communication in Advertising: Persons, Products, and Images of Well-Being*. London: Methuen, 1986.

Litvin, S. W., and J. D. Brewer. "Charleston, South Carolina Tourism, and the Presentation of Urban Slavery in an Historic Southern City." *International Journal of Hospitality & Tourism Administration* 9, no. 1 (2008): 71–84.

Loewen, J. W., *Sundown Towns: A Hidden Dimension of American Racism*. New York: The New Press, 2005.

Lollar, S. A., and C. Van Doren. "U.S. Tourist Destinations: A History of Desirability." *Annals of Tourism Research* 18, no. 4 (1991): 622–638.

Lowe, J. "From 'Flag in the Dust' to Banners of Defiance: Tales of a Symbol's Transformations." *Callaloo* 24, no. 1 (2001): 117–122.

Lowery, J. V. "A Monument to Many Souths: Tourists Experience Southern Distinctiveness at Stone Mountain." In *Destination Dixie: Tourism and Southern History*, edited by K. L. Cox, 223–243. Gainesville: University Press of Florida, 2012.

Lowry, B. "Old South's 1st White House to Celebrate Its New Look." *Montgomery Advertiser*, November 28, 1976.

MacCannell, D. *The Tourist: A New Theory of the Leisure Class*. New York: Schocken Books, 1976.

"Madison, Treasure Chest for Cherished Memories." *Outdoors in Georgia*, July 1978.

Magnotta, V., and A. Magnotta. "Visit Georgia's Stone Mountain Park." *Daily Record*, February 20, 1977.

Main, E. C., and G. S. Gryski. "George Busbee and the Politics of Consensus." In *Georgia Governors in an Age of Change: From Ellis Arnall to George Busbee*, edited by H. P. Handerson, 261–278. Athens: University of Georgia Press, 1988.

Martin, J. "Ed Hall's Job Is Telling the Story of Alabama Tourism." *Selma Times-Journal*, March 3, 1983.

Maxwell, A. *The Indicted South: Public Criticism, Southern Inferiority, and the Politics of Whiteness*. Chapel Hill: University of North Carolina Press, 2014.

McDaniel, R. *An Irresistible History of Southern Food: Four Centuries of Black-Eyed Peas, Collard Greens, and Whole Hog Barbecue*. Charleston: History Press, 2011.

McIntyre, R. *Souvenirs of the Old South: Northern Tourism and Southern Mythology*. Gainesville: University Press of Florida, 2011.

McPherson, T. *Reconstructing Dixie: Race, Gender, and Nostalgia in the Imagined South*. Durham, N.C.: Duke University Press, 2003.

Meyers, C. C., ed. *The Empire State of the South: Georgia History in Documents and Essays*. Macon, Ga.: Mercer University Press, 2008.

Mickey, R. *Paths out of Dixie: The Democratization of Authoritarian Enclaves in America's Deep South, 1944–1972*. Princeton, N.J.: Princeton University Press, 2015.

Minis, M. "Savannah, Charleston Wage Gracious War Befitting Southern Belles for Tourist Dollar." *Atlanta Constitution*, May 3, 1981.

Mississippi Economic Growth Programs: Hearing before the Subcommittee on Economic Growth of the Joint Committee, 94th Cong. (1976).

Mitchell, J. A. "Executive Cites

'New Realism' Between Business, Government." *The State*, January 26, 1979.

Mohl, R. A. "Miami: The Ethnic Cauldron." In *Sunbelt Cities: Politics and Growth since World War II*, edited by R. M. Bernard and B. R. Rice, 58–99. Austin: University of Texas Press, 1983.

Mok, M. "African King Has Six Wives and Rules a Tribe of 90 . . . in S. Carolina." *San Antonio Star*, August 21, 1977.

Molina, A., and A. Esteban. "Tourism Brochures." *Annals of Tourism Research* 33, no. 4 (2006): 1036–1056.

Monaco, J. *American Film Now: The People, the Power, the Money, the Movies*. New York: Oxford University Press, 1979.

Morgan, R. "Atlanta Makes Headway as 'Gateway City.'" *Atlanta Constitution*, September 28, 1980.

Morse, J. "Politics Provoking 'Georgia on Minds.'" *Albuquerque Journal*, January 30, 1977.

Murphy, R. "The South as the New America." *Saturday Review*, September 4, 1976, 8–11.

"My Position on Tourism in Mississippi." *Clarion-Ledger Sun*, August 3, 1975.

Nash, J., and A. Taggart. *Mississippi Politics: The Struggle for Power, 1976–2006*. Jackson: University Press of Mississippi, 2006.

"Natchez Invites Visitors." *Ville Platte Gazette*, June 17, 1985.

Neal, R. S. "Charleston: Where America Really Began." *The Gazette*, January 10, 1976.

Nelson, E. "The Art of Queuing Up at Disneyland." *Journal of Tourism History* 8, no. 1 (2016): 47–56.

Newman, H. K. *Southern Hospitality: Tourism and the Growth of Atlanta*. Tuscaloosa: University of Alabama Press, 1999.

Niewiadomska-Flis, U. "(Re)imagined Souths." In *Ex-Centric South: Reimagining Southern Centers and Peripheries on Page and Screen*, edited by U. Niewiadomska-Flis, 13–29. València, Spain: Publicacions de la Universitat de València, 2019.

"Noccalula Favorite of Tourists." *Anniston Star*, September 11, 1981.

Nolan, A. T. "The Anatomy of the Myth." In *The Myth of the Lost Cause and Civil War History*, edited by G. W. Gallagher and A. T. Nolan, 11–30. Bloomington: University of Indiana Press, 2000.

Nora, P. *Les lieux de mémoire*. 3 vols. 1984–1992. Paris: Gallimard, 1984.

Nordheimer, J. "Agnew Mellow in Talk Hailing Confederate Heroes." *New York Times*, May 10, 1970.

Nystrom, D. *Hard Hats, Rednecks, and Macho Men: Class in 1970s American Cinema*. New York: Oxford University Press, 2009.

O'Barr, W. *Culture and the Ad: Exploring Otherness in the World of Advertising*. Boulder, Colo.: Westview Press, 1994.

O'Brien, M. *The Idea of the American South: 1920–1941*. Baltimore, Md.: Johns Hopkins University Press, 1979.

Ohmann, R. M., *Selling Culture: Magazines, Markets, and Class at the Turn of the Century*. New York: Verso Books, 1996.

"Old Homes Take Limelight." *Morning Call*, April 4, 1971.

Ownby, T. "Nobody Knows the Troubles I've Seen, but Does Anybody Want to Hear about Them When They're on Vacation?" In *Southern Journeys: Tourism, History, and Culture in the Modern South*, edited by R. D. Starnes, 240–250. Tuscaloosa: University of Alabama Press, 2003.

Page, S. J., and J. Connell. *Tourism: A Modern Synthesis*. New York: Routledge, 2020.

Pallister, M. "How to Live a Life of Luxury in Dixieland." *Evening Times*, January 9, 1982.

Palmer, C. "An Ethnography of Englishness: Experiencing Identity through Tourism." *Annals of Tourism Research* 32, no. 1 (2005): 7–27.

Pan, S. "Tourism Slogans: Towards a Conceptual Framework," *Tourism Management* 72 (2019).

Pearce, P. L. *The Social Psychology of Tourist Behaviour*. Oxford: Pergamon Press, 1982.

Peirce, N. R. *The Deep South States of America: People, Politics, and Power in the Seven Deep South States*. New York: W. W. Norton, 1974.

Percy, W. *Signposts in a Strange Land: Essays*. Open Road Media, 2011, ebook.

Phillip, S. F. "Race and Tourism Choice: A Legacy of Discrimination?" *Annals of Tourism Research* 21, no. 3 (1994): 479–488.

"Plains Businessmen Hope Tourists Will Return with Carter." *Atlanta Constitution*, December 23, 1980.

"Plains Draws Visitors from 28 Lands." *Atlanta Constitution*, September 7, 1978.

Polner, M. "Vicksburg at Peace Nurtured by Its River, Obsessed with Its Past." *New York Times*, February 20, 1977.

Polovitz Nickerson, N. *Foundations of Tourism*. Upper Saddle River, N.J.: Prentice Hall, 1996.

Popp, M. "Africa-American Style Village in South Carolina Imitates West African Culture." *Ebony*, January 1978.

Poston, D. L., and R. H. Weller, eds. *The Population of the South: Structure and Change in Social Demographic Context*. Austin: University of Texas Press, 1981.

Pretes, M. "Tourism and Nationalism." *Annals of Tourism Research* 30, no. 1 (2003): 125–142.

"Processing of State Products Waller Goal." *Clarion Ledger*, October 17, 1973.

"Promote Tourism." *Clarksdale Press Register*, January 16, 1981.

Prunty, M. C. "Two American Souths: The Past and the Future." *Southeastern Geographer* 17, no. 1 (1977): 1–24.

Rahier, J. M., and M. Hawkins. "*Gone with the Wind* versus the Holocaust Metaphor: Louisiana Plantation Narratives in Black and White." In *Plantation Society and Race Relations: The Origins of Inequality*, edited by T. Durant and J. D. Knottenerus, 205–220. Westport, Conn.: Praeger, 1999.

Raines, H. "Todd and Stabler Offseason Game: Living It Up on 'Redneck Riviera.'" *New York Times*, June 21, 1978.

Rawls, P. "Hank: Musicians to Honor First 'Outlaw' Music." *Advertiser-Journal*, June 2, 1979.

"Rebel Soldiers Charge North." *Pensacola News Journal* (South Alabama edition), September 25, 1981.

Reed, J. S. "The Heart of Dixie: An Essay in Folk Geography." *Social Forces* 54, no. 4 (1976): 933–934.

Reed, J. S. *Minding the South*. Columbia: University of Missouri Press, 2003.

Rees, E. "Plains and Simple: The Influences of Plains, Georgia, and Small-Town Nostalgia on Jimmy Carter's Public Persona." In *Presidents and Place: America's Favorite Sons*, edited by T. Cobb and O. Akroyd, 197–212. Lanham, Md.: Lexington Books, 2023.

Reeves, A. S. "Mayor Rebuffs Attacks on Cyclorama Project." *Atlanta Constitution*, February 6, 1979.

Reilly, M. D. "Free Elicitation of Descriptive Adjectives for Tourism Image Assessment." *Journal of Travel Research* 28, no. 4 (1990).

Richter, L. "Political Instability and Tourism in the Third World." In *Tourism and the Less Developed Countries*, ed. D. Harrison, 35–46. London: Belhaven, 1992.

Rogers, W. W., R. D. Ward, L. R. Atkins, and W. Flynt. *Alabama: The History of a Deep South State*. Tuscaloosa: University of Alabama Press, 1994.

Roland, C. P. "The Ever-Vanishing South." *Journal of Southern History* 48, no. 1 (1982): 3–20.

Roland, C. P. *The Improbable Era:*

The South since World War II.
1976; rpt. Lexington: University
Press of Kentucky, 2013.

Roland, C. P., *A History of the South.*
New York: Alfred A. Knopf, 1947.

Romine, S., and J. R. Greeson, eds.
Keywords for Southern Studies, Athens:
University of Georgia Press, 2016.

Rugh, S. S. *Are We There Yet? The
Golden Age of American Family
Vacations.* Lawrence: University
Press of Kansas, 2008.

Saggus, J. "A&I Board Announces
Tourist Guide Plans." *Clarion-
Ledger*, August 1, 1973.

Salter, C. "Andersonville Has
Grim Kind of Beauty." *Atlanta
Constitution*, February 10, 1980.

Salter, C. "History, Recreation Blend
at Stephens State Park." *Atlanta
Constitution*, December 9, 1979.

Sanford, O. "The Blues 'King'
Paid His Dues." *Clarion
Ledger*, November 7, 1975.

Santangeli Valenzani, G. "Advertising
the Deep South in 2018: An Analysis
of Destination Image through
Louisiana, Mississippi, Alabama
and Georgia Travel Guides." In *Ex-
Centric South: Reimagining Southern
Centers and Peripheries on Page and
Screen*, edited by U. Niewiadomska-
Flis, 211–230. Publicacions de la
Universitat de València, 2019.

Santangeli Valenzani, G. "La sfida
sul ruolo del turismo negli Stati
Uniti. Lo scontro dimenticato dei
turbolenti anni settanta." *Ácoma* 16
(Spring/Summer 2019): 132–149.

Scarles, C. "Mediating Landscapes:
The Process and Practices of
Image Construction in Tourist
Brochures of Scotland." *Tourist
Studies* 4, no. 1 (2004): 43–67.

"Scarlett's Atlanta: Racing with the Wind."
Outdoors in Georgia, July 1978.

Schulman, B. J. *From Cotton Belt to
Sunbelt: Federal Policy, Economic
Development, and the Transformation
of the South, 1938–1980.* Durham:
Duke University Press, 1994.

Schulman, B. J. *The Seventies: The Great
Shift in American Culture, Society, and
Politics.* New York: The Free Press, 2001.

Schultz, J. D., J. G. West, and I. Maclean,
eds. "Utopianism." In *Encyclopedia
of Religion in American Politics.*
Phoenix, Ariz.: Oryx, 1999.

Scranton, Ph., ed. *The Second Wave:
Southern Industrialization from
the 1940s to the 1970s.* Athens, Ga.:
University of Georgia Press, 2001.

"See the USA." *Black Enterprise*, May 1973.

Selwyn, T. *The Tourism Image: Myths
and Myth Making in Tourism.*
New York: Wiley, 1996.

Shackel, P. A. *Memory in Black and
White: Race, Commemoration, and
the Post Bellum Landscape.* Walnut
Creek, Calif.: Altamira Press, 2003.

Shaffer, M. *See America First:
Tourism and National Identity,
1880–1940.* Washington, D.C.:
Smithsonian Books, 2001.

Shipp, B. "Think of Autumn
Colors and Sea Breezes." *Atlanta
Constitution*, September 8, 1977.

Sibley, C. *Peachtree Street USA.* Atlanta,
Ga.: Peachtree Publishers, 1986.

Silver, T. "The 'Deliverance'
Factor." *Environmental History*
12, no. 2 (2007): 369–371.

Simon, B. *Boardwalk of Dreams: Atlantic
City and the Fate of Urban America.*
Oxford: Oxford University Press, 2004.

Sirkaya, E., and A. G. Woodside. "Building
and Testing Theories of Decision
Making by Travellers." *Tourism
Management* 26, no. 6 (2005).

Slade, A., D. Givens-Carroll, and A.
J. Narro, eds. *Mediated Images of
the South: The Portrayal of Dixie
in Popular Culture.* Lanham,
Md.: Lexington Books, 2012.

Slotkin, R. *Gunfighter Nation: The
Myth of the Frontier in Twentieth-*

Century America. Norman: University of Oklahoma Press, 1998.

Smalhout, L., and A. K. Hoseman. "A Fond Salute to Dresses of Noble Women." *Clarion-Ledger*, November 1, 1978.

Smith, S. A. *Myth, Media, and Southern Mind*. Fayetteville: University of Arkansas Press, 1985.

Smith, V. *Hosts and Guests: The Anthropology of Tourism*. Philadelphia: University of Pennsylvania Press, 2012.

Smith, W. "Georgia Hopes to Capitalize on Carter's Tourist Draw." *Atlanta Constitution*, November 14, 1976.

Smyth, R. "Public Policy for Tourism in Northern Ireland." *Tourism Management* 7, no. 2 (1986): 120–136.

Souther J. M. "Making the 'Birthplace of Jazz': Tourism and Musical Heritage Marketing in New Orleans." *Louisiana History* 44, no. 1 (2003): 39–73.

Souther, M. J. "Making 'America's Most Interesting City': Tourism and the Construction of Cultural Image in New Orleans, 1940–1980." In *Southern Journeys: Tourism, History and Culture in the Modern South*, edited by R. D. Starnes, 114–137. Tuscaloosa: University of Alabama Press, 2003.

Souther, M. J. *New Orleans on Parade: Tourism and the Transformation of the Crescent City*. Baton Rouge: Louisiana University Press, 2006.

"The South Rises Again—as Draw for Tourists." *Orlando Sentinel Star*, July 31, 1977.

Stager, C., and M. Carver, eds. *Looking Beyond the Highway: Dixie Roads and Culture*. Knoxville: University of Tennessee Press, 2006.

Stanonis, A. J. *Creating the Big Easy: New Orleans and the Emergence of Modern Tourism, 1918–1945*. Athens: Georgia University Press, 2006.

Stanonis, A. J. *Faith in Bikinis: Politics and Leisure in the Coastal South since the Civil War*. Athens: University of Georgia Press, 2014.

Stanonis, A. J., ed. *Dixie Emporium: Tourism, Foodways, and Consumer Culture in the American South*. Athens: University of Georgia Press, 2008.

"Starkville Man Hired to Head New A&I Tourism Agency." *Clarion-Ledger*, October 13, 1976.

Starnes, R. D., ed. *Southern Journeys: Tourism, History, and Culture in the Modern South*. Tuscaloosa: University of Alabama Press, 2003.

"State Focuses Tourism Effort on Germans." *Magee Courier*, December 1, 1977.

Stillman, J. "46 Black Women Tour, Like South." *Fort Worth Star-Telegram*, August 12, 1972.

Stokes, B. F. *Myrtle Beach: A History, 1900–1980*. Columbia: University of South Carolina Press, 2007.

Sumners, C. L. *The Governors of Mississippi*. Gretna, La.: Pelican Publishing, 1998.

"Sunbelt South Emerges." *Clarksdale Press Register*, February 8, 1977.

Survey of State Travel Offices, 1977–1978. Washington, D.C.: United States Travel Data Center, 1977.

Survey of State Travel Offices, 1978–1979. Washington, D.C.: United States Travel Data Center, 1978.

Survey of State Travel Offices, 1979–1980. Washington, D.C.: United States Travel Data Center, 1979.

Survey of State Travel Offices, 1980–1981. Washington, D.C.: United States Travel Data Center, 1980.

Terrill, T. "No More Dixie? The Last Fifty Years of the American South." In *The United State South: Regionalism and Identity*, edited by V. Gennaro Lerda and T. Westendorp. Firenze: Bulzoni, 1990.

Tharpe, J. "1981 Becoming 'Gold Rush' for State Tourism," *Greenville News*, June 11, 1981.

Tiede, T. "'Oyotunji'—Voodoo for Ripoff." *The Sentinel*, August 17, 1977.

Tiede, T. "The King: Presley Fans Listen Intently to Tales of His Childhood." *The Columbian*, August 16, 1978.

Timothy, D. J., and G. P. Nyuapane. *Cultural Heritage and Tourism in the Developing World: A Regional Perspective*. Abingdon: Routledge, 2009.

Tolf, R. "Charleston's Great Gardens." *Fort Lauderdale News*, March 2, 1980.

"Tourism Efforts Are Paying Off." *Greenville News*, June 13, 1981.

"Tourism Official Says Potential Is $1 Billion." *Daily Herald*, January 2, 1977.

"The Try-Harder State Shoots for the Positive." *Clarion-Ledger*, November 7, 1980.

Tullos, A. *Alabama Gateway: The Political Imaginary and the Heart of Dixie*. Athens: University of Georgia Press, 2011.

Tunbridge, J. E., and G. J. Ashwort. *Dissonant Heritage: The Management of the Past as a Resource in Conflict*. New York: Wiley, 1996.

U.S. Census Bureau, *1967 Census of Transportation*. Vol. 1. Washington, D.C.: U.S. Department of Commerce, 1970.

U.S. Travel Service. *Program Report of the United States Travel Service: January–June 1966*. Washington, D.C.: U.S. Department of Commerce, 1966.

U.S. Travel Service. *Publications and Materials of the United States Travel Service: 1968*. Washington, D.C.: U.S. Department of Commerce, 1968.

U.S. Travel Service. *Publications and Materials of the United States Travel Service: 1977*. Washington, D.C.: U.S. Department of Commerce, 1977.

U.S. Travel Service. *A Regional Analysis of International Travel to the United States*. Washington, D.C.: U.S. Department of Commerce, 1979.

U.S. Travel Service, *Summary and Analysis of International Travel to the U.S.* Washington, D.C.: U.S. Department of Commerce, 1978.

Urry, J. *The Tourist Gaze: Leisure and Travel in Contemporary Societies*. London: Sage Publications, 1990.

Vandiver, F. E. "The Confederate Myth." In *The Old South*, edited by P. Gerster and N. Cords, 147–154. Vol. 1 of *Myth and Southern History*. Urbana: University of Illinois Press, 1989.

Vann Woodward, C. "The South Tomorrow." *Time*, September 22, 1976.

Vann Woodward, C. *Origins of the New South*. Baton Rouge: Louisiana State University Press, 1971.

Vinitzky-Seroussi, V. "Commemorating a Difficult Past: Yitzhak Rabin's Memorials." *American Sociological Review* 67, no. 1 (2002): 30–51.

Violi, P. *Paesaggi della memoria. Il trauma, lo spazio, la storia*. Firenze: Giunti, 2014, ebook.

Volkart, C. "Surrey Zoo Success Seen by Expert U.S. Showman." *Vancouver Sun*, November 10, 1977.

Wall, B. H. "An Epitaph for Slavery." *Louisiana History* 16, no. 3 (1975): 229–256.

Weathers, D. "Travelling through the Lowlands of the South." *Black Enterprise*, April 1977.

Webb, S. L., and M. E. Armbrester. *Alabama Governors: A Political History of the State*. Tuscaloosa: University of Alabama Press, 2014.

Weeks J. *Gettysburg: Memory, Market, and an American Shrine*. Princeton, N.J.: Princeton University Press, 2003.

Wells, F. "Andersonville Stirs Sad Memories of War." *Atlanta Constitution*, June 25, 1977.

Wesley, P. "Music Highlights Festival." *Montgomery Advertiser*, May 8, 1977.

"West: Tourism Has Large Impact on S.C. Economy." *Aiken Standard*, November 2, 1973.

White, G. "Greetings . . . from Stone Mountain." *Atlanta Constitution*, May 27, 1978.

White, L., and E. Frew. "Exploring

Dark Tourism and Place Identity." In *Dark Tourism and Place Identity: Managing and Interpreting Dark Places*, edited by L. White and E. Frew, 1–10. London: Routledge, 2013.

Wickenberg, B. "Natchez Pilgrimage: The Old South Under Siege." *Clarion-Ledger*, March 26, 1978.

Wicks, B. E., and M. A. Schuett. "Examining the Role of Tourism Promotion through the Use of Brochures." *Tourism Management* 12, no. 4 (1991): 301–312.

Wiener, J. "Civil War, Cold War, Civil Rights: The Civil War Centennial in Context, 1960–1965." In *The Memory of the Civil War in American Culture*, edited by A. Fahs and J. Waugh, 237–257. Chapel Hill: University of North Carolina Press, 2004.

Williams, J. A. *This Is My Country Too*. New York: New American Library, 1965.

Williford, S. "Traveling America's South Just Isn't What It Used to Be for Blacks—and That Is Good." *Los Angeles Times*, December 2, 1979.

Wilson, C. R. "Carter Era." In *Encyclopedia of Southern Culture*, edited by C. R. Wilson and W. Ferris, 3:501–502. New York: Anchor Books, 1991.

Wilson, C. R. "The Myth of the Biracial South." In *The Southern State of Mind*, edited by J. Nordby Gretlund, 3–22. Columbia: University of South Carolina Press, 1999.

Wilson, C. R. "Tourism, Cultural." In *Sports and Recreation*, edited by C. R. Wilson, 227–230. Vol. 6 of *The New Encyclopedia of Southern Culture*. Chapel Hill: University of North Carolina Press, 2011.

Wolf, B. "These Southerners Just Love Yankees." *Saturday Evening Post*, September 5, 1953.

Wolcott, V. W. *Race, Riots, and Roller Coasters: The Struggle over Segregated Recreation in America*. Philadelphia: University of Pennsylvania Press, 2012.

Yuhl, S. E. *A Golden Haze of Memory: The Making of Historic Charleston*. Chapel Hill: University of North Carolina Press, 2005.

Zaretsky, N. *No Direction Home: The American Family and the Fear of National Decline, 1968–1980*. Chapel Hill: University of North Carolina Press, 2007.

INDEX

Aaron, Hank, 138
Africa, 30, 132, 133
African Americans: black history in promotion and advertising, 80–81, 84, 87–88, 97–98, 101, 112–113, 121, 135–138, 151; black tourism and, 29–33; stereotypical representations in advertising, 7, 32, 79, 135, 137
Agnew, Spyro, 115
Alabama: image problems, 56–58; international promotion, 53, 98–101; major tourist attractions, 72–73; promotional and advertising themes, 70–71, 75–82, 87–93, 96–97, 101; social and economic situation, 48–50; target of promotion and advertising, 55; tourist industry development, 48, 50–51, 53, 54; visitors' place of origin, 56
Alabama (rock band), 86
Alabama Bureau of Publicity and Information, 23, 51, 62, 70, 71, 76–77, 79, 80, 86, 87, 92, 98. *See also* Cavanaugh, Caroline
Alabama Historical Commission, 82
Ally, Carl, 14
Andersonville (prison camp), 65–67, 120
Antebellum homes: as American symbol, 11; pilgrimages, 73, 75, 81, 83, 96; in promotion and advertising, 37, 58, 71, 75, 78, 81, 82, 91, 93–94, 97–98, 109–110, 134, 180n157; as symbol of southern tourism, xv, 4, 8, 28, 146
Aquila, Richard, 11
Arkansas, 21, 26, 28, 43–44, 55–56; advertising and, 35, 36, 39, 93
Armistead, Bill, 57–58
Ashmore, Harry S., 17
Atkinson, Paul M., 118
Atlanta, Ga.: in advertising, 65, 104; black tourism, 30, 33, 112, 113, 150; as destination, xvii, 21, 26, 61–62, 144; economic development and, 44–45; *Gone with the Wind* image, 109–112; as southern port of entry, 25, 98

Atlantic Beach, S.C., 131
Atlantic City, N.J., 7, 129
Autry, Robyn, 115

Bartley, Numan, 44
Bates, Christopher, 12
Bates, Denise, 88
Beauvoir (Biloxi, Miss.), 72, 73, 114, 117
Benson, Alvin, 87
Benton, Doug, 51, 162n75
Birdsall, Stephen, 28
Blight, David, 8
Bolton, Charles, 47
Boone Hall (Mt. Pleasant, S.C.), 126. *See also* Antebellum homes; Plantations
Borglum, Gutzon, 113
Brinkley, Jack (U.S. congressman), 67
Brinkman, Fred P., 48. *See also* South Carolina Department of Parks, Recreation, and Tourism
Brown v. Board of Education, 13
Brundage, Fitzhugh W., 4, 7, 15, 40, 128
Brussels, Belgium, 98
Buchanan, Burt, 90
Busbee, George: Georgia economic development and, 44; Georgia tourism promotion and, 45, 53–54, 60, 104, 142

California, 41, 42, 52, 54, 56
Callaway Gardens (Harris Country, Ga.), 63
Canada: as target of promotion and advertising, 24–25, 27, 34, 51, 53, 54, 101, 112, 142, 165n106, 180n148; tourists in South, 23–24
Caribbean, 30, 133, 134
Carter, Billy, 64
Carter, Jimmy: in advertising, 65, 105, 142; election's impact on tourism in Georgia and South, xvii, 27, 56, 60–62, 68; as symbol of national reunion, xiv, 16–20, 65–67; as tourist attraction, 62–68. *See also* Plains, Ga.
Carver, George Washington, 78, 80, 81–82

199

attractions, 105–106; promotional and advertising themes, 103–110, 134–139; social and economic situation, 44–45; target of promotion and advertising, 54–55; tourist industry development, 45–46, 53; visitors' place of origin, 56

Georgia Tourism Division, 45. 55, 65, 104, 106, 111, 112, 113, 137, 144, 149. *See also* Spivia, Ed

Germany, as target of promotion and advertising, 34, 53, 98, 164n83

Gilmore, Calvin, 131

Golden, Harry, 12

Golden Isles, Ga., 65

Gone with the Wind, 2, 58; as metanarrative, 122; in promotion and advertising, 26, 58, 60, 109, 110–112, 121, 126, 142; Tara, 110. *See also* O'Hara, Scarlett

Gorgas Home (Tuscaloosa, Ala.), 91. *See also* Antebellum homes

Grand Strand, S.C., 19, 61–62. 123, 128, 131, 142; Canadian visitors to, 24; in promotion and advertising, 105, 134

Greensboro, Ala., 81

Greenville, Miss., 84, 86

Greenville, S.C., 128

Gregory, James, 16

Griffin, Marvin, 113

Gunn, Clare, 2

Hackett, William, 59

Hall, Ed, 43, 87

Handy, W. C., 37, 78, 80–82, 86–87

Hartsfield, William, 118

Hawkins, Michael, 122

Hayes, Bernetta, 24

Heart of Dixie. *See* Alabama

Hillyer, Reiko, xiii

Hilton Head Island, S.C., 122. 134

Holton, Abner Linwood, 48

Horseshoe Bend National Military Park, Ala., 72

Houston, Tex., 30

Huntsville, Ala., 86, 88, 96; NASA Center, 72, 89, 90

Jackson, Andrew, 63

Jackson, Maynard, 119

Jackson, Thomas Jonathan "Stonewall," 113, 117

James, Forrest Hood "Fob," 50–51, 80, 86

Janiskee, Robert, 8

Japan: Japanese tourists in South, 22, 72; Japan National Tourism Organization, 50; Southeast U.S./Japan Association, 44; as target of promotion, 53, 141–142

Jenkins, Olivia, 1

Johnson, Andrew, 63

Judd, Denis, 59

Kammen, Michael, 9

Kentucky, 34, 35, 39; as target of promotion, 55

Kern-Foxworth, Marilyn, 137

King, B. B., 83

King, Martin Luther, Jr., 114, 116; in advertising, 79, 80, 135; Dexter Avenue Baptist Church, 79, 80, 81; National Historic Site, 112, 137

King, Nicole, 48

King, Stephen A., 84

Ku Klux Klan, 114

Kytle, Ethan, 128, 129, 131

Ladd, Barbara, 153

Lechner, Zachary, 146

Lee, Robert E., 17, 80, 113, 117; in promotion and advertising, 58, 112, 116

Liberty Hall (Crawfordville, Ga.), 116–118

Liming, Robert, 127

Little White House (Warm Springs, Ga.), 63

Los Angeles, Calif., 21, 30

Lost Cause: black heritage tourism and, 32–33, 121; as part of American memory, 11; in promotion and advertising, 37, 39, 63, 66, 83, 94, 101, 103, 116, 120–121, 143, 149; as symbol of South, 3, 6–7, 9, 12, 67, 74, 112, 117

Louisiana, 20, 41, 122; promotion and advertising by, 6, 32, 34–36, 39, 53, 93; as target of promotion and advertising, 55

Magnolia State. *See* Mississippi

McDaniel, Rick, 38

McIntyre, Rebecca, xiii

McNair, Robert E., 47–48, 144

McPherson, Tara, 146

McQueen, Butterfly, 113

Mexico: as target of promotion and advertising, 51, 53; tourists in South, 24, 51

Miami, Fla., 25, 30; Miami Beach, 25, 30, 134

Politics and Culture in the Twentieth-Century South